TRUMP IN EXILE

TRUMP
IN
EXILE

MERIDITH MCGRAW

RANDOM HOUSE
NEW YORK

Copyright © 2024 by Meridith McGraw

All rights reserved.

Published in the United States by Random House, an imprint and division of
Penguin Random House LLC, New York.

RANDOM HOUSE and the HOUSE colophon are registered trademarks of
Penguin Random House LLC.

Library of Congress Cataloging-in-Publication Data
Names: McGraw, Meridith, author.
Title: Trump in exile / Meridith McGraw.
Description: First edition. | New York, NY: Random House, [2024] | Includes
bibliographical references.
Identifiers: LCCN 2024016297 (print) | LCCN 2024016298 (ebook) |
ISBN 9780593729632 (hardback) | ISBN 9780593729649 (ebook)
Subjects: LCSH: Trump, Donald, 1946– —Homes and haunts—Florida—Palm
Beach. | Trump, Donald, 1946– —Impeachment. | Ex-presidents—Florida—
Palm Beach. | Presidents—United States—Election—2024. | Capitol Riot,
Washington, D.C., 2021. | Presidents—United States—Election—2020. |
Impeachments—United States. | United States—Politics and government—
2021– | United States—Politics and government—2017–2021. |
Mar-A-Lago National Historic Site (Palm Beach, Fla.)
Classification: LCC E913.3 .M39 2024 (print) | LCC E913.3 (ebook) |
DDC 973.933—dc23/eng/20240429
LC record available at lccn.loc.gov/2024016297
LC ebook record available at lccn.loc.gov/2024016298

Printed in the United States of America on acid-free paper

randomhousebooks.com

1st Printing

First Edition

Book design by Susan Turner

To my parents

So we beat on, boats against the current, borne back ceaselessly into the past.

F. SCOTT FITZGERALD, *The Great Gatsby*

CONTENTS

AS YOU WILL SEE IN THE COMING PAGES, EACH CHAPTER HAS BEEN TITLED after a favorite song of Donald Trump's, one that has been a part of his campaign playlist for years.

But the dozens of songs on Trump's playlist are not just a deafening backdrop at his rallies; they make up the soundtrack of Trump's daily life. While out on one of his golf courses Trump will pull out his iPad to play his latest favorite song, and when at dinner on the patio at Mar-a-Lago, Trump will scroll through Spotify to play DJ for his guests.

He sticks mostly to a playlist ranging from Andrew Lloyd Webber's Broadway hits to songs by Elvis Presley, Elton John, and the Rolling Stones. It's a chaotic mix of classics that everyone knows but that are rarely found on the same playlist, like Luciano Pavarotti's performance of "Nessun Dorma" and Kid Rock's "All Summer Long." The songs are at once pugnacious and comforting, celebratory and nostalgic, but always jarring when put on shuffle.

Many artists have issued cease-and-desist letters to Trump and his campaign after learning that their songs are being blasted at MAGA rallies. But Trump and his campaign have ignored their pleas.

The crowd loves the incoherent mix, dancing to "YMCA," singing along to "Tiny Dancer," and sharing looks of bewilderment when "Phantom of the Opera" is blasted at a thundering decibel level over the speakers inside a rally arena.

When I think of Trump rallies, I think of one song in particular: "Gloria," the 1982 disco anthem by Laura Branigan. It would often play over the speakers as I packed up my laptop and belongings and trudged through dusty fields turned parking lots illuminated by the headlights of rallygoers trying to depart and the bright beams of Trump's stadium lights. *Are the voices in your head calling, Gloria? Gloria, don't you think you're fallin'? If everybody wants you, why isn't anybody callin'?*

The songs here serve as guideposts for the theme of each chapter. It would be foolish to read *too* much into the lyrics of Trump's favorite songs, but they have at times appeared to send subtle messages.

Recent additions to the playlist have included Sinéad O'Connor's "Nothing Compares 2 U" and Elvis Presley's "Suspicious Minds." James Brown and Pavarotti's "It's a Man's Man's Man's World" duet played as Trump beat 2024 Republican rival Nikki Haley in the South Carolina primary.

In 2016, after Trump gave his victory speech after winning the presidential election, the choral beginning of the Rolling Stones' "You Can't Always Get What You Want" started as he made his way down the line of family and advisers, who looked both happy and shell-shocked that he actually won.

Hall of Mirrors

WE ARE LIVING THROUGH AN ACUTELY FRACTIOUS TIME IN THE UNITED States. Culturally and politically, consensus is almost impossible to come by among Americans; objective reality itself has become the primary political battle space; and just as leaders once drove consensus, so do they now drive our dissolution. We often seem to be in a state of cold war: rural against urban, red states against blue.

The attack on the United States Capitol on January 6, 2021, has become a bizarre American Rorschach test, subject to a remarkable degree of interpretation and argument. In the days after the attack, a brief consensus emerged that it was meant to disrupt and set aside the constitutional processes of presidential succession so a defeated president could remain in power in defiance of the will of voters. But over the following months, despite that initial revulsion and an astonishing amount of video evidence leaving no real confusion about the facts of the day, January 6 has been subject to a remarkable degree of interpretation and argument. An alternate theory, from a different universe, holds—with no evidence whatsoever—that the presidential election of 2020 was somehow stolen, and that the attackers of January 6 were not the constitutional vandals that they appeared to be but were, rather, constitutional defenders. Americans have taken refuge in their separate, siloed realities, in spite of our initial clarity about the attack.

The villain becomes the hero, the criminal becomes the political prisoner, and just like that, reality becomes not shared facts that we broadly agree on, but a version of events to which one subscribes.

At the center of this battle between reality and its alternate sits Donald Trump, who was president of the United States on the day that the Capitol came under siege by a sizable group of his loyalists.

In Trump's farewell address at the White House, he said that "all Americans were horrified by the assault on our Capitol."

"Political violence is an attack on everything we cherish as Americans. It can never be tolerated," he continued.

But since then, his rhetoric has changed. He has described January 6 as a "beautiful" and "perfect" day, and the participants of the attack as "loving and patriotic." He has promised to pardon many of the rioters if he becomes president again. A recording of January 6 defendants singing the national anthem—as images of them storming the Capitol were displayed onscreen—kicked off Trump's first rally of 2024, in Texas. He has called his former vice president, Mike Pence—whom he tried to pressure to overturn the results of the election—"delusional" and "not a very good person." The two have not spoken in years, and Pence declined to endorse his former running mate.

"For four years, we had a close working relationship. It did not end well," Pence wrote in his memoir. "When the president returned to the rhetoric that he was using before that tragic day and began to publicly criticize those of us who defended the Constitution, I decided it would be best to go our separate ways."

THIS BOOK IS NOT ABOUT the attack on the Capitol, nor is it about the effort to change the 2020 election results to keep Trump in office.

Rather, this book is a chronicle of the thirty-month period of

Trump's exile to his mansion in South Florida that those events set in motion—the years 2021, 2022, and much of 2023. Our narrative begins exactly two weeks after January 6, 2021, on the day that Joe Biden was sworn in as the forty-sixth president and moved into the White House, just hours after an outgoing president—for the first time in American history—was essentially forced from office, neither conceding the election that he lost nor attending the inauguration of his successor.

Since retreating to Mar-a-Lago, Trump has continued to maintain that he was deprived of reelection as the result of massive vote fraud in several states, assertions for which there is no evidence whatsoever. That belief is now held by a majority of Republican voters, according to polling data.

During his term in office, Trump would often project the belief that the well-being of the American people was inextricably intertwined with his own well-being—the personalization of presidential power, heretofore anathema in American politics. In exile, that impulse has been supercharged with the grievance of an allegedly stolen election.

FIRST AT ABC NEWS AND then at *Politico,* I covered Trump's presidency and was one of the few reporters who continued to chronicle his time out of office. I have been to Mar-a-Lago over half a dozen times, have traveled with Trump on Air Force One and his private plane, and have gotten to know the people and organizations who contributed to his return. And I also know, quite personally, the people who continue to be drawn to Trump and his vision for the country.

In this book, we take a close look at Trump's time out of the White House and go inside the pink stucco walls of Trump's beachside mansion, where Trump has rarely been challenged by the outside world or reminded of the fact that he was, at least when he arrived back in Palm Beach, a significantly diminished figure.

There are no parallels to this moment, although Trump's arrival in South Florida was immediately fashioned by commentators as a kind of modern-day Napoleon-at-Elba moment. At Mar-a-Lago, with its grandiose architecture copied from palaces in Venice, hand-carved ceilings, tapestry-lined walls all sparkly from the glow of sofa-sized chandeliers and gold candelabra like a modern-day Versailles, Trump was a self-described "king of Palm Beach" looking to come back to power as he watched the Biden administration's poll numbers slide thanks to high inflation and Biden's handling of the Afghanistan withdrawal.

Mar-a-Lago and the ritzy enclave of Palm Beach were essential to Trump's mythmaking and his grand designs to return. Steve Bannon, Trump's former chief strategist, who helped propel Trump's America First movement after he left the White House, described it as Trump's "center of gravity—a kind of court in exile."

And exiles, he added, "historically, if you do it right, have had tremendous therapeutic power and emotional and organization power for groups that get thrown out of power. People will look back [on him like] the lion in winter," Bannon said. "I think [that's happened] only one or two times in a democracy, maybe in France with de Gaulle, or something like this. It's unheard of."

If Mar-a-Lago was the cradle for Trump's return, the guiding political philosophy was fidelity to the stolen-election theory, which has become a litmus test for anyone with ambition to hold office or party position in the contemporary Republican Party.

The theory has rendered GOP elected officials of long service and good reputation stammering, unable to say publicly whether President Biden was fairly elected and legitimately serves, for fear of Trumpian retribution. Those who are most faithful to the theory have been plucked from obscurity and made into stars in the narrow Republican House majority.

Trump's own belief that the election was fraudulent—and his desire to seek revenge on those who impeached him over his actions on January 6—have defined most of Trump's own activities since January 20, 2021, as he involved himself in the campaigns of allies and planned his campaign for the Republican nomination in 2024.

This two-and-a-half-year period is of historic importance, vital to our understanding not only of this man and his political movement, but of this moment in the life of America—and made all the more important because we don't yet know how the story ends.

Meridith McGraw
May 2024

TRUMP IN EXILE

Goodbye Yellow Brick Road

DONALD TRUMP STARED AHEAD PAST THE WHITE ARCHWAY THAT LEADS from the White House residence and out to the South Lawn, where Marine One was waiting. It would be the last time he stepped through the double doors, flanked by guards, and onto the pavement, where press anxiously waited for him to say goodbye.

Wearing a navy topcoat and signature red silk tie, Trump held hands with First Lady Melania Trump, fashionably dressed for their political funeral, and stopped to give his parting words. "Goodbye, hopefully it's not a long-term goodbye," Donald Trump said as he stood in front of a huddle of reporters, there to document his exit from the White House as president.

The morning of January 20, 2021, was a characteristically chilly winter day in Washington, D.C. But for a city that was out of breath and exhausted, the blandness that washed over it was a welcome reprieve.

Just a few hundred yards away, at Blair House, Joe Biden was getting ready for his inauguration, hoping that the day would go more smoothly than the last few weeks in the capital. No clashes between protesters, no violent mobs assaulting the police. All over the city there were still signs of the chaos and violence that had recently erupted over Trump's insistence—his fantasy—that the presidential election had been stolen from him and his supporters.

"It's been a great honor," Trump said to the gaggle of reporters he typically would have taunted, as he made his way to a send-off ceremony at Joint Base Andrews in Maryland. "We've had an amazing four years. We've accomplished a lot. We love the American people, and again, it has been something very special."

But at that moment, any accomplishments were overshadowed by the way Trump's presidency ended: with the U.S. Capitol under siege, Capitol Police officers dead, a runaway pandemic, and the norms of presidential tradition shattered. But neither the press nor Trump was eager to fight one last time as they often did in that very spot. There was a collective sense of fatigue. It was time to go. And yet Trump left the pared-back crowd of staff and reporters gathered on the South Lawn, smaller than usual in the COVID era, with a message: He would be back.

"The movement we started is only just beginning," Trump had said in a farewell address at the White House the day before.

In some small ways, Trump's exit from the White House was ordinary. But in all the ways that mattered, it was handled in the same dramatic, chaotic way he had conducted his presidency. Trump watched as boxes of personal items, papers, and White House memorabilia were packed up and put inside moving trucks. The day before Trump left, he reached out to House Minority Leader Kevin McCarthy, who returned the call late that night. "What are you doing?" McCarthy asked. Trump responded that he had just finished writing a letter to the new president to put inside the Resolute Desk—a tradition McCarthy urged him to follow, and one of the very few Trump would observe as he left. McCarthy never asked Trump what he wrote to Biden. He didn't want to dwell on it. Following that tradition was one of the few positive, normal gestures at the end of Trump's presidency.

Trump was not welcome at Biden's inauguration. After January 6, Senate Majority Leader Mitch McConnell, House Speaker Nancy

Pelosi, and Senate Minority Leader Chuck Schumer planned to write a letter requesting that Trump not attend. McCarthy told Trump about the letter and refused to sign on—but it showed the extent to which the president was now persona non grata at the Capitol. Trump saved congressional leadership from having to disinvite him, though, when he announced on Twitter that he planned to skip out on Biden's inauguration. At his own inauguration, Trump had stood at a lectern while his predecessor, Barack Obama, and his 2016 challenger, former secretary of state Hillary Clinton, sat respectfully behind him per tradition as he described the "American carnage" he saw across the country.

But this time Trump, who relished nothing more than extravagance and pomp and being at the center of attention, declined to attend a celebration that symbolized what makes the United States of America unique. This time, though, the extravagance and pomp would not be for Trump. Besides, attending the inauguration of someone other than himself might convey the impression that he had conceded the election. That, of course, was something he did not want to do.

"To all those who have asked, I will not be going to the Inauguration on January 20th," read Trump's final tweet before he was suspended for "glorification of violence" in violation of the social media site's rules. At the time, his suspension was to be permanent, though it would later be rescinded.

His absence was met with a collective sigh of relief by party heads and a majority of the country that was still reeling and rattled by the horrific riots on the steps of the Capitol just two weeks before.

This inauguration felt and looked different. America, being neither monarchy nor dictatorship, allows herself only so much pageantry. But because of the pandemic, this change of government was modest even by American standards. By design, fewer people were in the audience, and on the National Mall, where throngs of people would normally have stood, miniature American and state flags were placed instead to represent the thousands who could not attend on account of the pandemic. Days before, on the West Front balcony, where Biden would place his hand on the Bible to take the oath of office, Trump-supporting insurgents had bloodied police officers and shattered windows as they pushed into the building and ransacked offices in a last-ditch effort to prevent Biden from becoming president.

Washington, D.C., remained in a state of emergency. To protect against a repeat of the violence of January 6, there were unprecedented security measures in the capital: newly erected fences with razor wire, National Guard troops stationed across the city. The security surrounding Biden was compared to the protection provided for the inauguration of Abraham Lincoln in 1861, just as the country was descending into civil war.

Trump suddenly found himself in a diminished position: a president shunned, effectively forced from office, his social media megaphone taken away owing to the danger that he posed to the country he had led just hours before.

In the days prior, Trump's bare-bones team at the White House, including Chief of Staff Mark Meadows, had discussed with the president his options for an exit. At this point, staffers and cabinet officials alike, including Education Secretary Betsy DeVos and Transportation Secretary Elaine Chao, had quit over the events of January 6, and those who remained were fretting over their limited employment options in Washington.

Those left surrounding Trump at the White House decided on a farewell ceremony at Joint Base Andrews ahead of Biden's inauguration, allowing the outgoing president to take Air Force One for the last time to Palm Beach, Florida. He could walk down a red carpet to "Hail to the Chief" and give a speech to the only people left in Washington who would listen, tying a bow on one of the most tumultuous ends of any American presidency.

In a sign of just how hurried Trump's team was—and just how desperate they were to fill seats—some of Trump's most outspoken employees turned enemies, like his former national security adviser John Bolton, his short-tenured communications director Anthony

Scaramucci, and former reality TV star and White House aide Omarosa Manigault Newman, were all invited to attend and even to bring as many as five guests. Invitations did not indicate that this event was any kind of farewell; rather, it was billed simply as a ceremony "featuring President Donald J. Trump."

The crowd of a few hundred people included the Trump family and some of Trump's most loyal aides, like his chief of staff, Mark Meadows, his deputy director of national intelligence, Kash Patel, and senior adviser Stephen Miller, all of whom would be among the few voices to defend their former boss in the coming months.

But there were also notable faces missing from the crowd.

Ronna McDaniel, the newly reelected chair of the Republican National Committee, wasn't there. She was recovering from surgery that required her to use a knee scooter to get around, as she had done just weeks before at the RNC's annual meeting in Florida; some in Trump circles saw the injury as a convenient coincidence that allowed her to stay away after January 6.

Mike Pence, Trump's vice president, wasn't there. January 6, when he had refused to go along with Trump's plot to overturn the election and as a result had been threatened by a feral crowd that beat down police officers and doors to try to stop the electoral process, had represented a final break in his relationship with Trump. Pence chose to attend Biden's inauguration instead, standing in the cold with his wife and applauding his successor, Vice President Kamala Harris.

Neither McCarthy nor McConnell was there, as they too were attending the inauguration.

But the crowd at Joint Base Andrews seemed blithely unaware that just a few minutes' drive away, a change of government was taking place.

From a VIP room at the passenger terminal at Joint Base Andrews, Trump aides and family—Ivanka Trump and Jared Kushner, Eric and Lara Trump, Donald Trump Jr. and Kimberly Guilfoyle—watched Fox News coverage of Donald and Melania leaving the White House.

"He will get on many more helicopters in his lifetime, but he will never get on Marine One again," said Fox News host Steve Doocy.

"There he is, turning around, looking at the White House for the last time as president," said Ainsley Earhardt of Fox.

Teleprompters were set up on a stage, but were taken down before Trump began to speak. "Don't Stop Believin'," the Journey classic that had long been a mainstay at Trump rallies, played before Trump and Melania Trump were announced onstage. While it seemed Washington and much of the country was withdrawing from Trump's undeniable forces—he was once able to command the attention of the world with a simple tweet or answer at a microphone—this crowd was made up of loyal aides ready for closure and true believers who felt it should be Trump up on the Capitol steps that day.

Chanel Rion, a Trump sycophant at the right-wing network One America News, broadcast live from his farewell speech and described it as only a "temporary goodbye."

"The fight has only just begun," she said.

Trump scanned the mix of fans, staff, and media. He had begun his presidency obsessively fixating on characterizations of his inauguration's crowd size. Now, as he stood onstage one last time as president, it was a disappointing final turnout.

The send-off offered him a last taste of the kind of patriotic grandeur Trump loved about the office. Standing in front of a line of American flags and behind the presidential seal, Trump rattled off a list of his proudest accomplishments. Space Force. The vaccine. The border wall. Three Supreme Court justices. Trump noted that his was "not a regular administration."

"Remember us," he said.

"I wish the new administration great luck and great success. I think they'll have great success. They have the foundation to do something really spectacular. And again, we put it in a position like it's never been before," Trump said.

Melania Trump gave her well-wishes to the crowd, but by the end there was little she would miss about her time in the White House.

She cherished her routine and her privacy and felt she had been afforded neither as First Lady.

"So, just a goodbye. We love you. We will be back in some form," Trump said, as if he was standing up from the table at the end of a long dinner party.

It was as close as Trump would come to admitting defeat.

IT WAS A ROUGHLY TWO-HOUR flight from Joint Base Andrews to Palm Beach International Airport, and a flight pattern the crew aboard Air Force One had come to know well. Trump spent as many weekends as possible in Florida when the weather in D.C. became dreary. He was restless for golf and for the serotonin hit that came not just from the sunshine, but from the endless stream of adoring fans who filled his clubs each day to offer praise or to get in his ear about some idea or another.

He had not spent much time contemplating what his life after the White House would look like, although he did have anxieties about his presidential legacy. Trump was obsessed with his image and would often reference his own legacy and how his presidency would impact his family, according to aides. Advisers in the White House, including Ivanka Trump and Jared Kushner, would sometimes bring up Trump's legacy as a way to encourage him to consider certain presidential actions.

Usually the first major task for an ex-president is the daunting mission of conceiving of a presidential library and figuring out how to fundraise and finance the entire operation. But post-presidency plans were put on a back burner as this ex-president pushed to reverse an election he believed had been stolen.

Some haphazard plans for a presidential library had been discussed behind the scenes by people close to him, with rumors swirling he could buy property for it somewhere near West Palm Beach. Those around Trump at the time understood they weren't supposed to talk about a presidential library, which Trump equated to a kind of cemetery for his career. He hadn't made clear he wanted to run again in 2024, but if there was talk of a library, one aide said, it would mean he was done. Trump never brought it up.

Trump boarded Air Force One with a smile and a wave, but feeling intensely frustrated—and strangely alone. He was surrounded by his family, including Don Jr., Ivanka Trump and Jared Kushner, and his youngest daughter, Tiffany Trump, who had gotten engaged just the day before to Michael Boulos in the Rose Garden of the White House. But not all of them would join for the ride down to Palm Beach.

Jared, Ivanka, and their kids decided not to take the flight down to Palm Beach, though that came as no surprise to some of Trump's aides, as they had made clear they needed to pack up their mansion in the Kalorama neighborhood of Washington and were ready to move on and start their separate post–White House lives in Florida. They had narrowed their search down to a property listed by Julio Iglesias on an exclusive private island near Miami and looked forward to being welcomed back by old social circles. They watched from the tarmac as the plane took off to Frank Sinatra's "My Way"—the same song Trump had chosen for his first two inaugural balls in 2017.

The remaining members of Trump's family and staff settled in for the trip. Two aides on the flight said it felt "weird" and "bittersweet."

While aboard Air Force One, Trump received a phone call from Ronna McDaniel, the RNC chairwoman who had stood at Trump's side—holding her breath the entire time, ready to adapt and handle every unpredictable impulse—throughout his presidency.

When McDaniel caught him on the phone, he was calm—but he wasn't happy about the current scenario. Among the few things they discussed in their brief phone call were recent reports that Trump, frustrated by what he viewed as insufficient support for him in the waning days of his presidency, mused about forming a third party and leaving the GOP entirely. But there were few, including McDaniel, who took that threat seriously. After years of McDaniel and her top lieutenants tending to his mercurial whims, the threat seemed toothless. But they also knew that while most of the country was currently working to move on from Trump, Trump and the party at that point were one and the same. For all the wishful thinking that the party was on the verge of moving on from Trump and Trumpism, there was an acute awareness among those at the top that the impeachments and legal fights had only emboldened Trump, any effort to push him out was foolish, and whether they liked it or not, he was still the former president and leader of the party.

The episode would set the tone for Trump's relationship with the GOP as he embarked on his next chapter.

On the flight, Air Force One staff served a brunch of steak and eggs with grits at the long table where Trump and his team would at times hold senior staff meetings.

For part of the flight, Trump remained in the front office of the plane by himself, at his corner desk, next to a presidential seal. He was focused on how his exit was playing out in the media.

Trump invited Jason Miller, his loyal, goateed campaign adviser, up to his private cabin for an update. Miller had a long history with Trump. In the final weeks of Trump's presidency as aides stepped away from the White House or tried to distance themselves from Trump and everything that transpired on January 6, Miller continued to work as a communications adviser and did not hesitate when asked if he would join on the final flight on Air Force One.

Trump had always obsessed about what the newspaper headlines and network chyrons were saying about him, favorable or not. And he was still sensitive to how the press perceived him, even after decades of embarrassing stories about his love life and his bankruptcies.

"How's this playing?" Trump asked.

"Well, everyone's covering it," Miller replied. "But you're not going anywhere. You're still the big dog," he tried to reassure Trump. "Your valuation is not gonna be determined by ABC, NBC, CBS, nor is it going to be determined by Republican Party officials or inside-the-Beltway types."

Trump's personal measure of performance and success still had

more to do with the metrics used by entertainers—ratings—than anything else. A natural performer in the reality TV realm, he had
learned that once introduced, conflict had to be continually escalated
and could never be allowed to de-escalate, even if continually fanning
the flames could eventually burn everything down. It was just as his
mentor and lawyer Roy Cohn had taught him back in New York
when he was hustling to become famous: *There is no such thing as bad
publicity.*

Even though he had been on the world stage for years now, since
his surprise takeover of the Republican Party and ascent to the most
powerful office in the world, the press still had not figured out how to
effectively cover Trump, who called journalists the "enemy of the
people," made a particularly adversarial relationship with the press a
calling card of his presidency, and eroded his supporters' confidence
in the media.

Trump had survived plenty of scandals before, but the violent attack on the Capitol on January 6 challenged Cohn's axiom. Maybe
trying to overthrow the lawful results of the 2020 election and failing
to stop his own supporters from attacking the Capitol was the kind of
bad publicity that not even the most shameless self-promoter of all
could survive.

It was so bad that Trump's own allies in Congress had been fighting to censure him in a vain attempt to prevent his second impeachment, which was akin to asking that he be sent to purgatory rather
than hell. But even that failed and he was impeached on January 13,
just seven days after he had invited a mob to descend on Capitol Hill,
and seven days before this lonely flight home to an uncertain future.

For Trump, though, being ignored by the news would be the true
definition of hell and more painful than any media pile-on. If he
wasn't visible, he didn't exist. And Miller tried to assure the president
that he was not flying down to Florida to face obscurity. Knowing that
crowds would be waiting for him in Palm Beach, Miller said, "Your
determination of how this will land will be when *we* land."

Miller did his very best to dispel Trump's fears, but on board the plane it was clear just how much Trump's universe had shrunk in a very short period of time. There was a sense that, as one person on the flight described, this was a last trip for the "dead enders."

The sparsely staffed plane was a shocking change from the huge groups that would typically travel with Trump on official trips to different corners of the country or far-off lands. He was used to dozens of people flowing in and out of the White House and Oval Office each day as if it was a bus station, with each person trying to get his attention or capture a second of his time.

The print pool reporter on board, the *Daily Mail*'s Rob Crilly, noted in his pool report that the plane made a low-level pass over Mar-a-Lago as it approached the airport.

Trump's bid for the presidency had begun with a media spectacle and a ride down a golden escalator, and that presidency was ending with the spotlight turned away and a quiet last ride on Air Force One.

TRUMP LANDED IN PALM BEACH a former president, looking like a deflated Dorothy in *The Wizard of Oz,* bewildered and a little crestfallen, but still pleased by the fanfare that greeted him in his technicolor Palm Beach world.

Melania Trump, who often sparked tabloid fashion cryptology into the hidden meanings of her outfit choices, whether she wore a "pussy bow" blouse, a suffragist-white pantsuit, or a parka with "I really don't care do U?" graffiti painted on the back, had changed during the flight in her last fashion statement as First Lady.

When she and her husband emerged from the plane, she had changed out of the entirely black Jackie Kennedy–esque skirt suit that she had been wearing when she left Washington and was now sporting a retro Gucci caftan with a brightly colored psychedelic print— ready-made for a tropical club, not the East Wing of the White House. The First Lady, who had at times barely contained her contempt for Washington and the scrutiny of a highly public life, had turned the page, announcing her arrival in Florida.

And for this one brief moment, almost all of Washington seemed united in the belief that the Trumps ought to stay there, for good. And that belief was perhaps most intensely held by some of Trump's fellow Republicans. For the first time since 2010, the Republicans were out of power in the White House, the House of Representatives, and the Senate. And for now, leaders of the party, most of the Senate, and even many of those who had stood by Trump's side after his 2020 election loss were fine with him potentially leaving Washington for good.

It seemed that the Republican Party was ready to break free of the MAGA movement and a man who had turned not only the GOP but the entire country on its head. It was a fateful moment, a hinge of history, and no one knew what might happen.

The chorus of high-profile abandonments turned on a loop in the news. On the evening of January 6, the Republican senator from South Carolina and one of Trump's closest confidants and most frequent golf partners, Lindsey Graham, had stood on the Senate floor and declared, "Trump and I, we've had a hell of a journey. I hate it to end this way. Oh my God, I hate it. From my point of view, he's been a consequential president, but today, first thing you'll see. All I can say is count me out. Enough is enough."

"Chaos, anarchy. The violence today was wrong and un-American," said Senator Rand Paul from Kentucky.

"There is nothing patriotic about what is occurring on Capitol Hill. This is 3rd world style anti-American anarchy," Florida Senator Marco Rubio tweeted.

Republican minority leader Kevin McCarthy, who had repeatedly called on Trump to stop the violence that day, would emphatically say in a private call with his GOP colleagues, "I've had it with this guy." And on the House floor, he laid responsibility for the attack at the feet of Trump.

"Those who are responsible for Wednesday's chaos will be brought to justice. . . . The president bears responsibility for Wednesday's attack on Congress by mob rioters," McCarthy said.

Shunned by key allies on Capitol Hill. Struggling to find lawyers to defend him in his second impeachment trial. All the doors were closing on Donald Trump, and the most powerful man in the world was suddenly quite powerless.

And then, in perhaps one of the most upsetting personal blows to the former president, came the coup de grâce: On January 10, the PGA announced that Trump's Bedminster golf club would no longer host the 2022 PGA Championship tournament.

But when Trump's motorcade made its last weave in and out of traffic from the airport in West Palm Beach, down Southern Boulevard, and across the bridge to Mar-a-Lago, he was greeted by a much different scene.

The streets were full of Trump superfans wearing MAGA hats, holding giant homemade signs, and waving Trump flags and American flags to welcome him home, as if he had just splashed down from a space voyage or won the World Series rather than being jettisoned in disgrace from the nation's capital. It was a hero's return. The motorcade crept along the road so he could read the signs, flash a smile, and give a thumbs-up to the hundreds assembled to hail his arrival.

And when he stepped out of the presidential SUV at Mar-a-Lago, a mix of club members and fans chanted "U-S-A!" and "We love you! Welcome home!"

"It was packed with people the whole way," a Trump aide said. "And I think at that moment, I think he realized: *They're still with me. The people are still with me.*"

The scene in Palm Beach was in some ways more reflective of Trump's political prospects than anything written in the *Wall Street Journal* editorial pages. A Quinnipiac poll released after January 6 found that only 17 percent of registered Republican voters held Trump responsible for the attack. Another *Washington Post*–ABC News poll found 66 percent of Republicans thought he acted responsibly following the election. Trump still had the support of millions of Americans.

It seemed fitting—and predictable—that in his final official act as president, Trump had announced a full pardon of Albert J. Pirro Jr., who once worked for Trump, was convicted in 2000 on conspiracy and tax evasion charges, and happened to be the ex-husband of Fox News host Jeanine Pirro. It finished off a flurry of last-minute pardons and commutations Trump issued to loyalists like Steve Bannon and celebrities like rapper Lil Wayne in the last hour of his presidency. Although he never went through with it, Trump had reportedly even floated the legally ambiguous action of pardoning himself.

That night, Fox News hosts—the Greek chorus of Trump's administration—began to foreshadow Trump's return.

"Make no mistake: The 75 million Americans who voted for President Trump, they are not going away. I'm one of them, I'm not going away either, although many on the left would probably love that. Our conservative values, they are not going away. Our dedication to the Constitution, that's not going away. Our love of freedom and justice for all, that's not going away either," said Sean Hannity, the Fox News host whose nightly monologues while Trump was in the White House were often viewed as a direct reflection of Trump's thinking, as the two would constantly talk on the phone.

Laura Ingraham, who was spotted regularly at the White House, predicted that "over the next four years the 74 million Americans who voted for Donald Trump will be reenergized and recommitted to protecting and defending the American values that we love."

"I just think the President is probably going to go back to Mar-a-Lago. He's going to unwind, not tweet because he can't tweet. Maybe that'll be good. He can reflect and think about how he's going to cut some deals overseas to rebuild the Trump Organization and make a mint with the memoir and some speaking deals," said Fox News's Jesse Watters.

Trump may have been banished to his rich enclave in Florida, but the crowds—and the sympathetic voices who began that very day to call for Trump's return—softened his landing in Palm Beach.

The billionaires and celebrities of the wealthy beach town weren't impressed by a former president and planned to leave him alone at home. Trump rarely left his own property to explore the fancy shops and fine dining along the ritzy designer shopping strip of Worth Avenue, and with the exception of occasional house calls to his billionaire neighbors, he chose to eat at home most evenings.

But home for the Trumps, like everything in their lives, was not normal.

MAR-A-LAGO WAS ONE OF TRUMP's prize properties: a decadent, sprawling, gilded mansion on the sea, and now home to the former president, his wife, a rotating cast of aides and assistants, and the constant buzz of wealthy and at times uncouth guests who would gawk at the Trumps as they enjoyed their steak and chocolate cake. Like two goldfish in a gold-encrusted fishbowl, Trump and Melania would sit on display at dinner, sometimes alone and sometimes with a member of Congress, a celebrity, a political adviser, or any other person who happened to be welcomed into Trump's world.

For that reason, depending on who you talked to, Mar-a-Lago was described as either the epicenter of Trump's political universe, where local millionaires and Trump fans could mingle with Fox News talking heads and conservative stars, or akin to the bar from *Star Wars*—colorful, eclectic, and unlike any of the other clubs on the island, such as the Everglades Club and the Bath & Tennis Club, which for decades had attracted blue-blood, old-money members.

Before Trump was president, Mar-a-Lago would regularly attract A-list celebrities at charity events and holiday galas. Billy Joel and Celine Dion have performed at the club, Rod Stewart and Martha Stewart could be seen sashaying about, Michael Jackson and Lisa Marie Presley honeymooned there, and Sean "Puffy" (as he was then known) Combs and Jennifer Lopez turned heads when they spent an Easter weekend at Mar-a-Lago. In the nineties, before he became a convicted sex offender, Jeffrey Epstein was frequently seen partying with Trump, and it was at Mar-a-Lago that Ghislaine Maxwell found Virginia Giuffre—who would later accuse Epstein and Max-

well of trafficking her to several men for sex—working as a spa atten-
dant. Trump and Epstein eventually had a falling-out over a real
estate deal in Palm Beach just weeks before allegations against Epstein went public, according to *The Washington Post*.

The scene—stars with their scandals, stiff old money and flashy
new money, a showcase for the gaudy, the brassy, and the surgically
enhanced—may not have been the "winter White House" that the
mansion's first owner, the cereal heiress Marjorie Merriweather Post,
had had in mind when she donated the Palm Beach property in 1973
to the U.S. government with the stated purpose that it be a summer
escape—a luxe Camp David—for presidents and their families. In
1974, just one month before President Richard Nixon resigned over
the Watergate scandal, he took a helicopter from his compound in
Key Biscayne to Mar-a-Lago to "determine its potential use for U.S.
presidents for foreign dignitaries," according to Nixon's diaries.

Called "Xanadu" by the press, Post's crescent-shaped Mar-a-Lago
mansion was inspired by the stucco villas found along the Mediterra-
nean. A long, coconut-palm-lined driveway led to a porte cochere and
an entrance hall with Spanish lanterns hanging from a painted carved
wood ceiling and niches with sixteenth-century Roman marble busts
depicting Cicero and Antoninus Pius. The living room was drenched
in gold, with a gold-leaf ceiling meant to look like the Accademia
Gallery in Venice, a large marble fireplace, and crystal chandeliers,
and the dining room's murals and moldings were a copy of those
found in the Chigi Palace in Rome.

The estate was eventually returned to the Post family over its ex-
orbitant $1-million-a-year upkeep costs, but where the government
saw a burden, Trump, ever the real estate mogul, saw an opportunity.

As Trump himself would tell it in his book *Trump: The Art of the
Comeback*, he asked his limousine driver in Palm Beach what in town
was on the market. A detour turned into Trump's realization that "it
had to be mine."

Buying the oceanfront estate, Trump believed, would launch his
outer-borough family into the ranks of the Vanderbilts, Whitneys, Pu-

litzers, Hiltons, and other one-name-and-you-know-their-story dynasties.

Trump snagged the estate in 1985 for a song, in his telling—$5 million for the property plus an additional $3 million for its gilded antique furniture. Ten years after Trump purchased Mar-a-Lago, he converted the property into a sprawling seaside club with ballrooms, a pool, tennis courts, a spa, and restaurants for its elite members who could help the cash-strapped Trump pay the bills and for the upkeep of the estate. Membership costs hundreds of thousands of dollars up front, plus annual fees of $14,000, according to a member. That gets you access to the ex-president and amenities of the property including tanning beds, which some have speculated is where Trump gets his perennial tan—although a regular application of bronzer is now how he gets his glow.

Even as Trump was holding on to office until the very last minute, preparations were being made behind the scenes to get the club ready for his arrival. The family's private quarters at the club were updated, and an office, above the club's lavish ballroom, was being set up so that Trump and staff would have a workspace away from the gawking club members.

Melania Trump had toured private schools in the area for their then-fourteen-year-old son, Barron, to attend once they resettled in Florida, and there was local buzz—especially among the wealthy New Yorkers who had moved their families to South Florida during the pandemic—about which ritzy school the Trumps might choose.

Shortly after arriving home, Trump retreated up to his residence. As the clock struck noon and the Trump presidency officially came to an end, aides watched as the president's security transitioned from a presidential detail to the smaller post-presidential detail that would now attend him for the rest of his life.

Much like the tapestry-covered walls of Mar-a-Lago, Trump's aides, club staff, and club members formed a kind of cocoon around Trump. He was surrounded by old familiar faces at his club and in his office, which was built out above the main ballroom of Mar-a-Lago to conduct post-presidential business. To get to the office, Trump would have to meander through his club and climb one flight of gilded stairs, passing briefly through the grand foyer of his club's largest, most opulent ballroom, where luncheons, charity events, fashion shows, and weddings are regularly held.

He loved to drop in on a happy couple's special day to take selfies and offer some generic well-wishes to the crowd. Whenever he and Melania Trump would walk out to the patio for dinner each night, they would be greeted by a round of applause from women dripping in diamonds and men with tanned skin from leisurely afternoons on yachts or the golf course. Later on, he would open a private Spotify account on his iPad to DJ for members on the terrace and pick from his selection of opera, Elton John, and the Rolling Stones.

With the constant attention from club attendants, rounds of applause and affirmation from guests and friends, Trump was wrapped in a world inside the walls of Mar-a-Lago that reinforced everything he believed about himself.

AT THE BEGINNING OF 2020, a small group of senior officials in his administration had begun crafting a second-term agenda. Brooke Rollins, his domestic policy adviser, Larry Kudlow, his top economic adviser, and Robert O'Brien, his national security adviser, teamed up, sometimes working from whiteboards in Rollins's office in the West Wing. At times they were joined by Ivanka Trump, Kellyanne Conway, and Russ Vought, his Office of Management and Budget director, along with other policy aides.

By that summer, they had built out a two-page framework for their ideas called "Vision 2025" that covered everything from the economy and healthcare to immigration.

Rollins had reserved Camp David for the week after the election in order to hit the ground running. But once November 3 passed, and attention had shifted from planning a second term to disputing the election, the Camp David plans were canceled, and the second-term blueprint was put on pause.

The ex-president swaddled himself instead in the constant adulation of his Mar-a-Lago members and paid aides and was comforted by his daily routine of morning golf and nightly applause.

If anything was to be mentioned, it was those plans for a second term. But implementing those plans seemed about as likely as taking a rocket ship across the universe. For once, there was no place for him to go. Not even Fox News was welcoming him on its airwaves—he would often turn on OAN or Newsmax instead—and for the first time ever both Trump and his tiny cohort of aides saw value in keeping a low profile. Trump would still let his frustrations seep out into the press through unnamed sources who would talk about bitterness and anger about his circumstances and what he viewed as disloyalty in Washington. But to the relief of his aides, the Twitterless Trump mostly kept quiet.

In the following months Trump would go on to build out a new media company, defend himself against another impeachment in the Senate and increasingly serious federal and state investigations, transform his delusions about the 2020 election into a loyalty test for his party, restart his political career, and catapult himself once more to the top of Republican politics.

But for now, Trump was unmoored, unsettled, unpopular, and in exile.

2

You Can't Always Get What You Want

THE MONTHS AFTER LEAVING THE WHITE HOUSE HAVE BEEN DESCRIBED BY previous former presidents as a strange, disorienting, but liberating time after years of making daily, economy-shifting, world-changing, head-spinning decisions.

Bill Clinton settled into suburban life in Chappaqua, New York, by unboxing hundreds of books, wearing blue jeans to the local café for lunch, watching basketball, and binge-watching television on his TiVo. He described how nice it was to wake up at whatever time he felt like and pay little attention to the news. "Most days, I just glance at the newspaper," he told *The Atlantic*. "It's amazing how oblivious you can get to whatever's going on." He then got to work on a memoir and setting up his foundation in Little Rock, Arkansas.

George W. Bush moved down to his 1,600-acre Prairie Chapel Ranch in Crawford, Texas, and promised his wife, Laura Bush, that he would get back to domestic chores like mowing the lawn and taking out the trash. He took up painting, inspired by the pastime of Winston Churchill, and started thinking about writing a book. A city house was bought in a ritzy part of Dallas, and there were already plans for a $300 million George W. Bush Presidential Center and think tank on the campus of Southern Methodist University. He dreaded having to fundraise again.

Barack Obama began his return to private life by jet-setting and writing. He kicked off his post-presidency with a trip to the British Virgin Islands as a guest of the British billionaire Richard Branson, followed by a stint on the French Polynesian island of Tetiaroa to write his memoir and trips to Tuscany and Bali with his family. By May, he and Michelle Obama had revealed plans for their own Obama Presidential Center in Chicago.

Donald Trump bitterly retreated to Palm Beach, where he was angry, frustrated, staring down a second impeachment, unsure of how to fill his days, and without a plan for his political future.

Even though Trump himself had given little thought to what his next chapter in Florida would look like, his staff at Mar-a-Lago had been renovating Trump's private apartment inside the club and making preparations for his move. Trump wasn't interested in going through the boxes that came with him from the White House, and as they stacked up in piles all over the mansion, his aides complained about having to shuffle them around.

While Trump played golf, a small group of young staffers who moved down to Florida to work for him—a mix of entry-level communications officials and advance aides who did not have experience with the behemoth logistical task of moving out of a White House— started putting together the office space above the large ballroom at Mar-a-Lago that would become his official workplace.

But even during his presidency, the entire Mar-a-Lago property had essentially functioned as Trump's office. Trump would take phone calls from the patio within earshot of guests, regularly showing off his phone with Fox News host Sean Hannity on the line, and would hold meetings on the gold brocade couch in the main room of the club or in the wood-paneled library bar.

Once, shortly after taking office in 2017, Trump had infamously held a high-stakes, high-level meeting about a North Korean missile launch with Japanese prime minister Shinzo Abe and his team in the middle of Mar-a-Lago's outdoor patio. Over chocolate cake and in front of gawking guests who posted photos of the visit to their personal social media pages, Trump's and Abe's senior advisers frantically examined documents and made calls back to Washington and Tokyo. Although their table was roped off, Mar-a-Lago guests were free to approach it and take photos of the scene as it unfolded. Trump smiled for the cameras.

In many ways, Palm Beach was the perfect location for an exiled former president. The thin strip of land that makes up the island was teeming with some of the wealthiest and most powerful people in the world. They mostly shrugged at the prospect of Trump's return, so long as his security didn't impede traffic on South Ocean Boulevard, which runs the length of the island, and interfere with cocktail hours and tee times. Besides, Trump rarely ventured beyond the gates of his own properties.

He kept to his own world within the walls of Mar-a-Lago, where he was surrounded by smiling portraits of himself, a staff ready to refill his Diet Coke, and guests who paid hundreds of thousands of dollars to be there, eager to see him.

Mar-a-Lago was a sustaining force for Trump as he fumed over headlines about Congress debating how to properly punish him for his actions in the final weeks of his presidency, and considered how viciously he would fight back against those he believed were disloyal and had crossed him.

In the first days of his exile, there were fewer guests around during the day than there would normally be—the COVID pandemic was still raging, after all, and January 2021 would see record mortality in the country, with more than ninety-five thousand dead. But club members would still shuffle through in their dinner jackets and jewels for the wedge salad and Trump's favorite family recipe meatloaf.

It seemed notable that when Trump bought the club he kept all the antique furniture and some of Marjorie Merriweather Post's more personal touches, like the Latin inscription over the fireplace, IN ME MEA SPES OMNIS, "All my hopes rest in me." It was the motto of Marjorie Merriweather Post, who had it carved into the pink granite monument at the opulent Hillwood Estate in Washington in which her ashes are now enclosed. The phrase had suited Post, a larger-than-life character who in her time owned her own plane and the world's largest private sailing yacht, threw lavish parties, and, it is said, may have been an inspiration for F. Scott Fitzgerald's *The Great Gatsby*.

But the motto could just as well have been coined for Trump. His self-obsession had made him the star of his own show, and in its last act, he was determined to seek revenge.

While there was never any question that Trump would continue to haunt the Republican Party after he left the White House, there were questions about how—and how soon—he would reemerge. Most former presidents observe the tradition of maintaining a respectful silence after their terms in office have come to an end, sometimes for years, allowing their successors to govern without interference, and perhaps in tacit recognition that their time commanding the spotlight is over. But it took little more than forty-eight hours after Joe Biden's inauguration for Trump to make his first foray back into national politics.

On the first Friday night of his post-presidency, from his outpost at Mar-a-Lago, Trump recorded a robocall and offered his "complete and total endorsement" for another term for Arizona Republican Party chairwoman Kelli Ward, a controversial and fiercely loyal Trump foot soldier who went to war with the state's Republican governor and promoted conspiracies about election fraud. Just days before Trump left the White House, Trump personally called Ward to encourage her to seek a second term as party chair. It would be vital during the years ahead to have loyalists running state parties, with loyalty at times being more important than either competence or success. Ward's track record as leader of the Arizona GOP was less than stellar: Under her leadership, Republicans in Arizona had lost both Senate seats and given Democrats their first presidential win in the state in twenty-four years.

But Ward had become a standard-bearer for the MAGA movement and ticked the box for Trump in two essential ways: In general, she placed loyalty above reason or reality, which in the end was the only principle that truly mattered to the former president. And in particular, she preached Trump's false message that the presidential election had been stolen from him, loudly and without evidence or compunction.

The following day, ahead of the voting, Ward played Trump's recorded endorsement for her fractured state party.

"I've been told by a couple of national radio hosts that the lobbyists, the slime, the consultants in Washington, D.C., thought they were finally going to be rid of me, that they were finally going to be rid of Trump, that they were going to finally be rid of America First. Well, I've got news for you, folks: I'm still here," Ward said in a video message posted by the Arizona Republican Party after her win. "President Trump was very closely watching this race. I hadn't realized that this is the first race he endorsed since he left the White House and so it was very important. It's a message, really, to our state and to our nation that the America First agenda is alive and well."

In a sign of where the Arizona GOP was heading—and how broken the party was—the same night that Ward won reelection to her party post, the Arizona state party voted to censure prominent Republicans in the state including Governor Doug Ducey, former senator Jeff Flake, and Cindy McCain, John McCain's widow. The crowd that had assembled to celebrate Ward booed loudly at the mention of McCain and Flake, both of whom had supported Biden over Trump in the 2020 election, and Ducey, who was criticized for using emergency orders to protect public health during the pandemic and for defending the state's election process.

The purges were under way.

As Republicans clung ever harder to Trumpism and conspiracies of a stolen election in Arizona, in Washington the national party found itself in a full-bore existential crisis. Leaders in Congress were negotiating the terms of Trump's second impeachment and grappling with the prospect that Trump—who had never been anything more than situationally loyal to the Republican Party, using the Party of Lincoln only as an accessory to his ambition—might actually step out on the GOP and form his own MAGA-centric third party.

Trump had mused about this new party, which he said would be called the Patriot Party, and had brought it up again with RNC chairwoman Ronna McDaniel on his flight down to Palm Beach on Inauguration Day. Trump's aides didn't take it all that seriously, and interpreted the idea as mostly about seeking revenge and dangling the potential for political chaos over the Trump-weary Republican senators who were going to be holding his fate in their hands in his second impeachment trial. Trump's official campaign committee even filed a notice with the Federal Election Commission that it disavowed any new political groups affiliated with the "Patriot Party."

Jason Miller, who was working as Trump's unofficial communications manager, went on Fox News that weekend to assert that Trump "made clear his goal is to win back the House and Senate for Republicans in 2022." Regarding third-party threats, Miller added, "There's nothing that's actively being planned regarding an effort outside of that, but it's completely up to Republican senators if this is something that becomes more serious."

It was a nudge and a wink ahead of the impeachment trial, a not-so-subtle warning to Republican senators whom Trump vowed to primary if they voted to convict him. But privately that weekend, Trump was also sending a back-channel message to a select group of senators. Upon returning to Mar-a-Lago, Trump asked Brian Jack, the former White House political director, to spread the word with senators on Capitol Hill that while he had no serious plans to create a new party, he fully intended to maintain his grip on the GOP.

Jack was one of Trump's most trusted and reliable aides, who worked on the campaign in 2016 and in the White House as deputy political director, then political director. Originally from Georgia, with a Southern gentleman's demeanor to match, Jack served as national delegate director for the Trump campaign in 2016 after having begun the election season working for Ben Carson's campaign. He bonded with Trump over a shared interest in professional boxing and other sports, and he had such a good working memory of who's who in the political world that Jared Kushner, Trump's son-in-law, would refer to him as the "ESPN of politics."

Jack spent the first post-presidential weekend working the phones, reaching out to Senators Roger Marshall, Bill Hagerty, and Kevin Cramer to try to lower the temperatures around Trump on Capitol Hill. Trump instructed him to tell senators he had no intention of forming a third party. The upcoming impeachment was not part of any of their conversations, but the upcoming vote hung over senators. Even as some of them had begun to publicly distance themselves from Trump and his conduct and his claim that the election had been "stolen" from him, they still feared him, and did not want to face his wrath or the wrath of his MAGA constituency when they ran for re-election.

"The president wanted me to know, as well as a handful of others, that the president is a Republican, he is not starting a third party and that anything he would do politically in the future would be as a Republican," Cramer told *Politico*. "The Republican Party is still overwhelmingly supportive of this president."

But Ward's win in Arizona, the impending impeachment trial of Trump, and the potential that he could blow up the entire GOP in Washington laid bare the dilemma the Republican Party faced.

Even as some in the party believed that Trump should step aside for the good of the country and American democracy, there was a grassroots movement aiming to overhaul voting systems in the name of "election security"—a solution without a problem, all in response to Trump's lies about the election, which, while rejected by the vast majority of the country, were becoming something close to orthodoxy to the MAGA base of the Republican Party.

Nearly two-thirds of the Republican Party now believed that Biden was not legitimately elected president, polling suggested, and that figure would continue to grow as Trump's brazen defiance of reality continued unabated. Trump's falsehoods about the election resulted in dozens of bills in Republican state legislatures that restricted voting—drastically limiting systems for voting by mail and in Florida even establishing an Office of Election Crimes and Security.

Representative Marjorie Taylor Greene, the brash new Republican congresswoman from Georgia who was fiercely loyal to Trump and was steadily gaining a following in the far-right corners of the party, spelled out on Twitter exactly where a large segment of the party stood: "Here's the warning the GOP needs to hear," she wrote. "The vast majority of Republican voters, volunteers, and donors are no longer loyal to the GOP, Republican Party, and candidates just because they have an R by their name. Their loyalty now lies with Donald J Trump."

TRUMP HAD LONG CLAIMED TO be the "Hemingway of 140 characters," and each day he would provide on Twitter what amounted to a diary, showcasing his anger, delight, rage, and commentary about news of the day, his latest fight or fixation. By pressing Send, Trump could sink the stock market, spook allies, and ruin a reporter's or lawmaker's day. His fans loved his brash, uncensored take on the world, a take not filtered through journalists, while his critics saw his tweets as a grotesque reflection of a man who regularly blew up and rejected norms.

Trump would command news cycles by tweeting or calling in to cable TV shows, or making outrageous statements to divert or deflect from whatever the latest headlines happened to be. At the White House, aides would note his delight in firing off a tweet and seeing headlines change in real time on his many televisions. But that superpower was stripped away when Twitter and Facebook suspended his accounts after January 6. It was a sudden crackdown on Trump after years of criticism that the social media companies did not do more to stop him from spreading false and incendiary claims on their platforms, and Trump was furious.

In an effort to evade the suspension, Trump tried using other official accounts to get his messages out, including the official President of the United States Twitter handle, under which he announced that he had been "negotiating with various other sites," would have a "big announcement soon," and would be looking at the "possibilities of building out our own platform in the near future." The posts were quickly removed.

Trump had been entertaining ideas of starting his own media company since he was elected president, but that wouldn't fix his immediate issue—without White House press releases and social media access, he had no way of talking to his supporters and dictating the news. The one thing he did have was an acting spokesperson in the early months of his post-presidency: Jason Miller.

Miller's history with Trump stretched back to when the Manhattan mogul was better known as a celebrity and a late-night talk-show punchline. Miller, then a former aide to Rudy Giuliani's 2008 presidential campaign, was recommended as a potential campaign manager for a Trump 2012 bid that never fully coalesced, instead winding down after injecting "birtherism"—the baseless claim that Barack Obama was not born in the United States—into the political conversation.

In 2016, Miller went down with the ship on the Ted Cruz campaign—and joined Trump's a month later as a communications adviser, a position he rode all the way to an infinitesimally brief tenure as White House communications director-designate, before allegations of an affair led to his withdrawal from any role in the incoming Trump administration. Instead, he joined CNN as a contributor until his departure in the fall of 2018 to focus on "clearing [his] name and fighting the false and defamatory accusations being made against [him]."

But truly permanent departures from Trumpworld are relatively rare, and staff with a personal rapport with Trump have something resembling nine lives. Miller had success as a Republican consultant and strategist, and stayed close to Trump and Trumpworld. Even if he wasn't defending Trump from inside the White House, he was one of Trump's biggest defenders in the media, teaming up with former Trump adviser Steve Bannon to co-host a pro-Trump podcast.

Miller joined the Trump reelection effort as a senior adviser in June 2020 to assist then campaign manager Brad Parscale, and was even offered Parscale's job following his ouster from the campaign (Miller declined).

When you work for an arsonist, it pays to be a firefighter, and that is how Miller spent much of his time—he was quick to return reporters' calls and provide on-the-record comments to bolster Trump and put out those fires. On the night of January 6, 2021, with the White House emptied out, it was Miller who reached out to reporters late into the night in a desperate attempt to put out the biggest fire of all. And he was one of the few aides who followed Trump down to Mar-a-Lago to help him navigate his desire to command the media spotlight without making things even worse for himself.

But Miller had no platform to work with. When Trump arrived in Palm Beach, the former president barely had an office, let alone a website the public could visit. At the very least, Trump's team needed a way to send out press releases and for Trump to blast out messages—although, aides hoped, not at the same frequency or volume as he had been able to with the click of a button on Twitter. Enter Brad Parscale.

Like many people in Trumpworld, Parscale floated in and out. In July 2020, he was demoted as campaign manager, and just a few months later found himself in the headlines after police were called to his home in Florida after his wife reported he was behaving erratically. He was involuntarily committed and officially stepped down from the campaign, although he stuck around as a digital and data adviser for the operation. In the aftermath of the campaign, he created a digital firm, Parscale Strategy, and a software start-up called Campaign Nucleus to provide data and communications services to campaigns that would be "uncancellable."

Parscale pitched using his Nucleus platform to blast out messages to his followers via an email list from Trump's official website—

essentially, a blog. On January 25, Trump announced he had "formally opened the Office of the Former President." The office, a statement from his team said, would "be responsible for managing President Trump's correspondence, public statements, appearances, and official activities to advance the interests of the United States and to carry on the agenda of the Trump Administration through advocacy, organizing, and public activism."

Notably, it was the first and only time that Trump or his office would refer to him as a "former president." In future missives Trump would call himself "the 45th president," as if to imply that his time in the White House had never officially come to an end.

But the blog backfired. Trump's new email messaging was immediately mocked in the press, and headlines read that the former president was now "blogging." Trump hated it.

Email lists were about as agile as flyers for the church bazaar. Trump needed a platform with the immediacy and reach of Twitter, but with standards and practices flexible enough to accommodate the Trumpian version of reality and comportment.

Soon after arriving in Palm Beach, Trump received a phone call from a Fort Lauderdale attorney named Bradford "Brad" Cohen. Back in 2004, Cohen was a contestant on *The Apprentice,* and was given the famous "You're fired" by Trump in the boardroom during the second week of the show for making some kind of strategic blunder. His reality TV career cut short, Cohen went back to working as a criminal defense attorney and lined up clients like Lil Wayne and Kodak Black—and eventually, Trump's former campaign manager Corey Lewandowski.

Late in the 2020 campaign, it was Cohen who connected Lil Wayne with Trump, who met with the rapper at his Doral golf course to discuss criminal justice reform and other policy initiatives aimed at the Black community and intended to improve Trump's dismal standing with Black voters. At the end of the meeting at Trump's club, Lil Wayne posted a photo on Twitter of the two standing together with thumbs up, a welcome endorsement for Trump.

Flash forward to January 2021, and both Lil Wayne and Kodak Black were granted clemency for recent convictions. Lil Wayne had pleaded guilty to a federal weapons charge just one month after his meeting with Trump and was staring down a prison sentence. Black had been sentenced to four years in prison for making false statements to purchase a firearm. Cohen worked connections in the entertainment world to help lobby for clemency for both of them, including rappers Gucci Mane and Vanilla Ice, who helped draw attention to their cases.

Cohen and Trump had stayed in touch over the years, and just days after Trump left the White House and pardoned two of his clients, he reached out to make an introduction to Trump. Two other *Apprentice* alumni, Wes Moss and Andy Litinsky, wanted a few minutes of Trump's time to pitch the former president on a Trumpcentric media company they believed could make them all very rich.

The idea for a new Trump media company had been in the works for months. But as soon as it became clear that Trump wasn't going to win the election, Moss and Litinsky realized they could build something that would harness Trump's popularity with conservatives and the growing skepticism among people on the right toward mainstream media and social media platforms. Of course, his MAGA constituency's contempt for traditional sources of information had been well conditioned by Trump himself—every news report that was disagreeable was "fake news," and the only information that could be trusted came from Trump himself. So Moss and Litinsky's idea was to capitalize on the captive audience that Trump himself had created. The proposition made sense, so much so that the Moss and Litinsky pitch wasn't the first attempt to corner the Trump market on social media. Parler, an alt-right Twitter clone that had been launched to great fanfare in the summer of 2018, catering to a far-right audience and featuring a mix of Trumpian disinformation and pornography, had tried to negotiate a deal with Trump while he was in the White House, a flagrant ethics violation that was slapped down by the White House counsel's office.

Just three days after the election, Moss and Litinsky started pitching potential investors. First they called up Mark Burnett, the influential producer and creator of reality television hits like *Survivor, The Apprentice, The Voice*, and *Shark Tank*, who declined to get involved. Next, they flew out to Las Vegas in December to meet with Dana White, the Ultimate Fighting Championship president, about coming on board, but nothing ever came of it.

Then January 6 happened. The small team working to put together a Trump media company knew that they had to act fast—Trump had been deplatformed, and Moss and Litinsky told themselves that he was likely hearing similar pitches from other people.

For two weeks at the end of January, the small team worked on dreaming up their idea for a Trump media company and drew up display boards, printed at a Florida FedEx office, that they could show to Trump.

One board read "Trump's New Media Empire," and the Trump Media Group (thereafter to be known as TMG) would include a "Trump Digital Subscription," "Trump Radio/Podcast," "Trump Live Events," "Trump Newsletter," "Trump Documentaries," "Trump Book Publishing," "Trump Faith/Classic Films," and the potential acquisition of right-leaning companies like Parler, Discord, Rumble, and even the OAN and Newsmax news networks. "Trump Technology," another potential arm featured on the whiteboard, would include digital advertising, Trump Payment Processing, and a new social media platform for Trump and his supporters.

The concept was tailor-made to appeal to a man who seemed to find great pleasure in life affixing his name to virtually anything. Moss and Litinsky were onto something. And as they worked on their presentation, Cohen called with news. He had lined up a meeting with Trump. The very next day, Wednesday, January 27, just one week after Trump had fled Washington and landed in Palm Beach to a very uncertain future, they were going to give their pitch at Mar-a-Lago.

On that Wednesday afternoon, Cohen, Moss, and Litinsky arrived at Mar-a-Lago to make a presentation they believed could be worth billions. Trump listened as they went through their ideas and a business plan. Most important to their pitch was that even though it was called Trump Media, Trump would not have to invest a penny in the company—a detail Trump loved. Over hamburgers with ketchup, followed by ice cream for dessert, they talked about a potential business formation, legal contracts, media consulting, discussions with potential investors, and a hiring plan. By the end of the meeting, an oral agreement was made. Trump would own a 90 percent stake in the company, and the only capital he'd be investing would be his name— the value of which was highly debatable by the end of January 2021. If owning a 10 percent stake and paying for the entire operation seemed like a bad deal for Moss and Litinsky, that's because it was a bad deal. They would not be the first to discover that there was no such thing as a successful, smooth-sailing business venture with the former president. Like so many before them who had done business with Trump, it wouldn't take his new partners long to discover that in deals with the devil, the benefits all go one way.

Less than a week later, Trump officially signed an agreement for the formation of Trump Media LLC, and the parent company of what would eventually be Truth Social was born.

TRUMP WAS STILL IN A dealing mood when, on Thursday, January 28, the day after he had negotiated the deal for his nascent media empire, Representative Kevin McCarthy paid him a visit.

Trump's aides had reached out to McCarthy, asking him to come to Mar-a-Lago. McCarthy had already planned to be in Palm Beach for a political fundraiser at the home of Wilbur Ross, Trump's wealthy former commerce secretary, and he told Trump's team that while he could not make dinner work, he could swing by for lunch.

Over the years, McCarthy and Trump had developed what one close aide described as a "familial" relationship. Trump would call McCarthy "my Kevin," a gesture of public tenderness and possessiveness that he used for anyone ranging from "my generals" and aides like Stephen Miller to Egyptian president Abdel Fattah al-Sisi. "Where's my favorite dictator?" he joked at the Group of Seven summit in 2019.

McCarthy had perfected the art of dealing with Trump, and was known for overtures like presenting him with a gift of his favorite cherry and strawberry Starburst candies, and serving as a kind of interpreter on Capitol Hill for lawmakers who were endlessly perplexed and vexed by the mercurial Trump and his whims.

And perhaps for the first time since Donald Trump's hostile takeover of the Republican Party, the relationship was a two-way street. In the weeks since January 6, in rare displays of independence, Beltway Republicans had been openly hostile toward Trump, but McCarthy was in a bind. He was forced to reckon with Trump's political mess, placate the more unruly faction of his party, prepare for Democratic plans to impeach Trump, and prove that he was capable of righting the ship. And then there was the problem of how to mend fences with Trump.

As rioters stormed the Capitol, McCarthy had desperately pleaded with Trump to call off the mob and had even gone on television in an effort to get his attention and have him understand the grave danger people were in.

Having received a firsthand view of the consequences of Trump's inaction that day, McCarthy discussed with colleagues the possibility of censuring Trump or even encouraging him to resign to stave off impeachment. But in a short period of time, he made an about-face on the subject of January 6, from saying Trump "bears responsibility" to claiming that "everyone across the country"—Democrats, rude people on social media—should also be blamed for the violence that day.

"I don't believe he provoked it if you listen to what he said at the rally," McCarthy told reporters at a news conference on January 21. In an interview with Greta Van Susteren the next day, he further distanced himself from coherence, saying, "I think this is what we have to get to the bottom of, and when you start talking about who has responsibilities, I think there's going to be a lot more questions, a lot more answers we have to have in the coming future."

Even though McCarthy did not support impeaching Trump, the former president fumed over McCarthy's earlier comments on the House floor. But for once the two men needed each other, and McCarthy's overture was seen as a peace offering by Trump aides and a chance for them to press Restart on their relationship.

Those close to McCarthy brushed aside the idea that it was a strategic meeting. McCarthy, they said, was known for reaching out to other party members and checking in on people when there was a loss in the family, or a big life event. Inciting a riot on Capitol Hill wasn't exactly akin to a wedding or the loss of a loved one, but McCarthy felt it was the right thing to do even if his own colleagues on Capitol Hill felt otherwise. After all, if Republicans were going to win back the majority in the House in 2022 and the speakership, they needed Trump not only to get on board but also to help fundraise and back candidates who could win.

But while McCarthy never planned to have news of the meeting leak out, Trump seemed eager to tell the world about their lunch date.

As soon as McCarthy arrived at Mar-a-Lago, Trump wanted to take a photo together, but his photographer was nowhere to be found. So McCarthy used his personal phone to commemorate the moment before Trump led him through the main living room of his club to the wood-paneled library bar for lunch. They ordered hamburgers and fries, although Trump made a point that he was trying to lose the weight he had put on at the White House. With an oil painting of Trump posing in tennis whites smiling down on them, Trump and McCarthy discussed the future of the party and Republican support for Trump among members on the Hill—a subject Trump was keenly interested in as he tracked members' support, serving as his own whip. By the time they finished their burgers, Trump had given McCarthy an assurance he would help win back the House in 2022 and thereby pave the way to McCarthy's speakership.

At the end of their lunch, a photographer had arrived to snap a photo of the former president grinning as he stood beside McCarthy. Trump's team didn't consult McCarthy before blasting the message out to reporters along with a statement about the visit that said it was a "very good and cordial one," adding the claim that the former president's "popularity has never been stronger than it is today." Trump delighted in the visit and the opportunity to show off the photo to his detractors. Even when he was in exile and facing the disgrace of a second impeachment trial, the photo was evidence that the party leadership would come back around.

McCarthy also got what he needed, his initial principled response to the attacks of January 6 all but erased from memory. "Today, President Trump committed to helping elect Republicans in the House and Senate in 2022," McCarthy said in his own separate statement. "A united conservative movement will strengthen the bonds of our citizens and uphold the freedoms our country was founded on."

Back in Washington, a few Republican members wanly called the visit "inappropriate" and were dumbfounded by McCarthy's willingness to fly down to meet with Trump and, with the photo, appear to offer his endorsement.

Liz Cheney, who was the Republican face of efforts to punish Trump and prevent him from ever holding office again, appeared on *Fox News Sunday* and said the party should not be "embracing the former president."

"I think that when you look at [Trump's] actions leading up to January 6, that he was impeached in a bipartisan fashion, the fact that he lost the presidency, the fact that we lost the Senate. We have to be in a position where we can say we stand for principles, for ideals," she said.

But her position on Trump—while shared by a majority of Americans—was not held by the party. McCarthy asked Cheney to apologize for her vote in an attempt to gain some goodwill with the conference, an overture she refused.

The same day as Trump's meeting with McCarthy, Representative Matt Gaetz, a Trump loyalist from Florida, flew to Wyoming, where he rallied hundreds of Trump supporters on the state capitol steps against Cheney, and the Wyoming Republican Party voted to censure her over her impeachment vote.

"We are in a battle for the soul of the Republican Party, and I intend to win it," said Gaetz. "You can help me break a corrupt system. You can send a representative who actually represents you, and you can send Liz Cheney home—back home to Washington, D.C."

TRUMP TOLD ADVISERS HE WANTED to do something completely uncharacteristic upon arriving in Palm Beach—keep a low profile.

He played golf with a rotating cast of partners that included Kid Rock. He dialed up allies on the phone. And the Sunday before his impeachment trial, Trump attended the Super Bowl party at his golf club, where he chatted with Sylvester Stallone and left at halftime. It was all meant to project the image of an ex-president who had better things to do than worry about impeachment—even if privately, Trump was concerned about who would vote for his conviction.

As the trial approached, Trump and his team were confident not only that he would be acquitted by the Senate, but that the results of the trial would send the message that in spite of the historic violence and chaos that had attended the end of his presidency, the GOP was still Trump's party.

Their confidence came largely from the fact that the trial centered on a debate over whether it was constitutional to impeach a former president—and even some of Trump's critics found themselves agreeing that while Trump's behavior was dangerous and reprehensible, the legal foundation for impeaching someone no longer in office was dubious. Testing that advantage, a week before the trial began, Kentucky senator Rand Paul brought a motion to the Senate floor attacking the constitutionality of impeaching a president who was no longer in office. "Private citizens don't get impeached. Impeachment is for removal from office, and the accused here has already left office," he said. Forty-five Republican senators voted in support of Paul's measure. It was an ominous sign to the House impeachment managers, given the two-thirds necessary for conviction.

But for all of the Trump team's posturing and premature faith in the outcome, they were striking out on finding qualified counsel who would be willing to represent Trump, who wanted his lawyers to focus their defense on his claims of election fraud rather than questions around whether impeaching a former president was constitutional.

The team Trump leaned on during his first impeachment as president, which had included Jay Sekulow, White House counsel Pat Cipollone, and his deputy Pat Philbin, declined to represent Trump this time around.

Desperate, Trump aides and allies made a plea for help in lining up legal representation for the upcoming trial. Lindsey Graham, who said he had seen enough after January 6, immediately returned to his role as Trump's top ally in the Senate and referred Trump to prominent South Carolina attorney Butch Bowers, who initially agreed to lead the defense. But shortly before the trial started, Trump's team of lawyers—including Bowers—abruptly quit when it became clear that the former president expected them to perpetuate and push the lie that the election had been stolen from him.

Eric Herschmann, a former White House lawyer who was close to Trump's son-in-law Jared Kushner, helped Trump and his team patch together a group of attorneys at the last minute who were willing to stand on the Senate floor just days after the January 6 insurrection and defend what most Republicans—even those who had no plans to support the impeachment—deemed indefensible.

Among them were Bruce Castor, an attorney from Pennsylvania and former Philadelphia prosecutor who most famously had declined to press charges against disgraced entertainer Bill Cosby; David Schoen, who represented Republican mischiefmaker and Trump ally Roger Stone during special counsel Robert Mueller's Russia investigation; and Michael van der Veen, a personal injury lawyer from Philadelphia.

Trump's legal team had no background in constitutional law, no chemistry, and no real experience in the kind of high-profile television showmanship that Trump expected from his attorneys. And some of their ideas for adopting Trumpian ways were viewed as ridiculous by Trump's aides. At one point during their very brief trial preparations, rather than devoting every moment to who would give which presentations and to acquittal strategies, Trump's team held an internal debate over whether Castor should make a splash by driving his Corvette right up to the Capitol and emerging with bravado—presumably to project confidence.

But for all the dysfunction, the Trump team had one major advantage that was overlooked by many in Washington—that the results of the Senate trial against Trump were assumed, and beyond the Beltway, most of those who had voted for Trump still supported him. Seeking to speak to that sizable cohort of Americans, Trump's team worked with the Republican National Committee to draw up talking points to be shared during the trial.

And Senator Pat Toomey of Pennsylvania, one of the Republican Senators that Trump's team were concerned might vote to convict Trump, said in an interview ahead of the trial that he believed a conviction would be "very unlikely."

For weeks, Trump's team had been warning Republicans about grassroots GOP backlash to impeachment. In the final days of Trump's presidency, John McLaughlin, one of Trump's pollsters, found that a majority of voters in battleground states opposed the impeachment. Jason Miller blasted out the two-page polling memo from McLaughlin to reporters.

"It's a massive miscalculation by the Democrats and the Liz Cheneys of the world who are massively disconnected from the grass roots that votes in primaries," Miller wrote. "That's really what matters. Washington is a very fickle town, and President Trump has never staked his strength as being in the nation's capital. It's always been out with the real people."

Trump watched the second impeachment trial—tailor-made for a TV audience with dramatic video clips—unfold from Palm Beach

and was annoyed with his own legal team's lengthy and boring opening presentation. He checked in with allies in real time and watched
as criticism rolled in about his attorneys' apparent lack of preparation
or passion, particularly compared to the Democratic team of
prosecutors—led by Representative Jamie Raskin of Maryland, who
was a professor of constitutional law before entering Congress—
whose arguments were razor sharp.

The start of the trial was brutal for Trump. Raskin opened with a
horrific montage of the violence that transpired on January 6, still
fresh in the minds of the senators who lived through that day and of
the audience watching at home. Senators could be seen wincing and
squirming at the sight of officers being bloodied and pummeled by
rioters and the Capitol being defaced.

When Bruce Castor and Trump's other impeachment attorneys
followed, they rambled through dry constitutionality and process arguments that lacked any of the emotion shown by the House impeachment team. Trump, watching as his attorneys were mocked and
criticized for their lackluster performance, was furious, relaying his
anger in a phone call with Jason Miller and Justin Clark, a longtime
lawyer and political adviser.

His critique wasn't just about the quality of the legal advocacy
that he was getting. He hated how his lawyers looked on TV. In particular, he growled over the boxy, untailored look of Castor, who wore
an oversized black pinstripe suit. "He looks like one of those old-time
movies, like Dick Tracy or something!" Trump bellowed over the
phone to Miller and Clark.

So the next morning, before the second day of the trial got under
way, Miller called up a suit shop in Washington, which, to his relief,
happened to be open. Around 8:30 A.M. a tailor arrived at the Trump
Hotel conference room on the first floor, where Trump's legal team
had been working, to take Castor's measurements. Van der Veen put
down his credit card, and a few hours later—just ahead of the 1 P.M.
start time on the Senate floor—Castor had a suit that fitted.

But it wasn't just the suit; Trump told Miller and Clark that he didn't want to see Castor go on television ever again. When the message was conveyed to Castor by Clark inside the conference room, fireworks erupted. Castor raised his voice and said it was wrong to have him sidelined, and the moment rattled some of Trump's bare-bones legal team so much that they considered quitting. Trump's aides were worried that in the middle of the trial, they would have to find replacement lawyers.

Arguments over suits and television appearances illustrated just how madcap Trump's defense team was behind the scenes, all in response to their mercurial client watching on TV hundreds of miles away.

Meanwhile Democratic prosecutors painted a ghastly picture of Trump as a leader who used violence and emotional language and promoted conspiracy theories to whip his followers into a frenzy and inspire them to storm and deface the Capitol, ruthlessly attack police officers, and threaten American democracy.

The House impeachment managers repeatedly referred to Trump's tweet on December 19—stating "Big protest in D.C. on January 6th. Be there, will be wild!"—as a "save the date" for the protests on January 6. And they connected the dots between that and other tweets, like a December 26 message from Trump that read: "The 'Justice' Department and the FBI have done nothing about the 2020 Presidential Election Voter Fraud, the biggest SCAM in our nation's history, despite overwhelming evidence. They should be ashamed. History will remember. Never give up. See everyone in D.C. on January 6th."

"He incited this attack, and he saw it coming," Representative Jamie Raskin said. "To us, it may have felt like chaos and madness. But there was method in the madness that day."

The impeachment managers zeroed in on a group of senators they believed were particularly persuadable, but one of the biggest unknowns was how Mitch McConnell would vote. He was notoriously hard to read, and had already voted in favor of Paul's measure, but some Democrats held out hope that McConnell could potentially lead the way to an impeachment vote that could end Republican bel-lyaching over Trump for good. People close to McConnell had sig-naled his support for the impeachment effort. But hopes that he would follow through with a guilty vote proved to be overly optimistic.

ON FEBRUARY 13, IN A historic bipartisan vote, fifty Democratic and seven Republican senators found Trump guilty of inciting the Janu-ary 6 insurrection on the U.S. Capitol. It was not enough to reach the conviction threshold of sixty-seven votes, and Trump was acquitted of all charges.

Toomey, who had predicted ahead of the trial that Trump would not be found guilty, voted "guilty," along with six other Republicans: Senators Richard Burr, Bill Cassidy, Susan Collins, Lisa Murkowski, Mitt Romney, and Ben Sasse. They each had some political cover for their votes. Toomey had already announced his retirement. Cassidy and Collins had just won reelection and had a six-year cushion before they might face voters again. Burr and Sasse later left the Senate, and the two least surprising Senate GOP impeachment votes came from Romney and Murkowski, both longtime Trump critics.

McConnell, meanwhile, went along with his conference and voted "not guilty." Democrats—and Republicans who wanted to see McConnell hold Trump to account—were stunned by the Republi-can leader's decision. While McConnell privately waffled over what to do, he ultimately followed the majority of the Republican confer-ence in deciding to give Trump a pass for having sparked the violence that engulfed the Capitol. Even if they believed Trump was guilty, it was clear that some feared alienating his base of supporters, who had elected them and would be relied on in the 2022 midterms.

So instead of voting to convict and giving permission to the rest of his conference to follow suit, McConnell decided to focus on damaging Trump's legacy in a blistering speech on the Senate floor. "January sixth was a disgrace. American citizens attacked their own government. They used terrorism to try to stop a specific piece of domestic business they did not like. Fellow Americans beat and blood-ied our own police. They stormed the Senate floor. They tried to hunt down the Speaker of the House. They built a gallows and chanted about murdering the vice president. They did this because they had been fed wild falsehoods by the most powerful man on earth—because he was angry he'd lost an election," McConnell said.

"Let me just put that aside for a moment and reiterate something I said weeks ago: There is no question—none—that President Trump is practically and morally responsible for provoking the events of the day," McConnell continued. "The people who stormed this building believed they were acting on the wishes and instructions of their president.

"The leader of the free world cannot spend weeks thundering that shadowy forces are stealing our country and then feign surprise when people believe him and do reckless things. Sadly, many politi-cians sometimes make overheated comments or use metaphors—we saw that—that unhinged listeners might take literally. But that was different.

"This was an intensifying crescendo of conspiracy theories, or-chestrated by an outgoing president who seemed determined to either overturn the voters' decision or else torch our institutions on the way out."

In the end, McConnell qualified his "not guilty" vote by saying, "I believe the Senate was right not to grab power the Constitution doesn't give us."

In that moment, McConnell was done with Trump—something he made clear in his speech—and echoed what many Republicans were saying privately about the actions of the former president fol-lowing the 2020 election. But the speech angered Democrats and frustrated Republicans who knew Trump was guilty but watched him, once again, get off scot-free.

House Speaker Nancy Pelosi called a press conference after McConnell's remarks to slam him and other Republicans for acting "cowardly." "That the President of the Senate, Mike Pence—'Hang

Mike Pence' was the chant and they just dismissed that. Why? Because maybe they can't get another job. What is so important about any one of us? What is so important about the political survival of any one of us that is more important than our Constitution that we take an oath to protect and defend?" Pelosi said.

And she called McConnell's bluff for refusing to expedite an impeachment trial while Trump was in office only to turn around and say that he wouldn't convict because Trump was no longer in office.

"For Mitch McConnell—who created the situation where it could not have been heard before the twentieth, or even begun before the twentieth, in the Senate—to say all the things he said, oh my gosh, about Donald Trump and how horrible he was and is, and then say, 'But that's the time that the House chose to bring it over'—Oh, no. We didn't choose. You chose not to receive it," Pelosi said.

McConnell's speech aside, his vote that day and the overall sentiment of the Republican Party demonstrated just how intertwined the fate of the GOP had become with Trump. Republicans did not want to cross the former president or alienate his supporters, whom they would need in order to win in the upcoming primaries.

McConnell was asked two weeks later by Fox News's Bret Baier if he would support Trump for president again if he were the party's nominee in 2024. McConnell did not hesitate for a second.

"The nominee of the party? Absolutely."

IF TRUMP'S NEXT POLITICAL STEP wasn't clear immediately after he left the White House, it had crystallized by the end of Trump's impeachment trial: taking down Representative Liz Cheney in the 2022 midterm election.

Cheney, the number three House Republican and daughter of former vice president Dick Cheney, had become the face of opposition to Trump, his behavior following the 2020 election, and his baseless allegations of election fraud.

Cheney had a target on her back for over a month. During

Trump's speech in front of the White House on the morning of January 6, Trump specifically called for her removal from office. "We got to get rid of the weak congresspeople, the ones that aren't any good, the Liz Cheneys of the world," Trump said to a cheering crowd.

The moment was so disturbing to Cheney's father, the former vice president, that he called her while she was in the cloakroom of the Capitol to tell her about Trump's comments. His message to his daughter, just hours before rioters stormed the Capitol: "You're in danger."

Cheney represented Wyoming, a state Trump won with almost 70 percent of the vote. She stood by Trump as the Republican nominee after the *Access Hollywood* tape came out in 2016, saying that what Hillary Clinton did by handling sensitive emails on a private server was worse, and Cheney endorsed Trump's reelection in 2020. She even served as a surrogate for Trump during the Iowa caucuses in 2020. Trump returned the favor over the years, praising Cheney as "a friend of mine, and a wonderful person, and somebody that has, I don't know, a pretty unlimited future."

But that quickly changed in the aftermath of the 2020 election, when she watched with disgust as Trump bucked democratic norms and spread "the big lie"—that he had not lost the election. Cheney wrote a twenty-one-page memo to fellow House Republicans warning them against objecting to Electoral College votes, and she called on Republicans to listen to Trump's "deeply troubling" call with Georgia secretary of state Brad Raffensperger during which he asked him to "find" enough votes to overturn the election results.

On January 13, Cheney joined nine other Republicans—Reps. Peter Meijer of Michigan, Fred Upton of Michigan, Tom Rice of South Carolina, Anthony Gonzalez of Ohio, Adam Kinzinger of Illinois, John Katko of New York, Jaime Herrera Beutler of Washington, Dan Newhouse of Washington, and David Valadao of California—in voting to impeach the president over the events of January 6.

After the House officially voted to impeach Trump and set the stage for the Senate trial, the president was briefed on the votes—one by one—by his political director, Brian Jack. But of all the Republicans who voted to impeach Trump, it was Cheney whose decision stung the worst.

"The President of the United States summoned this mob, assembled the mob, and lit the flame of this attack," Cheney said in a statement. "Everything that followed was his doing. None of this would have happened without the President. The President could have immediately and forcefully intervened to stop the violence. He did not. There has never been a greater betrayal by a President of the United States of his office and his oath to the Constitution."

The former president and his team zeroed in on her reelection campaign as the best way to seek revenge.

Trump's team and his Save America PAC commissioned new polling that showed how Cheney's impeachment vote made her vulnerable in the 2022 midterm election. A decisive defeat of Cheney, they believed, would not only send a message to any other Republican who decided to cross Trump, but would pave the way for his 2024 return.

I Want It That Way

DONALD TRUMP'S LIFE HAD ALWAYS BEEN GUIDED BY CHAOS, AND AT MAR-a-Lago he was like a spinning top losing momentum, without any clear sense of direction. Being erratic and constantly in motion often worked to Trump's advantage—no one was ever able to pin him down before he would spin off to the next thing. But it was clear to the very small group of people still orbiting Trump that no one was in charge and that someone needed to impose some semblance of order on his post–White House life.

Trump had found himself in low places before. In the 1980s he fashioned himself as a great titan of real estate and business, and yet he would file for bankruptcy multiple times in the 1990s. In his 1997 book *The Art of the Comeback,* he outlined ten rules for bouncing back from personal and business failures: play golf, stay focused, be paranoid, be passionate, go against the tide, go with your guy, work with people you like, be lucky, get even, and always have a prenuptial agreement.

Now at his personal and political nadir, "play golf," "be paranoid," and "get even" seemed the most relevant to Trump. "During the bad times, I learned who was loyal and who wasn't. I believe in an eye for an eye," he wrote in *The Art of the Comeback*. "A couple of people who betrayed me need my help now, and I am screwing them against the wall!"

Back in Palm Beach, he was torn between wanting to launch his reputational rehab, exacting revenge on the GOP, and simply keeping a low profile, cosseted in his club. As the horrors of January 6 continued to dominate headlines, he told aides that for the time being he was content to keep to his typical Florida routine.

In the mornings, Trump would pile into a black SUV for a short drive off Palm Beach island to Trump International Golf Club in West Palm Beach. As he zipped around the course in a golf cart wearing his signature red hat, he would dial up friends between holes to brag about how far he was hitting his drives, or stop to gossip with club members or take a photo. After lunch with his golf partners—a rotating cast of club members and New York financiers, lawmakers who had made the pilgrimage to kiss the ring, and even celebrities like Kid Rock—he would change out of his golf polo and into a sport coat and return to Mar-a-Lago. From the ornate gilded living room where he was on display for the rich and perfectly coiffed old blond ladies who showed up early for dinner, Trump would take phone calls or quiz staff about renovation details and membership numbers.

During this period, Trump evinced no interest in the duties that have in the modern era become associated with a former president. Never one to feel the pull of public obligations or the need to observe conventions, Trump in exile seemed to adopt an almost hostile disregard for both.

The disarray in Palm Beach had been months in the making. Preparing for Trump's post-presidency had been an afterthought during the chaotic final days in the White House. As provided for by the Presidential Transition Act of 1963, $2.6 million was made available by the General Services Administration to Trump and Vice President Mike Pence to pay for staffing, office space, and miscellaneous office needs like printers and postage in the first six months post–White House.

Mark Meadows, Trump's chief of staff—who had been preoccupied with efforts to overturn the election—had delayed signing the necessary paperwork to release funds to lock down transition office space for Trump's and Pence's teams until January 11.

And so the bulk of the post-presidency logistics fell on the shoulders of junior staff—Trump's scheduler Molly Michael, Desiree Thompson Sayle, a White House aide who had also worked in the Bush administration, Trump's former personal aide Nick Luna, and White House operations aide William "Beau" Harrison, one of the young aides who would move down to Palm Beach to be a part of the "45 Office" staff. Working with the General Services Administration, Harrison, Michael, Luna, and Sayle tried to stand up an office and tend to basics, like payroll, computers, and places for everyone to sit.

When Trump arrived in Palm Beach, there was no official space where he could work, or even designated Wi-Fi for his staff. There wasn't anyone ready to unload moving trucks at Mar-a-Lago. Trump's private living quarters were a mess, with boxes upon boxes of personal items from not only the White House but Trump Tower and racks of clothing lined up in hallways throughout the residence. It was all described by one Trump aide as "unsettled, chaotic, unplanned, sad—all of that on steroids."

Michael and Luna were credited by aides with working around the clock to try to make some kind of order out of the chaos and set up Trump's office. Trump initially balked at the idea of creating a work space at Mar-a-Lago one flight of stairs above the ballroom, where charity events and weddings were regularly held and band sound checks would vibrate the walls. Michael and Luna picked out furniture and designed the space with an eye to creating an office that looked like an extension of the West Wing.

A large wooden desk—almost as large as the Resolute Desk in the Oval Office—sat in front of a window overlooking palm trees and Trump's property, with family photos and a collection of challenge coins displayed on nearby tables. On the walls were oversized framed photos of Air Force One flying over Washington and the presidential helicopter flying past Mount Rushmore during a July 4 celebration; once on display in the West Wing, they represented the power and pomp of the presidency, which Trump loved.

But there was no valet or special button that would immediately bring him a Diet Coke. There was no switchboard operator who would dial his calls. (One person close to Trump recalled their cell-phone ringing with an unknown Florida number. They did not pick up, but later learned it was Trump.) He no longer had access to Air Force One. And he was surrounded by a bare-bones staff of paid and unpaid advisers, as many of his close aides had taken other jobs and were no longer at his beck and call. One of the few signs that a former president lived at Mar-a-Lago was a model of Air Force One—bearing his new, never-to-be-implemented color scheme—prominently on display in the main living room of the club.

Trump would get a nightly boost from attention on the patio. On Valentine's Day, he received a standing ovation as he and Melania walked into the room, then allowed club guests to take selfies with him, along with Donald Trump Jr. and his fiancée, Kimberly Guil-foyle, the former Fox News personality.

But he still craved the daily sparring and self-generated headlines from engaging with the press. In the early months, Trump repeatedly asked his team to summon a press pool—a group of reporters and photographers who travel with a president—to Mar-a-Lago. An aide asked a former Trump White House reporter if they could come down to Mar-a-Lago to cover Trump, and if there was still a Trump pool, and then had the perilous task of informing the former president that no, press pools are for presidents, not formers.

During the presidency, those around Trump knew that a bored Trump could be a restless and reckless Trump. Aides would come to fear the early morning hours, particularly on a Saturday, when the president was alone and prone to tweeting out his thoughts and some-times market-moving ideas or complaints into the ether while much of America was still asleep. The world would wake up to the news cycle that Trump had made. But down in Palm Beach, stripped of Twitter, where would his energy go?

To keep Trump connected to the world beyond club walls, Trump's aides would set up dinners with political advisers and allies. John McLaughlin, a longtime Republican pollster, and former Florida attorney general Pam Bondi were early guests, as was Trump's former Florida senior adviser, Susie Wiles.

He would pepper them with questions about polling or his political rivals. But with Wiles, what he wanted to know was quite specific: How did they win Florida, but lose so many other states? And how could he win again?

ON A WARM FEBRUARY EVENING, Susie Wiles arrived well prepared for dinner with Donald Trump.

During the 2020 election, Wiles was put in charge of winning the state of Florida. She had held the same role in 2016, and the second time around managed to help Trump widen his margin in the state by two percentage points. Following the election, Wiles put together an exhaustive after-action report on Florida, chock-full of data and information about how people and resources were used throughout the state. Businesslike and organized, Wiles wanted to have detailed documentation of the campaign.

Sitting at Trump's table on the patio at Mar-a-Lago, Wiles went page by page through her findings with Trump over dinner and Diet Coke.

Wiles was a shrewd political operator, but disarming in her appearance and demeanor. A grandmother in her sixties, she had short blond hair and a warm smile, and liked to bring up her dog and grandson in conversation. She was known for checking in on people working around her, was quick to give credit, and developed a loyal following among several top political operatives in the state— relationships Trump would later benefit from in his 2024 bid.

Throughout 2020, she had been the only state director during the campaign to send nightly reports on the state of play in Florida. Still trying to make sense of the election, Trump spent their two hours together asking detailed questions about what had worked, but also about what had gone wrong.

The former president was eager to understand at a granular level why he was no longer in the White House. And even though their dinner took place in early 2021, the subtext of his line of questioning was *How can I do this again and win?*

Wiles believed the conversation would be one of the few opportunities she had to be blunt about the 2020 campaign, so she laid out what she thought was a critical weakness in their operation.

One of the main reasons they had been successful in Florida, she said, was that she was from the state and knew the laws and the people. In the 2020 campaign, she explained, there were too many staffers who were dispatched to places where they didn't understand their own environment, let alone the electorate, and so when things inevitably went wrong, they did not have the connections or resources to fix them.

And she would know. Doing just that—knowing who the players are and building relationships in the world of politics—was something Wiles had worked hard at for decades.

By the end of their dinner, Trump told Susie Wiles that he was getting ready to start another super PAC.

"Would you like to be on its board?" Trump asked Wiles. She agreed.

The daughter of Pat Summerall, the former NFL player turned legendary sportscaster, Wiles grew up in the world of sports and fame. She cut her teeth in politics in 1979, working for Representative Jack Kemp, a New York Republican and former teammate of her father's, before joining Ronald Reagan's 1980 presidential campaign. In the first year of Reagan's White House, Wiles was a scheduler before moving over to the Labor Department.

At the very start of her career, she got a front-row seat to the masters of crafting a political image. Among the people Wiles worked closely with in the White House was Michael Deaver, a close aide to Reagan who was known as a "visuals guru" and "media maestro" and who changed the modern presidency with his carefully choreographed photo ops and meticulous attention to the president's image.

Wiles went on to work for the presidential campaign of George H. W. Bush before settling near Jacksonville, Florida, to be closer to her family.

She took the lessons she learned working for Reagan and Bush to start her own public affairs firm, where she gained a reputation as a top political consultant for the northeastern part of the state. She ran Republican representative Tillie Fowler's office in Jacksonville and later managed the successful campaigns of several Jacksonville mayors. She was never wed to any particular type of Republican and worked for every stripe under the "R" tent.

In 2010, Wiles was introduced to Rick Scott, a wealthy healthcare executive and Tea Party favorite who planned to use his millions to propel a long-shot, last-minute bid for the governor's mansion, and signed on as his campaign manager. There were others from Scott's campaign who would come back to serve in top roles for Trump, including pollsters Tony Fabrizio and John McLaughlin. After Scott won his race, she jumped to the presidential campaign of Jon Huntsman Jr., a businessman and former governor of Utah, before bowing out after one month, eventually signing on with the Florida campaign of the 2012 GOP nominee, Mitt Romney. Romney would narrowly lose the state to Barack Obama.

She worked with the Florida lobbyist Brian Ballard before taking her next step—joining Trump's presidential campaign in 2016. Trump did not have anyone in Florida when he announced his 2016 run for president, and he had asked Ballard if he knew someone for the job. He did: It was Wiles, who, coincidentally enough, had recently reached out to Ballard after seeing Trump's announcement and said she thought Trump had something special and could win the presidency. After a meeting with Trump at his eponymous high-rise in Manhattan, Wiles joined his campaign.

The move raised eyebrows in national Republican circles. Wiles went from working for two members of Mormon GOP royalty to working for Trump at the encouragement and recommendation of some close to Trump, including then-governor Rick Scott. It was a trajectory that Wiles herself felt the need to explain away.

At the time, Wiles wrote in an email that was published by *The New York Times,* "As a card-carrying member of the GOP establishment, many thought my full-throated endorsement of the Trump candidacy was ill advised—even crazy."

And yet Wiles signed on, giving his outsider campaign serious bona fides among the political class in Tallahassee. And when Senator Marco Rubio ran for reelection after being humiliated by Trump, it was Wiles who was a conduit between the two as the Trump and Rubio camps tried to bandage the wounds.

Wiles once came close to quitting. During a dinner with Trump, former New York mayor Rudolph Giuliani, and campaign aides at Trump National Doral in Miami, Wiles asked for a large check to help with direct mail as they chased ballots in the state. The news that he was behind and the request that he write a hefty six-figure check set Trump off. He berated Wiles in front of everyone at the dinner, in a blowup that left Wiles shocked and rattled, and aides wondering if Trump was going to fire her.

The next day, Trump was holding his last fundraiser of 2016 at Mar-a-Lago and saw Ballard, who he knew was close to Wiles. "Your girl doesn't have it," Trump said. Ballard told Trump he was wrong. Wiles needed the check—and badly—for direct mail. "Okay," Trump said. "But if I lose Florida it's on you," he added, pointing his finger at Ballard.

That 2016 hiccup aside, Trump had an affinity for Wiles. He liked that her father was the celebrity television sportscaster, and respected her opinion as someone who had won in Florida before. And it was because she was a successful person in her own right that Wiles was of particular value to Trump. She didn't need him the way that so many in his orbit did—often desperately. And because she wasn't a sycophant, she seemed to understand him with a rare clarity, as the strange and complicated human he was. Unlike so many others around Trump, she wasn't afraid to tell him bracing truths that he didn't want to hear.

It wasn't the first time she had confronted a powerful man. She had watched as her famous father, who died in 2013, struggled with his own demons. In 1992, she was part of an intervention that her father credited with saving his life from alcoholism. In his autobiography, he wrote about his close friends and daughter describing his embarrassing behavior when he was drunk. She told him in words that, he wrote, made him weep "tears of regret" that his alcoholism made her feel "ashamed we shared the same last name." His daughter's words prompted Summerall to check into the Betty Ford Clinic in Palm Springs, California, for treatment and get sober.

Wiles continued her winning record in Florida when she stepped in to run the campaign of Ron DeSantis, a young Florida congressman who had set his sights on the governor's mansion but was floundering after an unexpected primary victory. Florida Republican representative Matt Gaetz, a Trump loyalist through and through, recommended Wiles for the job, and with just one month remaining before Election Day, she delivered DeSantis a win.

If Wiles made one mistake, it was sticking around the Florida Republican Party after successfully installing DeSantis in Tallahassee. She stayed on with Ballard Partners, the lobbying and public affairs firm, and was set to play a critical role in Trump's reelection efforts in the state. But DeSantis and his wife, Casey DeSantis, had other plans. According to multiple people working in Florida politics at the time, they were deeply suspicious that Wiles had so much influence in the state party and believed she was more loyal to Trump than to them. They were also suspicious of political advisers making money off their proximity to the governor.

To prove their point, the DeSantises ordered an audit of the Republican Party of Florida and hired an investigator with close ties to billionaire Ike Perlmutter, the former chair of Marvel Entertainment. The report wasn't published because nothing was found.

In September 2019, the *Tampa Bay Times* broke a story about an internal DeSantis campaign committee memo that outlined ways the governor could raise money and make powerful connections with lobbyists in the state, including $25,000-per-person golf fundraisers. The story wasn't a good look for the young governor who had higher ambitions. Without any evidence, DeSantis and his wife blamed Wiles for leaking the memo to the paper. She had written the fundraising memo that was splashed across the front page of the paper, but vehemently denied playing a role in the story.

Two people close to Wiles suggested that the DeSantises were still annoyed by a different memo Wiles had presented to them at the governor's mansion outlining the laws and ethics of gifts, especially because there had been issues with the family accepting inappropriate gifts from GOP donors, such as a golf simulator that was installed in the governor's mansion in 2019.

But Wiles's denials didn't stop the DeSantises from going out of their way to try to make her unemployable in Florida politics. The new governor started a whisper campaign about her, making it clear that as long as he was governor, Ballard Partners would have a hard time retaining clients if she remained employed there. Seasoned Florida political hands were astonished at the degree of DeSantis's vindictiveness. He was blackballing Wiles, trying to kill her ability to earn a living anywhere in the state.

Wiles eventually stepped down from Ballard Partners, citing personal health reasons. "Due to a nagging health issue, it's time for me to focus on taking care of myself, so out of fairness to the firm and its clients, I have decided to separate from Ballard Partners," she wrote in a statement shared with the Sunshine State political blog Florida Politics. One person close to Wiles said that she simply understood that the friction between her and the governor was a distraction, and she was personally feeling the stress and pressure from it all.

But the DeSantises' crusade against Wiles continued. The same month that the *Tampa Bay Times* story broke, DeSantis personally called Trump to ask him to fire Wiles.

The episode left her shell-shocked. But that thin-skinned heavy-handedness would come to mark DeSantis, and soon enough would become his fatal flaw. After all, Wiles had worked in Florida politics for decades before DeSantis had come on the scene.

Wiles kept a low profile for the next several months. But when Trump's campaign was losing juice in Florida in the summer of 2020, Trump asked his closest advisers, people like Bill Stepien, Kellyanne Conway, David Bossie, and Michael Caputo, about who they should bring on to recreate the "magic" of 2016. Only one name kept coming up: Susie Wiles. And yet DeSantis would try to block her again.

In a phone call, DeSantis told Trump that he'd heard the Trump campaign was thinking about hiring Wiles. You shouldn't, DeSantis said.

Stepien, Trump's campaign manager, was patched in to the call and said yes, it's true. "We are thinking about hiring her."

DeSantis told Trump and Stepien that he thought Wiles lied and leaked to the press. "Fair enough," Stepien replied. "But you won, and so did Donald Trump in Florida in 2016."

Trump made the final decision. "We're hiring Susie." She was back in the fold by the beginning of July.

THE MOST IMMEDIATE PROSPECT FOR reasserting control over his party—which would also double as a test of rank-and-file fidelity to him and his MAGA movement—would be picking and choosing among the GOP candidates announcing for office in 2022 and issuing a battery of his trademark "complete and total" endorsements. But without any kind of process in place for Trump to make endorsements, he had already begun to endorse candidates haphazardly, doling out his support to Republicans that Donald Trump Jr. and some of his aides viewed as "squishy," or not sufficiently MAGA, like Kansas senator Jerry Moran, who in their view had been too critical of Trump's trade policies and was not sufficiently loyal.

At the end of February, his closest remaining political advisers were summoned to Mar-a-Lago to start charting out how they would approach things like endorsements.

It was a strange and empty time at Trump's club. COVID-19 had scared off some of its members (the next month, the club would be temporarily shut down by an outbreak of the coronavirus). Other members had left after Trump's 2020 loss and January 6, when it became clear to them the hefty membership fee was worthwhile only when Trump was in power. At the time, being associated with someone who inspired a bloody attack on the Capitol didn't have the same social clout as being associated with a president.

The meeting was held in the empty tea room at Mar-a-Lago, a dining room just off the main living room. Trump's former campaign managers, Brad Parscale and Bill Stepien; Justin Clark, a lawyer and deputy campaign manager; trusted advisor Dan Scavino; Jason Miller; and Corey Lewandowski sat in banquet chairs around a table with a white tablecloth. After working in the White House and on Trump's 2020 campaign, they found the setup oddly informal.

There was no set agenda. No one was in charge, and—unusual for Trumpworld—no one was angling to be. Trump wanted to be a political Godzilla, but at the moment he barely had the capacity to send out an email, let alone fundraise. Among the top priorities they discussed that afternoon was sorting out who was going to do mail, and some kind of process for making endorsements, so as to block people from pushing their friends on Trump. Word had already gotten back to Trump Jr. that Senator Lindsey Graham, Trump's ally and golfing buddy, had been lobbying endorsements.

For those who had worked for Trump since 2016, having clearly delineated roles and responsibilities was a novel concept—an exciting change of pace, actually.

And even if not much came from the meeting beyond an online process for candidates to make endorsement requests and a weekly call, there was also the sense in the group that if Jared Kushner had run things in 2020, it was Donald Trump Jr. who was going to assume a larger role moving forward.

Kushner and Trump's son were both wealthy, Ivy League–educated men, born just three years apart, but they had different views of the world. After Kushner he served as a top adviser to Trump in the White House, he and his wife, Trump's daughter Ivanka, were eager to move on and reingratiate themselves with the jet-set New York crowd, while Trump Jr. looked forward to disappearing into the wilderness of Pennsylvania to hunt deer and was eager to make his own mark on the MAGA movement.

Don Jr., as he was referred to, made clear that when it came to his dad's political capital, they needed to be scrupulous: Unless Trump was getting something in return, or unless the candidate in question proved they were true believers or allies, Trump wasn't going to give out his endorsement.

One idea came from Andy Surabian, a Republican strategist who had worked on Trump's 2016 campaign as war-room director under Steve Bannon and went on to work closely with Don Jr. He suggested that candidates answer a one-page questionnaire about their positions on issues like immigration and foreign policy, and whether they would endorse Trump if he ran again in 2024. Everyone loved the idea, and questions were drafted. But the idea was later scrapped by Trump himself.

Trump's small team of advisers also needed to figure out fundraising vehicles that could drop money into upcoming midterm races. Save America, a leadership PAC, was formed right after the election, and Trump planned to use that to pay for staff and political expenses. In addition to Save America, a new super PAC, Make America Great

Again Action, was created to raise and spend an unlimited amount of money on advertising in upcoming midterm races.

Trump had just announced his first endorsements—for Sarah Huckabee Sanders, the White House press secretary turned gubernatorial candidate in Arkansas, and for Moran in Kansas—but he was eager to start endorsing more and was hell-bent on upending the campaigns of the Republicans who supported his impeachment or who he felt had crossed him in the 2020 election.

Trump endorsed Max Miller, a former White House aide who announced he was running against Representative Anthony Gonzalez of Ohio, one of the ten House members who had voted for Trump's impeachment. Miller was close to Trump and the entire Trump operation—in August 2022 he got married and received a toast from Trump at his Bedminster club. It kicked off an avalanche of endorsements Trump would roll out over the coming months, sometimes at random, and not always in complete agreement with his circle of advisers.

But one race and one endorsement emerged as top priority for Trump—where they couldn't afford to elevate the wrong person—and it was the Wyoming Republican primary against Liz Cheney. For the next year, it would be an all-hands-on-deck effort to identify and elevate a competitive candidate that could take down Cheney, the one Republican who dared to stand up against Trump and challenge the former president on January 6 and his falsehoods about the 2020 election. Trump's political fate, they believed, rested on taking Cheney down.

Two weeks after Wiles's dinner with Trump, he frantically called and asked her to return to Mar-a-Lago for another meeting.

Wiles, who lived four hours away in Ponte Vedra Beach, had gotten in her car for the long drive down the coast to Palm Beach when Trump called again.

"It's a fucking mess," Trump said, sounding exasperated. "I don't know who's in charge. I don't know how much money I have. I don't know if they're stealing from me. I don't know who's who. I need you to fix it."

The sudden job offer in early March took Wiles by surprise. Although she had worked for Trump twice, and had seen him a few times over the years while he was president, she didn't consider herself part of the inner circle, someone like Kellyanne Conway or Corey Lewandowski. She wasn't a household name or a regular on Fox News. And while she was always grateful to Trump for bringing her back into the fold in 2020, she currently had a job she didn't want to leave.

"It'll just take you a couple weeks," Trump explained. "Just get it straight."

Except that getting Trump's current operation in line, from fundraising to personnel, didn't take two weeks—it took around two months.

After Wiles did a thorough review of his political operation, she drove back down to Palm Beach for a meeting with Trump to brief him on everything she had put together on the money he had available to him, who he needed to hire, and who he didn't need working for him. If Trump ever needed someone who was experienced and competent, it was then. Trump agreed to all of her suggestions on the spot.

And there was the added benefit that unlike many of the people who had surrounded Trump for decades, Wiles never asked to be compensated for her work. According to CNN, she only requested reimbursement for her travel expenses when she accepted the job. It was a breath of fresh air for Trump and his family.

Wiles—much to the relief of Trump's family, who viewed her as trustworthy, and his longtime aides, who were happy to see an adult in the room—was now in charge.

WAITING BACKSTAGE AT THE Conservative Political Action Committee's annual conference in Orlando on February 28, Donald Trump looked in the mirror and fixed his hair with a puff of hairspray. Next to him, a man working the event wore a medical-grade face mask, a reminder that the deadly coronavirus pandemic was not over.

Trump typically checked his look in a mirror before heading into an event, and on windy days would don one of his trademark red hats to protect his carefully constructed coif. But this evening there was a bit more pressure than usual to make sure everything was just right.

It was Trump's first public appearance since leaving the White House. And Trump and his team were concerned, of course, about crowd sizes and the optics of the event.

As Trump rode down the highway from the Orlando airport to the Hyatt Regency Orlando, where CPAC was being held, he was surprised to see that the state police had closed down the roads for his arrival, even though he was no longer president. "It put a little wind in the sails" before the event, according to an aide. It was the first time Trump had traveled beyond Palm Beach County, and he was impressed that his presence could still require the heightened security he had become accustomed to in the White House.

Trump was expected to talk about his vision for the GOP and attack President Joe Biden's agenda. What many Republican leaders and even some in his own circle did not want him to do was hark back to his unfounded claims of 2020 being a "rigged" election, or anything that could possibly make him even more of a target for prosecutors, who had started their investigations into the lead-up to January 6.

Even the Republican strategist Karl Rove—a frequent critic of Trump—tried to encourage him to focus on Biden, not on his grievances and gripes, in a *Wall Street Journal* op-ed ahead of the speech. "Leaders who come out of the wilderness after defeat do so by changing their approach and re-creating themselves. It's unclear whether Mr. Trump has the ability to change, especially after a defeat that left him embittered and isolated. What are the odds Mr. Trump takes the more constructive second tack? His choice Sunday will tell us a lot about his future and what the GOP will face in the next few years," Rove wrote.

But Trump was never going to heed anyone's advice and he rarely stuck to the script. At CPAC, it didn't matter.

CPAC during the Trump years had transformed from an essential conservative grassroots conference to a kind of Trumpfest. And at CPAC 2021, held in Florida instead of Maryland due to COVID-19 restrictions, Trump was still king. There was a giant golden statue of Trump that was moved around the Orlando venue and that fans wearing rhinestone-encrusted MAGA hats and Trump T-shirts would wait to have a chance for a photoshoot with. At almost every turn, there were signs supporting Trump.

For decades, the annual conference sponsored by the American Conservative Union set the tone for the conservative movement, and right-wing stars were made onstage. The first keynote speaker of the conference in 1974 was Ronald Reagan, and since then the confab has helped launch political careers with the mix of speeches, dinners, panels, and opportunities for grassroots organizers and talking heads to rub elbows with elected officials and aspirants.

Having claimed an interest in running for president since the late 1980s, Trump had made his debut at the conference in 2011, where he previewed some of the banner themes of his presidential campaigns, saying "our country will be great again," and was considered the most popular speaker of the weekend.

But this time, if the Republican leaders were looking for signs that the party was willing to move on, they would not find them in the sprawling convention halls in Florida.

Former vice president Mike Pence declined an invitation to speak at the conference after the violent mob at the Capitol threatened to hang him for breaking with Trump. Those who did speak—especially those with presidential ambitions—made sure to declare, like Florida governor Ron DeSantis, that the current movement would "never return to the Republican establishment of yesteryear."

"Let me tell you right now," said Senator Ted Cruz of Texas, "Donald J. Trump ain't goin' anywhere."

Before walking onstage, Trump took note of the CPAC straw poll results that had just been announced by John McLaughlin, his pollster. When those in the room were asked who they wanted to run for president in 2024, Trump won 55 percent, while DeSantis came in second with 21 percent.

And while the CPAC speech could have given Trump the opportunity to look forward, it was clear he did not listen to the warnings of some in the GOP to avoid talking about the 2020 election and widen the splits in the party. He wanted to assert that it was his party, and he had plenty of grievances to share—which were wholly embraced by the cheering crowd.

"Hello, CPAC. Do you miss me yet?" Trump said with a grin, as chants of "USA! USA!" filled the room.

The speech that followed showcased Trump's dominance over the party and his total disregard for trying to heal any old wounds. Instead he ripped them back open and for ninety minutes went one by one through his own enemies list, which included President Joe Biden, Democrats, Twitter and Big Tech, RINOs, and establishment Republicans Trump claimed were trying to stand in his way.

To the relief of party leaders like McDaniel and McCarthy, Trump announced that reports he would form a third party were "fake news" and predicted the GOP would "unite and be stronger than ever before."

But he went on to call the Republicans that voted for his impeachment "grandstanders" who "will destroy the Republican Party and the American worker, and will destroy our country itself." There weren't divisions in the Republican Party, Trump said, but divisions between "a handful of Washington, D.C., establishment political hacks, and everybody else all over the country."

One by one Trump read off the names of Republicans who had voted to impeach him as though it was a hit list, pausing to allow the audience boos to reverberate throughout the hall and adding particular emphasis to the name of the third-ranking House Republican, Liz Cheney. "Warmonger," Trump seethed. "The good news is in her state, she's been censured, and in her state, her poll numbers have dropped faster than any human being I've ever seen. So hopefully they'll get rid of her with the next election."

But, ignoring advice, Trump veered off script and fanned conspiracies about election fraud, the falsehood that the election was rigged against him and he had not lost.

"I may even decide to beat them for a third time. Okay? For a third time. True," Trump said, even though he lost the second time. "You cannot have a situation where ballots are indiscriminately pouring in from all over the country, tens of millions of ballots. Where are they coming from? They're coming all over the place, where illegal aliens and dead people are voting, and many other horrible things are happening that are too voluminous to even mention. I mean, it's being studied, and the level of dishonesty is not to be believed. We have a very sick and corrupt electoral process that must be fixed immediately. This election was rigged, and the Supreme Court and other courts didn't want to do anything about it."

The crowd erupted into chants of "You won, you won, you won, you won!"

"We did," Trump responded.

For Trump and the small team still working with him, the speech provided an important data point: Not only did he attract a large crowd and win the straw poll, he raked in serious money. The same day as his speech, online donations poured in.

"EVERYONE GO GET YOUR SHOT," Trump said to the crowd during his speech at CPAC. Trump hailed Operation Warp Speed, the public-private partnership that supported the fast development of COVID-19 vaccines, as a "modern medical miracle," and rattled off statistics about how many million Americans had received the coronavirus vaccine.

"We took care of a lot of people, including, I guess on December twenty-first, we took care of Joe Biden. 'Cause he got his shot. He got his vaccine. He forgot. It shows you how unpainful all that vaccine shot is. So everybody go get your shot," Trump said. "He got his shot, and it's good that he got his shot." What was left unsaid, but revealed the next day, was that Trump and the First Lady had also secretly received the vaccine.

While Trump was in the White House, it had remained a mystery whether he would get the shot his administration worked hard to produce. Trump had a severe case of COVID-19 as president that sent him to Walter Reed for days. White House reporters had been told it was unlikely Trump would get the shot while he was still president because he still had antibodies from his last infection. Besides, they admitted in private, Trump did not want the image of his bare arm being projected out to the world. Instead, other public officials like Vice President Mike Pence literally rolled up their sleeves to be vaccinated on camera.

It was notable, then, when just a few weeks later a new public service announcement was released featuring all the other living former presidents and First Ladies encouraging the public to receive vaccinations. Barack Obama, Bill Clinton, and George W. Bush met on the sidelines of Biden's inauguration to film a commercial encouraging the public to get a shot.

Trump advisers said he had never been formally asked to appear in the ad, but there had been ongoing discussions from the time he was in the White House and after about how to get him to engage on a subject that so many of his supporters had spun into conspiracies.

Trump tried to straddle both sides, saying positive things about the vaccines, a major breakthrough during his time in office, but not going so far as to alienate his supporters. Instead he started bucking mandates—and not vaccines.

During an interview with Fox Business host Maria Bartiromo in mid-March, Trump said that he would "recommend" that people get the vaccine. It was the first time he admitted that he was in fact inoculated.

"I would recommend it to a lot of people that don't want to get it and a lot of those people voted for me, frankly," Trump said. "But again, we have our freedoms and we have to live by that and I agree with that also. But it is a great vaccine. It is a safe vaccine and it is something that works."

Trump understood that the remarkable scientific achievement of the vaccine could be a significant part of his legacy—but he was also acutely aware that many in his base were vaccine skeptics. A healthy dosage of misinformation had been administered online since the start of the pandemic—some of it spread by Trump himself and close allies—and vaccination rates fell along party lines. A report by the Kaiser Family Foundation found that while vaccination rate gaps across ethnic and racial lines narrowed by the end of 2021, they widened according to political affiliation: Ninety percent of Democrats had been vaccinated, compared with 68 percent of independents and just 58 percent of Republicans.

FOR ALL OF DONALD TRUMP's talk of unity and his promise during his CPAC speech not to form a third party, there was one line that made Republican officials raise their eyebrows: "There's only one way to contribute to our efforts," Trump declared, "and that's through Save America PAC, and DonaldJTrump.com."

Trump was a fundraising juggernaut. After the CPAC speech, more than $3 million poured into Save America, Trump's leadership committee, in one of its biggest single-day hauls. The group already had over $80 million.

The marketing wiz who had slapped the Trump name on everything from steaks and wine to golf balls and hotel rooms had taken note of the fact that his face and name were showing up on materials sent out by three major arms of the GOP: the Republican National Committee, the National Republican Senatorial Committee, and the National Republican Congressional Committee.

Just days after Trump called for donations to be sent directly to Trump entities, his attorney Alex Cannon sent cease-and-desist letters to the RNC and the other committees. Using legalese, he made clear there would be no more fundraising off Trump's grinning smile and blond hair, his calls to "Make America Great Again," his impeachments or legal headaches.

But the request appeared to be mostly bark and no bite. In a phone call after the letter was sent, Trump assured McDaniel that in actuality, he still planned to support the RNC and wasn't trying to block any donations or donor outreach.

"The R.N.C., of course, has every right to refer to public figures as it engages in core, First Amendment–protected political speech, and it will continue to do so in pursuit of those common goals," the chief counsel for the RNC Justin Reimer wrote back to Save America. He added that Trump and McDaniel "enjoy a close relationship, and we understand that President Trump reaffirmed to her over the weekend that he approves of the RNC's current use of his name in fundraising and other materials, including for our upcoming donor retreat event at Palm Beach at which we look forward to him participating."

The episode illustrated the roller-coaster relationship between Trump, McDaniel, and the RNC that began soon after the 2020 election. She was hard at work to keep Trump placated and hold together a deeply fractured GOP.

Once she became RNC chairwoman, she developed a close working relationship with—and understanding of—Trump, even as that caused tensions with some RNC members and in her own family. McDaniel dropped her maiden name, "Romney"—her uncle was the Utah senator, frequent Trump critic, and former Republican presidential nominee Mitt Romney—after Trump's prodding. She also attributed the change to another, more personal factor: She wanted her name to give credit to her husband, who shouldered extra family responsibilities when she took on the job. She plowed past criticism from some Republicans who said she embraced Trump too much and let the MAGA movement and GOP become intertwined.

After the 2020 election, McDaniel called for state party leaders to investigate allegations of irregularities in the results. In late November, she was on a call with Trump during which he pressured two election officials in Michigan not to certify the results. In the call, reported by *The Detroit News*, Trump told the Republican officials, "We've got to fight for our country. We can't let these people take our country away from us."

McDaniel then chimed in to say the RNC would provide legal counsel if the officials did not certify the results. "We will get you attorneys," McDaniel said. Trump responded, "We'll take care of that."

And yet, McDaniel also made it known privately that she did not support some of Trump's wilder claims about election fraud. People close to McDaniel described her—like many at the top of the RNC—as feeling a "serious and solemn obligation" to make sure the GOP didn't go entirely off the rails. But of course, that horse had left the barn months, if not years, earlier. The leadership of the party was at times holding on for dear life, desperate not to alienate the party's new base— populist, angry, bent on conspiracy, loyal only to Trump, and utterly indifferent to the "establishment" Republican Party, its beliefs or traditions. "She was constantly trying to mediate with people," said a former RNC official. McDaniel was at once trying to "keep things moving" and "keep everyone happy—but as a result it left everyone unhappy."

DURING THE TRUMP ERA THERE was an entire genre of Republicans who ascended to the top ranks of Trump's administration, only to immediately begin a furious SOS back-channel to the outside world or leak to the media about how they'd prevented one catastrophe or another, or curbed some of Trump's worst impulses.

There was General John Kelly, who would later describe Trump as "pathetic" and "the most flawed person I have ever met in my life." Kelly attested that "the depth of his dishonesty is just astounding to me" and claimed that in addition to having to brief the president on who the good guys and bad guys were in World War II, during his eighteen months as White House chief of staff he routinely prevented Trump from doing rash things that he wanted to do.

Trump did not impulsively take military action against North Korea because Kelly persuaded Trump that he could be seen as heroic if he were to pursue peace with Pyongyang. Kelly's ruse worked, resulting in Trump's bizarrely gushing over the "love letters" that he and the dictator Kim Jong Un had exchanged, which was far preferable to the exchange of tactical nuclear weapons that Kelly feared Trump's bellicose "fire and fury" rhetoric was making increasingly likely.

White House counsel Don McGahn refused an order from Trump to fire Robert Mueller, the special counsel in charge of investigating ties between the Trump campaign and the Russian intelligence services, repeatedly telling Trump that he would sooner quit than fire Mueller. McGahn's resignation would have jeopardized Trump's program of judicial appointments, an effort that McGahn led. Trump relented in the face of reason.

But now that he was out of power, clear signals and principled stands might just have allowed the party to well and truly turn the page from the Trump era, as so many anonymous professional Republican "adults in the room" claimed they wanted and needed to do. Under normal circumstances, it is not unusual for a defeated president to remain the standard-bearer of his party until the wheels turn and another nominee rises to put his or her mark on the future. But for as much as the upper ranks of the party clamored for new leadership, they also recognized the power Trump and his "America First" agenda had over a core base of supporters that would decimate the GOP if they left.

For whatever reason, political lassitude or moral paralysis, as the winter of 2021 turned to spring, a vacuum formed. And two things thrive in a vacuum: chaos—and Donald Trump.

If one is inclined to entertain alternative outcomes, a fateful moment—or an example of why the Republican ranks could not let go of Trump—might be the winter RNC meeting, which was held at the beginning of January 2021 on Amelia Island, Florida. As the events of January 6 unfolded, Ronna McDaniel and the conference were distracted by party business they were conducting inside a ballroom at the Ritz-Carlton resort. McDaniel ran unopposed and won reelection, and members passed resolutions on voter fraud. They sipped cocktails and mingled poolside under palm trees.

But they weren't completely shut off from the mayhem unfolding that day. McDaniel and party officials were receiving updates from their security team back in Washington, where two pipe bombs had been found outside RNC headquarters, and they were stunned later that evening as they watched news coverage of what had transpired in the capital. The horrors there seemed a world away from their beach-front paradise, and RNC officials said that even as they watched the events on TV, it was hard to fully process in the moment what a black eye January 6 would be for the party.

The very next morning—January 7—McDaniel was onstage when she received a call from the president. He was mad. There were reports circulating—inaccurate, he said—that he was supposed to be at the RNC meeting, and despite everything else going on, that was what was aggravating him. McDaniel told him she would put him on speakerphone from the conference, and the party officials greeted him with a round of applause.

The response at the meeting by the RNC committee members in the aftermath of January 6 laid bare how the organization had evolved over the Trump presidency. With the exception of a handful of committee members, most were loath to criticize the president or his actions, and pushed for officials to do more to support his claims of voter fraud.

RNC members condemned the violence in a statement and McDaniel acknowledged the images from the Capitol were damaging to the party. But like the other members there, she did not cast blame on Trump and said the party should work to keep his supporters engaged. Privately, she insisted she would stay neutral in the party and welcomed potential 2024 contenders like former U.N. ambassador Nikki Haley, who said in a speech that Trump's actions "will be judged harshly by history." But Haley's comments were an outlier.

In her victory speech, McDaniel did not directly acknowledge

Trump's loss and thanked him for his backing. Like the rest of the party, she had learned the Trump choreography. A few steps to the right, forward, backward, but in lockstep, always together.

FOR MONTHS, THE RNC'S SPRING donor retreat had been scheduled for the Four Seasons resort in Palm Beach. The oceanfront five-star hotel, where rooms go for over $1,000 a night in the spring season, is a short drive from Mar-a-Lago and the ultra-exclusive properties along South Ocean Boulevard.

The retreats gave deep-pocketed donors and ambitious lawmakers the opportunity to get plenty of face time, and were particularly important for presidential hopefuls looking to make inroads with wealthy Republicans. And in the aftermath of a presidential election, they also served as the first official party get-together to discuss how to move forward.

When the multiday event was scheduled, there were no plans for it to be held at Trump's club. But just as Trump and the RNC at the time were in the middle of their public spat over using Trump's image and name in fundraising, a decision was made to bus all the donors over to Mar-a-Lago for the final night to hear the former president speak. The RNC decided that moving the event—a venue change that cost the committee almost $100,000—would make not only Trump happy but also some of the donors who were clamoring to have a chance to visit the famed club.

After all, in just a few short months he had turned his club into the hottest right-wing ticket in town and an easy way to make money. Lawmakers and event organizers liked to book an evening in the white gilded ballroom with the hope that Trump might offer to make some remarks or stop by on his way to or from dinner to speak off the cuff, or that some of his wealthy club members might be interested in attending and writing a check. And they believed Trump might be more enticed to endorse if they ponied up the cash for a Mar-a-Lago event.

Wealthy donors would pay thousands of dollars to be schmoozed by lawmakers and candidates like White House press secretary turned Arkansas gubernatorial candidate Sarah Huckabee Sanders and Kentucky senator Rand Paul, over hors d'oeuvres and Trump-brand wine and seated dinners with gold-rimmed plates.

But that weekend there was a competing event in town. The night before the RNC donor retreat, Trump spoke for over an hour at his club as part of a two-day meeting and fundraiser organized by Republican fundraiser Caroline Wren for a new GOP donor network sponsored by the Conservative Partnership Institute, a nonprofit that Trump's former chief of staff Mark Meadows had joined after his time in the White House.

In early 2021, Wren was one of the organizers for the Save America rally on the morning of January 6, at the Ellipse near the White House, and was accused by fellow rally organizers of trying to help far-right conspiracy theorists like Alex Jones and Ali Alexander become part of the official program. While they were not included in the eventual lineup, Wren's involvement in the event got her a subpoena from the January 6 committee.

But Wren was well-connected in GOP politics and within Trumpworld, and saw an opportunity after Trump left the White House for Republicans to band together and fundraise as a kind of counterbalance to Democracy Alliance, the well-funded Democratic donor network.

In early February, Wren drafted a pitch for what she called America Alliance, which she shopped around to wealthy Republican donors in the spring of 2021. Her pitch to donors hinged on the idea that Republicans could not win by super PACs alone, and without proper coordination among competing right-wing groups, Republicans would likely lose again in the next election.

First over Zoom, and later at Mar-a-Lago, Wren made her pitch to Trump's woman in charge, Wiles.

Wiles liked the idea, but thought it should be a Trump-aligned entity. And then there was the issue of Trump himself, who was skeptical of any group whose funds weren't being directly shoveled to him. But with Trump's blessing, they all agreed that they could essentially make the group an exclusive club of donors who would pool their money to distribute to candidates and across the constellation of new pro-Trump and Republican groups, many of which had been started by former administration officials who were not initially going to find an ideological home in many of DC's top conservative think tanks.

Meadows and the Conservative Partnership Institute had purposefully scheduled the meeting to coincide with the RNC's donor retreat to try to attract some of the disgruntled donors who were displeased with how money had been spent by the party in the 2020 election. The event annoyed the RNC team, who didn't appreciate that their first major donor event after the presidential election was effectively being counterprogrammed.

But among those who showed up for the event were Fox News personalities and top officials in the Trump administration, including former cabinet members Linda McMahon and Dr. Ben Carson. The event was viewed by Wren and some of those who attended as essentially an unofficial kickoff to a presidential campaign that was still two years away from being announced.

But the Trump-backed answer to the Democrats' Democracy Alliance never got far off the ground before it was killed by Trumpian infighting.

Corey Lewandowski, Trump's first campaign manager in 2016, had just been tasked with running a new Trump-blessed super PAC, MAGA Action. And word got back to him that Wren had discouraged donors from giving to super PACs and that she was receiving serious commitments from donors. He was in a bind. Many donors in 2021 were reluctant to hand over big checks to Trump, since they weren't certain he was going to run again and they weren't entirely on board with some of the candidates Trump had endorsed in the primaries. It quickly became clear there were too many competing forces in Trumpworld.

Not long after she locked in a $5 million donation to America Alliance, Wren received a cease-and-desist letter, firing her from the group she started. The Alliance disbanded.

But a few months later, Lewandowski was fired from MAGA Action PAC. Lewandowski had been accused of unwanted sexual advances toward a wealthy Trump donor's wife at a charity event in Las Vegas. "He will no longer be associated with Trump World," Trump spokesman Taylor Budowich wrote on Twitter. But, of course, they always come back.

SPEAKING AT CPAC IN FEBRUARY was a chance for him to address his grassroots supporters and base for the first time since leaving Washington. But speaking to donors at the events that spring also offered him a chance to flex his muscle in front of his wealthy peers and top lawmakers and, most important, those who might challenge him in 2024.

Some of Trump's allies hoped that in his prime speaking spot, he would offer a forward-looking vision for the party. Trump's team prepared a speech that was given to McDaniel ahead of time to preview. But there was no point. Trump had a lot to get off his chest.

"I have this long boring speech to read, so maybe we'll leave it," Trump said.

He kicked off his speech by teasing McDaniel.

"She has to be neutral, you know, she's supposed to be neutral," Trump said. "She's neutral like I'm neutral."

What followed was a nearly hour-long speech focused on grievances and falsehoods that viciously ripped into some Republicans on the Hill, like Mitch McConnell, whom he called a "dumb son of a bitch," Senator Mitt Romney, who was booed by the room, and Mike Pence, who "disappointed" him because he didn't have the "courage" to stop the certification of votes on January 6.

Trump called McConnell a "stone cold loser" and attacked

Elaine Chao—McConnell's wife and Trump's former transportation secretary—who had resigned over January 6 and later was subjected to racist taunts by Trump.

"I hired his wife. Did he ever say thank you?" Trump said. Trump had already started his attacks on McConnell; in February, he released a long statement calling the Kentucky senator "a dour, sullen, and unsmiling political hack."

Trump lit into infectious disease expert Dr. Anthony Fauci and claimed someone had called him up to suggest that he should name the COVID-19 vaccine after himself. "Somebody called up, Sir, would you please call it a Trumpcine from now on? Trumpcine," Trump recounted.

But mostly his speech was focused on the 2020 election results and all the ways he believed Biden's presidency was fraudulent. He found in his own ballroom a sympathetic audience.

"By the way, we won anyway. Because when you look at the dead people who voted, the illegal immigrants who voted, the machines, when you look at all of the things that happened. Does it matter? Because we won by a massive amount anyway," Trump declared. "Who in the room thinks we won the presidential election? Most within the Republican Party believe that."

It was one of the RNC's best-attended donor retreats to date.

4

All Summer Long

IN THE SPRING OF 2021, A NEW CONSPIRACY THEORY CAUGHT FIRE AMONG some of Donald Trump's most fervent supporters and fringe conservative media: Trump would be reinstated as president by August 13.

"Donald Trump will be back in office in August," Mike Lindell, the CEO of MyPillow, said during a March appearance on Steve Bannon's *WarRoom* podcast. "The election of 2020 is going bye-bye."

Lindell, along with Sidney Powell, the lawyer who had spread some of the most outlandish theories about the 2020 election results, and some of Trump's other allies claimed that by the end of the summer there would be enough evidence gathered from election audits to prove that Trump had won. Lindell said that after his election symposium in South Dakota at the beginning of August, their findings on the 2020 election would be so explosive that the matter would somehow be taken up by the Supreme Court, which would decide that Donald Trump, and not Joe Biden, should be in the White House.

That the Lindell/Powell scenario was impossible mattered not at all to those who believed it would come to pass. And this pattern would come to define the relationship between Trump and some of his loyal base during the first year of his exile. Conspiracists who understood little about how American federalism actually works preyed on die-hard MAGA adherents, who desperately wanted to believe in the Trumpian version of reality—that Trump either was in fact still president or would magically be restored to office by some heretofore unknown extraconstitutional process.

The CEO of MyPillow was a celebrity on the right. He constantly advertised on conservative television and radio, making his big mustache and wide smile instantly recognizable, and he had come on the political scene with an inspiring personal story. Lindell was a drug addict turned born-again Christian and multimillionaire entrepreneur. He was known to give away his products to charity, and he was a Trump superfan who was often seen at the White House and campaign events.

Lindell was a member at Bedminster and Mar-a-Lago. Trump loved his salesmanship and loyalty, and had even encouraged Lindell to run for office in his home state of Minnesota.

But after the 2020 election, Lindell transformed from being a benign MAGA mascot into one of the most extreme election conspiracy theorists. In the desperate and deranged last week of the administration, he was at the White House pitching Trump on bizarre election theories, and he financed last-ditch efforts to overturn the results of the election. On January 15, 2021, Lindell was spotted by a photographer heading into the West Wing of the White House holding a document that appeared to reference the "Insurrection Act" and "martial law."

Lindell had also pushed the conspiracy theories that Smartmatic and Dominion voting machines were somehow rigged by foreign governments who wanted to disrupt the election, a claim that had made him a defendant in a $1.3 billion defamation suit from Dominion Voting Systems. In early February, he purchased two hours of airtime from the right-wing network One America News to broadcast a documentary he had made, *Absolute Proof,* about his false claims of a stolen election.

But the more that legal scholars and even some of his own lawyers dismissed the idea as nuts, the more Trump himself became intrigued by the idea that for the first time in American history, a president could be deposed so that his predecessor could be restored to office. His stolen election theory, which had begun as a hash of outright fabrications and grossly misinterpreted videos of legitimate election processes, all as a salve to Trump's inability to accept that people might have actually chosen to vote against him, had hardened into belief, which would become orthodoxy, which would eventually become a litmus test—*the* litmus test—for his party.

If Trump could get a member of his party to either espouse his lies about the election of 2020, or dissemble when invited by a journalist or constituent to acknowledge the objective reality of what had happened, then that person was deemed loyal. On the other hand, if a prominent Republican objected to Trump's lies, that person was a RINO and would need to be banished.

By the early summer, Maggie Haberman, the well-sourced *New York Times* reporter, would tweet, "Trump has been telling a number of people he's in contact with that he expects he will get reinstated by August (no that isn't how it works but simply sharing the information)."

ABC News's Jonathan Karl asked Trump in July if he really believed the idea. Trump replied that he wasn't going to explain it. "You wouldn't either understand it or write it," Trump told Karl.

While conceding that the "landscape of conspiracy theories" is "definitely a part of our world," some of Trump's senior advisers insisted the former president never actually bought into the idea that he could somehow be reinstated (that was just the "crazy people talking," said one), and yet that summer, he started reaching out to allies and conservative writers to suggest the idea that he could still return to the White House.

The *National Review*'s Charles C. W. Cooke wrote, "I can attest, from speaking to an array of different sources, that Donald Trump does indeed believe quite genuinely that he—along with former senators David Perdue and Martha McSally—will be "reinstated" to office this summer after "audits" of the 2020 elections in Arizona, Georgia, and a handful of other states have been completed. I can attest, too, that Trump is trying hard to recruit journalists, politicians, and other influential figures to promulgate this belief—not as a fundraising tool or an infantile bit of trolling or a trial balloon, but as a fact."

One of the journalists Trump attempted—unsuccessfully—to convert was Rich Lowry, the editor in chief of the *National Review*. On a summer morning in 2021, Lowry was driving with his wife to one of their children's summer activities when he received a phone call out of the blue from Trump. The former president would sometimes reach out to the conservative columnist to offer his criticisms or thoughts on a recent story.

"Rich, you're doing okay, and the *National Review* is okay, but you could really be the hottest thing in the country if you just say the election was stolen, and just acknowledge the truth of this," Trump said. The former president then referred to the ballot audit then going on in Arizona as proof that the election was fraudulent.

"When a diamond is stolen from Tiffany's, it's not enough to know it's stolen. It has to be returned," Trump said.

Trump went on to tell Lowry that the stolen election was the only thing Republicans wanted to talk about. He said that if the election wasn't made right, no one was going to vote for Republicans again.

The call demonstrated the extent to which Trump was influenced by voices like Lindell's and how far he would push falsehoods about the election, even after his commitment to those falsehoods triggered a cascade of legal problems.

AT THE SAME TIME AS the reinstatement theory was taking root, Trump was obsessed with the partisan ballot review taking place in Maricopa County, Arizona.

Arizona was a sore spot for Trump. The race there had been close, and he continued to harbor frustrations with Fox News for calling the state relatively early on November 3, when the network's analytics indicated to them that the race was over and that, for only the second time since 1952, a Democrat had won the state. Biden won Arizona by a slim margin—just ten thousand votes, or 0.3 percent. But after two hand-count audits of the 2.1 million ballots cast in Maricopa County, the most populous part of Arizona, covering the city of Phoenix and its surrounding areas, no irregularities had been found, and the results were certified by Republican Arizona governor Doug Ducey.

Yet Trump—and some of the Arizona Republicans who had bought into his allegations of widespread fraud—claimed to be unconvinced. Not only was there evidence of voter fraud, that fraud was rampant, they claimed. If the votes were fairly counted, the scales would fall from skeptical eyes and all would finally see that the thing that Donald Trump had been saying over and over was actually true, the election results would be reversed, and all would be right with the world. In the absence of any forceful counter in the spring of 2021, this rejection of legal process in favor of a corrupt magical thinking seized some of the Republican Party.

Polling data began to reflect the grip of this alternate reality. The belief that the election was stolen by illegal voting and that Trump was the "true president" was held by a majority of the Republican Party by the spring of 2021, according to multiple surveys. Turbocharging this collective delusion was the Arizona audit.

Using the State Senate's subpoena power, Arizona's legislature seized county ballots and voting machines and hired a cybersecurity team out of Florida called Cyber Ninjas to conduct an additional examination and ballot count of the state's results.

Cyber Ninjas did not have any experience in elections. Its CEO, Doug Logan, had bought into the idea that fraud had turned the election, a fact that would undermine the audit even before it started, given that Logan's firm was seeking to affirm a conclusion that he had reached before counting a single ballot. That did not prevent Arizona Senate Republicans from moving forward with hiring Cyber Ninjas to oversee two other firms to scan ballots and perform a full, manual recount of the more than two million ballots cast during the 2020 election.

The entire audit was a political spectacle, and the Arizona Veterans Memorial Coliseum, which once hosted the Phoenix Suns, the Rolling Stones, and Elvis Presley, was transformed into ground zero for Trump's complaints about the 2020 election.

Each day, dozens of people, mostly Republicans, would sit at neat rows of tables wearing color-coded T-shirts, closely examining and photographing ballots as they spun around on a lazy Susan.

As they counted, the auditors were also looking for evidence to support details of the election conspiracy that had spread in dark corners of the Web. They used magnifying glasses to find evidence that the paper ballots were made with bamboo, which would prove that China had manufactured and "stuffed" some forty thousand illicit ballots in Arizona to tip the state to Biden. They were also using UV lights to look for any sign of watermarks on official ballots, part of another internet theory that Trump himself was particularly interested in knowing more about; QAnon-linked conspiracies suggested that official ballots are secretly marked to distinguish them from falsely cast ballots.

There were no bamboo ballots. And Maricopa County ballots are not watermarked.

The Republican-majority Maricopa County Board of Supervisors called the entire audit a "sham" and a "con" in a letter to Senate Republicans that defended the way the state had conducted its election, and called for an end to the audit. "Our state has become a laughingstock," the Maricopa officials wrote. "Worse, this 'audit' is encouraging our citizens to distrust elections, which weakens our democratic republic."

"It is time to make a choice to defend the Constitution and the Republic," they continued. The audit, they said, was "a spectacle that is harming all of us."

Despite the concerns raised by local Republican officials, Arizona

Senate president Karen Fann said the audit would proceed so that the public would know "that our next election will be 100 percent safe and secure."

Trump had become deeply invested in the outcome of the audit. He would frequently ask advisers and allies for updates on what was happening in Arizona, and was frustrated that mainstream channels weren't giving the audit the kind of attention he thought it demanded.

Trump asked his new spokeswoman, Liz Harrington, as one of her first tasks on the job, to call up Fox News anchors including Laura Ingraham and Tucker Carlson to say they needed to cover the audit and the 2020 election more. But Ingraham told Harrington that it was time for Trump to stop talking about 2020 and move on.

Later in the summer, Trump and Harrington's frustrations with Fox News coverage of his false election claims exploded when an interview he did for the Fox show *Unfiltered with Dan Bongino* was in fact filtered when posted later on YouTube. Unbeknownst to Bongino, Trump's comments about 2020 being a "fake election" were cut to comply with YouTube's content policy about the election.

Trump had his team teach him how to tune in to programs like former White House chief strategist Steve Bannon's *WarRoom* podcast livestream, or Right Side Broadcasting Network or OAN, so that he could watch the latest interpretation of what was happening on the floor of the Veterans Memorial Coliseum.

The coverage of the audit on the right was as conspiracy-laden and scrambled as it was breathless. Bannon's livestream set up the audit as a kind of Armageddon. At the top of his show, he would play Ralph Waldo Emerson's "Concord Hymn," written in 1837 for the dedication of a battle monument in Concord, Massachusetts, where in 1775 the Minutemen met the advancing British troops.

Trump paid close attention to this coverage and had reached out to top Arizona officials to thank them for "pushing to prove any fraud."

There was one reporter in particular that Trump would pay attention to—Christina Bobb.

Bobb was a fervent believer that the election had been stolen and became the unofficial face of the Arizona audit, where she would broadcast live for the far-right and pro-Trump One America News Network from the audit floor. A young lawyer from the Phoenix area, Bobb had served as a Marine before joining the Trump administration as executive secretary for the Department of Homeland Security. In the summer of 2020, Bobb joined OAN to cover the White House, filing sycophantic reports and hosting a weekly TV show.

Bobb constantly blurred the lines between reporting and advocating. As she reported on the 2020 election, for example, she was volunteering to work with Trump's lawyer Rudy Giuliani, and the Trump campaign's legal team, on overturning the results.

In Arizona, she gained special access for OAN on the floor of the audit, where she would discuss the nuts and bolts of what the group was trying to do, but then she would peddle conspiracy theories about the audit and even raise money to pay for it. "Join us in the fight for the AZ Election Audit. This audit is crucial to know the truth about 2020," Bobb wrote on Twitter.

But while partisans were funding the audit, Trump wasn't.

By the end of summer 2021, Trump's fundraising entities had amassed a war chest of more than $102 million from emails and texts calling for Trump supporters to "fight back" against the "rigged" election. None of that money would be spent on the Arizona audit.

There was no need for a cash infusion from Trump. In mid-July, Cyber Ninjas reported that in addition to the $150,000 Fann and the Arizona State Senate allotted, they had collected more than $5 million from pro-Trump groups to finance its operations.

The largest donation, over $3 million, was made by former Overstock CEO Patrick Byrne's organization, the America Project. Byrne had resigned from his position as CEO of Overstock after it was revealed he had had an affair with political activist and Russian agent Maria Butina, and he made bizarre statements about being coerced into the relationship by the government. Byrne was later part of the crew that pushed fraud claims and tried to put together a plan to flip the election results.

The wealthy financier became so obsessed with conspiracies about the election that he wrote a book, *The Deep Rig: How Election Fraud Cost Donald J. Trump the White House, by a Man Who Did Not Vote for Him*, and produced a film on election fraud that happened to feature the head of Cyber Ninjas, Doug Logan, who proclaimed in the film, "If we don't fix our election integrity now, we may no longer have a democracy."

Another large donation, $605,000, came from Voices and Votes, a fundraising effort led by Bobb, who called for donations on air as she reported on the audit.

"One America News (OAN), one of the fastest growing networks on television, and the 'hottest,' is doing a magnificent job of exposing the massive fraud that took place. The story is only getting bigger and at some point it will be impossible for the weak and/or corrupt media not to cover. Thank you to OAN and other brave American Patriots. It is all happening quickly!" Trump said in a May statement.

"I wouldn't be surprised if they found thousands and thousands and thousands of votes," Trump told a crowd at Mar-a-Lago in April. "So we're going to watch that very closely. And after that, you'll watch Pennsylvania and you'll watch Georgia and you're going to watch Michigan and Wisconsin. You're watching New Hampshire. . . . Because this was a rigged election. Everybody knows it. And we're going to be watching it very closely."

The audit, which was supposed to take sixty days, stretched on for nearly six months. It ended with an embarrassing whimper. The Cyber Ninjas firm issued a report that found not only did Trump lose Maricopa County, Biden's margin had actually been greater than originally counted; the audit ultimately added 360 votes to Biden's total.

Trump claimed vindication regardless, and pointed to the Arizona audit results noting "23,334 mail-in ballots, despite the person no longer living at that address. Phantom voters!" Except that those numbers could be accounted for by people moving within Maricopa County before the registration deadline.

By the time the report came out, the damage was done. Trump and his allies had successfully undermined confidence in the election among a majority of Republicans, and his unfounded complaints about 2020 would continue to be a rallying cry for his base, who launched similar efforts around the country.

DONALD TRUMP WALKED THROUGH THE double doors of his smaller ballroom at Mar-a-Lago, beaming. Standing in front of him were dozens of his former political advisers, Palm Beach club members dressed to the nines, and conservative media stars who clapped and cheered as he made his way to a podium.

They were gathered inside the shimmering mirror-paneled room under chandeliers the size of golf carts at Trump's palatial beachfront resort for the debut of one of many films released after the 2020 election designed to cast doubt on its results. And they were also there for the chance to see Trump, the center of the right-wing universe, whose grievances about the election had become a fixture of conservative culture.

"I really liked *Citizen Kane. Gone with the Wind* was fantastic. *Titanic* was fantastic. But this is the one I'm really looking forward to seeing," Trump said, as he explained just how excited he was about the film they were all about to watch.

Trump was talking about *Rigged: The Zuckerberg Funded Plot to Defeat Donald Trump,* a new film from David Bossie, the president of Citizens United and a Trump adviser and ally. The premise of *Rigged*—which featured interviews with Trump, Kellyanne Conway, former House Speaker Newt Gingrich, and Senator Ted Cruz—was that Meta's Mark Zuckerberg had given Democrats a boost by donating hundreds of millions of dollars that went toward voter turnout and funding drop-box ballot operations in predominantly blue counties in swing states.

"Some people say we shouldn't be talking about the 2020 election," Bossie said in his introduction, calling Trump the "forty-fifth and forty-seventh president of the United States." "I think it's vital that we do, because if we don't find out what happened in 2020, how are we going to stop it from happening again?"

And yet there was a very real conversation among people close to Trump—including some of those in the ballroom—about how the fixation on the 2020 election was not helpful. At a time when Trump and the GOP could be talking about Joe Biden's weaknesses and low approval ratings—literally anything else—they were instead relitigating the last election and reminding voters beyond Trump's base of the former president's penchant for saying things that are not true. Of course, this particular thing had by now created an entire counterculture—from books and films to conferences and TV segments—focused on trying to unearth the many methods by which the election was believed to have been stolen.

And this ballroom in Palm Beach had become the place for the cinéastes of election fraud to convene and to leave fortified for the next fight. For *Rigged* and a series of other films released since Trump had left the White House, the former president turned Mar-a-Lago into his own kind of Grauman's Chinese Theatre, with a red carpet, movie posters, Trump-branded champagne, popcorn, and puff pastry hors d'oeuvres.

Women in glittering gowns, including some emblazoned with American flags or MAGA, and men in tuxedos gathered around the large blue pool at Mar-a-Lago sipping cocktails and eagerly awaiting the arrival of Trump. After all, even though the movies did not center on Trump, he was the star around which the entire MAGA universe rotated.

For Trump, who once wanted to be a Hollywood director or producer, had made a cameo appearance in *Home Alone 2*, and regularly held screenings at the White House for his favorite flicks, the premieres demonstrated just how much he and his club had become the mecca for a conservative counterculture—a type of Hollywood hub for the decidedly anti-Hollywood crowd. Inside Trump's own *Truman*

Show set, he could live out unchallenged the alternate reality—over and over again—that he had won the election.

"President Trump shouldn't be here," remarked Kari Lake after the premiere of one of the election fraud films at Mar-a-Lago. The Trump-endorsed Senate candidate in Arizona had turned right-wing concerns and falsehoods about the election into a centerpiece of her campaign. "He should be in the White House."

Before the red carpet reception, Trump hosted a dinner at which a who's who of Trump's White House buzzed around the ballroom catching up and reminiscing on life pre-2020 as though they were at a high school reunion or, perhaps more aptly, a dysfunctional family reunion where those once on the outs were welcomed back with open arms.

There was former White House spokesperson Hogan Gidley, always tanned and wearing tailored suits, who was working on election integrity efforts at a Trump-aligned think tank. Hope Hicks, in a white sundress, chatted with Trump's former chief of staff Reince Priebus, who fetched cocktails from the bar for himself and Kellyanne Conway, who playfully teased the ex-chief about how he was going to be portrayed in the memoir she was working on. Corey Lewandowski, who had been briefly cast out of Trumpworld after he was accused of assaulting a top donor's wife, was back and giving interviews to conservative reporters from Newsmax and *Breitbart*.

"Jerry Nadler! If he wants a subpoena, bring the subpoena," Lewandowski could be heard telling a reporter across the room.

After dinner on Mar-a-Lago's gilded china, the guests were ushered over to another, larger ballroom that had been turned into a makeshift theater with red-and-white-striped tubs of popcorn for people to snack on while the movie played. Trump sat in the front row.

Over ominous music, people like Cleta Mitchell, the Republican election lawyer who was part of the conspiracy to overthrow the results of the 2020 election, along with Trump himself, claimed on-screen that Zuckerberg was trying to rig the election against him and Republicans.

In reality, the Chan Zuckerberg Initiative—a joint charitable effort by Zuckerberg and his wife, Priscilla Chan—donated nearly $400 million to the Center for Technology and Civic Life (CTCL) in 2020 to "to help ensure that they have the staffing, training, and equipment necessary so that this November every eligible voter can participate in a safe and timely way and have their vote counted."

The initiative was praised by some election officials who said it was necessary to help run elections during the pandemic. But right-wing critics said that the money was unfairly concentrated in heavily Democratic areas in swing states and ultimately skewed the results of the 2020 election.

The coronavirus pandemic scrambled every facet of American life, including elections, and numerous foundations gave grant money to help local officials with costs related to orchestrating a fair election and making sure the elderly, the quarantined, and those with health concerns were not disenfranchised. Because of the pandemic, less than one-third of all ballots in the 2020 election were cast in person at a polling place on Election Day. Instead, many people relied on early voting and at-will absentee or mail-in ballots, which were legal in battleground states like Pennsylvania, Georgia, Michigan, and Wisconsin even before the pandemic.

There was nothing illegal about Zuckerberg's initiative, but the donation—and the publicity it received from the Citizens United film—sparked a series of bills sponsored by Republicans in state legislatures to block outside funding for elections in the future.

A spokesperson for Zuckerberg said in a statement, "When our nation's election infrastructure faced unprecedented challenges in 2020 due to the pandemic, and the federal government failed to provide adequate funds to allow states and localities to conduct elections, Mark Zuckerberg and Priscilla Chan stepped up to close that funding gap with two independent, nonprofit organizations to help the American people vote."

Trump already harbored a deep animosity toward Zuckerberg for suspending him from Facebook, and the allegations in the film only deepened his resentment toward the social media giant for what he viewed as unfair interference in the 2020 election.

"It was a rigged election," Trump said in the documentary. "These are guilty people. And they have to be held accountable. Mark Zuckerberg is one of them."

The guests gave a standing ovation as the credits rolled at the end of the film. But after the lights came on and many of the stars left the ballroom, a prominent Trump political aide came over to the news media to vent frustrations about the fact that while there was a lot of talk about the 2020 loss, there was no real plan of action for the next election, no forward-looking vision.

"Until we have a reckoning and a conversation, I don't know what we are doing here," the aide said.

Republicans who privately admitted Trump lost would contort themselves to explain what Trump meant by widespread fraud. Most would point to mail-in ballots or the pandemic impacting how ballots were received or counted, and others would point to extremely rare cases of a ballot cast under a dead person's name, or someone voting twice after moving across state lines.

Just one month after hosting the debut of *Rigged*, Trump hosted another premiere for a film focused on election fraud falsehoods, this one by Dinesh D'Souza.

Once a policy adviser in the Reagan administration and rising conservative star, D'Souza had taken a dark and conspiratorial turn that turned out to be lucrative. He wrote a bestselling book—panned by conservatives and liberals alike—that claimed the left's treatment of Muslims was responsible for 9/11, and he pushed claims that Barack Obama and Hillary Clinton were guilty of a litany of crimes and misdeeds. In 2014, D'Souza himself was convicted of a felony. He pleaded guilty to making illegal campaign contributions by enlisting his friends to make $10,000 donations to a campaign and then reimbursing them in cash. As president, Trump pardoned D'Souza and claimed that like himself, he was "treated very unfairly by our government."

In *2000 Mules*, his new film, D'Souza promoted the idea that there was a vast and coordinated election fraud conspiracy to prevent Trump from winning reelection. The flick used debunked data and analysis of cellphone location data and selective surveillance footage near ballot drop box locations to suggest that ballot "mules" illegally collected and delivered ballots in states like Arizona and Wisconsin.

Trump hosted a similarly splashy poolside premiere for D'Souza's book of the same title, with guests like Representatives Matt Gaetz and Marjorie Taylor Greene, Michael Flynn, Jenna Ellis, Bernard Kerik, Rudy Giuliani, Lara Logan, Kyle Rittenhouse, Charlie Kirk, and Dan Bongino, who took selfies with fans and posed on the red carpet for right-wing media.

The filmmakers relied on the shoddy work of a group called True the Vote and left some gaping holes in their analysis. For instance, they did not provide video of people making repeat trips to ballot drop-off locations and they did not provide evidence that anyone was paid to make ballot drop-offs.

"I think the conclusion of the film is not justified by the premises of the film itself. There are a bunch of dots that need to be connected. Maybe they will be connected, but they haven't been connected in the film," said conservative commentator Ben Shapiro in his review for *The Daily Wire.* Ann Coulter, a Trump fan turned critic, slammed the film as a "conspiracy movie" that "doesn't show what it says it shows."

"In the five states where D'Souza deploys his hocus-pocus cell phone data—Arizona, Georgia, Michigan, Pennsylvania and Wisconsin—Trump lost 8% of white voters, and 12% of white men, compared to 2016," Coulter wrote. "How'd liberal vote-harvesters pull that off?"

Connecting the dots didn't matter—Trump's fans were hungry for an explanation as to why he wasn't in the White House. In less than twelve hours, *2000 Mules* grossed more than a million dollars streaming on Rumble, the conservative-leaning video platform.

ON SEPTEMBER 23, THE DAY before Cyber Ninjas released its report, Trump sent a letter to Texas governor Greg Abbott, calling for an

Arizona-style audit in a state he had won by more than six percentage points over Biden.

"Governor Abbott, we need a 'Forensic Audit of the 2020 Election,'" Trump wrote. "Texans know voting fraud occurred in some of their counties."

Just hours later, Texas officials claimed in a statement that audits in the state's two biggest Republican- and Democratic-leaning counties were already under way. But that was news to county officials who said they were just learning about all of this from the state.

Trump's letter had set off a mad dash inside Abbott's office to figure out if the ex-president was actually serious in his demands for an audit—the secretary of state's office was unoccupied at the time.

But the scramble behind the scenes to placate Trump and his Republican base demonstrated just how influential Trump was by the end of 2021 with GOP state leaders, who rushed to help undermine the 2020 results and avoid any confrontation with the ex-president. These events showed, too, just how powerful the belief was within Trump's Republican base of supporters that it was all rigged.

A CENTRAL FOCUS OF REPUBLICAN-LED efforts to recount or verify the 2020 election results was equipment from Dominion Voting Systems, a Denver-based company that sells and services voting machines.

Conspiracies about Dominion—false accusations that the company aimed to take down Trump and had ties to financier George Soros, to Venezuela, and to the software company Smartmatic—were shared by Trump attorneys after the election and repeated on Fox News. Unsubstantiated stories about connections to Hugo Chávez, the late socialist leader of Venezuela, inspired complaints across the country by voters who were falsely led to believe that many votes were not counted.

As part of the audit in Arizona, State Senate Republicans subpoenaed hundreds of Maricopa County's election machines, which were leased by Dominion, for review by the Cyber Ninjas team.

IN ANTRIM COUNTY, MICHIGAN, IN May 2021, a lawsuit was filed—and thrown out—calling for an audit over claims the 2020 election was fraudulent, and caught the attention of Trump.

"The major Michigan Election Fraud case has just filed a bombshell pleading claiming votes were intentionally switched from President Trump to Joe Biden. The number of votes is MASSIVE and determinative. This will prove true in numerous other States," Trump said in a statement.

And throughout the spring of 2021, similar challenges popped up in other counties in Michigan, among them Cheboygan and Houghton, and in New Hampshire and Pennsylvania, too.

Arizona's partisan review of ballots inspired Republican state senator Doug Mastriano of Pennsylvania, a Trump ally who would later go on to unsuccessfully run for governor, to call for a "forensic investigation" of the 2020 election. Mastriano had become one of the biggest purveyors of the claim that widespread fraud impacted the November election. He hosted Giuliani for a hearing in November in Gettysburg, soon after the 2020 election, during which Trump called in and asked for the election to be overturned. And Mastriano traveled to Washington, D.C., on January 6 to participate in the "Save America" rally, although he did not participate in the storming of the Capitol and publicly condemned the violence.

IN JUNE 2021, MASTRIANO BROUGHT a group of Pennsylvania delegates out to Phoenix to witness the audit and get ideas for how they could hold a similar ballot recount. Mastriano claimed, in a post to his campaign site, that a Pennsylvania audit would not be conducted to overturn election results but instead to "confirm the effectiveness of existing legislation on the governance of elections or to point out areas for potential legislative reform."

"Here in Pennsylvania, a cloud of suspicion hangs over the 2020

General Election. Hundreds of sworn affidavits from eyewitnesses alleging fraud, irregularities, and illegal behavior during the election have lain dormant," Mastriano wrote after visiting Arizona. "Those who think that there was zero voter fraud, no irregularities, and the elections were conducted perfectly will have the chance to be vindicated."

But like those of other Republicans who were lobbying their own state legislatures, Mastriano's claims of fraud were energized by Trump and his allies. U.S. Representatives Marjorie Taylor Greene and Matt Gaetz flew out to Phoenix to hold a rally nearby in support of "America First" principles and the "audit." "It's my belief that Arizona will be the launch pad for elections audits and election integrity efforts all over this great country," Gaetz told a crowd in Mesa, Arizona.

Even though the results in Pennsylvania had been certified, and two post-election audits were conducted in the state that confirmed the results, Trump pressed for Mastriano and Pennsylvania Republicans to support another partisan audit of the election. "The people of Pennsylvania and America deserve to know the truth," Trump shared in a statement. "If the Pennsylvania Senate leadership doesn't act, there is no way they will ever get re-elected!"

IN A SIGN OF SUPPORT for the Arizona audit, Trump flew out to Phoenix at the end of July to appear at a Turning Point Action gathering billed as the "Rally to Protect Our Elections." It was his first appearance in the state since 2020.

For nearly two hours, Trump gave an angry, rambling speech focused on the 2020 election and his baseless conspiracy theories. He cheered on the partisan audit. He ticked through a list of issues he had with polling, none of which were supported in lawsuits filed by allies after the election. He chided his former vice president Mike Pence, Senate Minority Leader Mitch McConnell, and Arizona governor Doug Ducey. And he praised Rudy Giuliani.

"I am not the one trying to undermine American democracy—I'm the one trying to save American democracy," Trump proclaimed, and called the election "a scam—the greatest crime in history."

"This is only the beginning of the irregularities," Trump told the crowd. "We're not talking about Arizona any more. We're talking about the United States of America."

Even though Trump was the main attraction inside the Arizona Federal Theatre that July, there was another rising star in MAGA world who captured the attention of the movement and of Trump. The event, led by Turning Point Action's Charlie Kirk, attracted Republican candidates for Senate and governor, including two who would go on to win Trump's support. One was Blake Masters, the protégé of billionaire Peter Thiel. The other was Kari Lake.

Lake was well-known in Arizona by the time she announced her gubernatorial run in June 2021. A local Fox anchor for two decades, Lake was a familiar face to millions who watched her deliver news and weather reports with her signature smooth voice, glowy complexion, and cropped hair. But she decided to turn her longtime career into a political springboard, and, taking cues from Trump, made the "fake news" and media industry her punching bag.

Trump took note of Lake's popularity at the event and asked Kirk backstage if he could meet the former reporter. One month later, Lake and her husband would fly out to New York to meet with the ex-president at Trump Tower for over an hour in his office.

"That wasn't a poll that you hire some pollster to do," Trump said to Lake about her reception at the Turning Point event, according to her book. "That was a real poll. That's the people telling you who they like."

By the end of their meeting, Trump told Lake she had his support.

Lake went on to win the Republican primary and take on Democrat and Arizona secretary of state Katie Hobbs in the race for governor, which would go on to be a lightning rod for election falsehoods and the Republican debate over the 2020 election.

Lake's commitment to talking about fraud in the 2020 election would make even Trump laugh at times. He would tell candidates they should be more like Lake when talking about the election, and would privately tell people just how fervent she was about the issue.

"It doesn't matter what you ask Kari Lake about—'How's your family?' And she's like, 'The family's fine but they're never going to be great until we have free and fair elections,'" Trump would tell friends and donors. One said, "He was like, 'You could ask her, how's the weather?' And she'll turn it into the election. 'Oh, the weather in Phoenix is OK, but you can never have great weather unless the election is fair.'"

Trump told Blake Masters, whom he endorsed in the Republican Senate race in Arizona, to be more like Lake in talking about the 2020 election.

"I heard you did great on the debate, but bad election answer, you've got a lot of support and you have to stay with those people," Trump said to Masters, in a call that was caught on camera for a documentary about Masters.

"If you want to get across the line, you've got to go stronger on that one thing, lot of complaints about it. Look at Kari, Kari is winning with very little money, and if they say 'How is your family?' she says, 'The election was rigged and stolen.' You'll lose if you go soft. You'll lose that base,'" Trump said.

Believing—or at least peddling—Trump's falsehoods about the election would go on to become a litmus test for a Trump endorsement. And Lake, like many of those Trump supported, went on to be one of the loudest standard-bearers for the election denialism movement.

THE CONSPIRACY THEORY THAT TRUMP would be reinstated on August 13 hinged on a three-day cybersymposium in South Dakota put on by Lindell himself.

At the event, Lindell promised to deliver "irrefutable" proof that China stole the election for Biden, and he promised to give $5 million to anyone who could disprove his data. It turned out to be a spectacular failure—starting with the inability to get the livestream for his event working, and blaming that glitch, without evidence, on a cyberattack.

From August 10 to August 12, so-called experts and die-hard election deniers filtered through a conference room in Sioux Falls, South Dakota. Lindell sat onstage, with a giant screen behind him, and teased blockbuster evidence of a stolen election. But the event revealed zero proof of fraud and nothing that would suggest that Trump could in fact be somehow reinstated. Even some of the experts Lindell hired to run the event said it was a sham.

"He gave us experts NOTHING today, except random garbage that wastes our time," wrote Rob Graham on Twitter during the event. Graham noted that the data came from someone named Dennis Montgomery, who had been behind several high-profile conspiracy theories, including the allegation that a deep-state supercomputer was used to alter ballots across the country.

As if the spectacular flop of a symposium wasn't bad enough, on the last day of the event, Lindell suddenly rushed off the stage. News had just broken that a judge denied his motion to dismiss Dominion Voting System's $1.3 billion lawsuit against him and his MyPillow company over claims the voting machines were rigged in the 2020 election.

On August 13, 2021, the day after the symposium, Trump was not reinstated as he and so many of his followers had hoped.

There had been such a frenzy among some Trump supporters that the Department of Homeland Security was monitoring online conversations about Trump being reinstated to make sure there were no threats of domestic terrorism.

But on that Friday, Trump got a visit from Lindell and some of the very people who had spun up the idea he could somehow be put back in the White House by the end of the summer.

Straight from the symposium in South Dakota, Lindell, pro-Trump lawyer Kurt Olsen, and New Mexico State University law professor David Clements, who traveled all over the country talking about claims of election fraud in 2020, met with Trump for dinner at his golf club.

Trump sat at the head of a long wooden table in the club's dining room, surrounded by some of the biggest election fraud conspiracy theorists in the country.

"Spent an unforgettable evening with the real President of the United States," Clements shared after the dinner on his Telegram page.

The symposium may have been a mess, and no evidence was put forward that would somehow, unconstitutionally, reverse the results of the election. But that did not stop Trump from pushing election conspiracies and touting Lindell's efforts. "I watched him over the last week at his symposium, which was really amazing. Some of the people he had were incredible, incredible people. Mike Lindell," Trump said the next week at a rally in Alabama. "It's true. He had some people up there, really—they were scientists, they were political scientists and beyond. They were incredible, what they said and what they understand."

Trump's aides insisted that the former president never actually believed Lindell's idea that he would somehow get sent back to the White House, even though he publicly entertained the idea. At the end of a statement he dictated to Harrington in June 2021, Trump included the phrase, "2024, or before." One former Trump aide said he was simply having "fun with things."

But no downplaying of the slogan changed the fact that it sent a dangerous message. Trump was sowing doubts about the 2020 results and feeding the falsehood his aides said he deeply believed: that he did not, in fact, lose.

Sympathy for the Devil

THERE WAS PERHAPS NO BETTER BAROMETER FOR DONALD TRUMP'S DOMInance over the GOP than the millions he raised and the near-daily parade of politicians lining up to get his endorsement.

Six months after Trump left the White House and was banished from social media, his team was still able to whip up donations from across the country with the click of a button. And a stamp of approval from Trump could knock out political rivals and all but guarantee his die-hard base would give their support.

A parade of Republican lawmakers marched through Mar-a-Lago and Bedminster to raise money with Trump from the time he landed in Palm Beach through the summer of 2021, including Senator Mike Lee, Governor Kristi Noem, Sarah Huckabee Sanders, Lynda Blanchard, Governor Ron DeSantis, Max Miller, Senator Marco Rubio, Representative Mo Brooks, Josh Mandel, Representative Billy Long, and Representative Ronny Jackson.

Even if some party leaders yearned to leave Trump behind, his millions of supporters continued to write checks and show up at the polls. Cutting off Trump would have meant cutting off their oxygen supply—and the very people now central to the party's identity.

When Trump tapped Susie Wiles to take charge in the spring of 2021, he laid out two top priorities: building out an endorsement process and sorting out his political organization and fundraising arms, which he felt were in disarray.

Trump made clear he wanted the Save America leadership PAC, formed two days after the 2020 election was called for Joe Biden, to get straightened out. The PAC allowed Trump to wield influence in the upcoming elections but also to fund his own team. According to election laws, Trump couldn't promote his own candidacy with the funds, but he could spend an unlimited amount of it on funding other candidates and use the money to pave the way for 2024 with consultants, travel, polling, lawyers, and his growing legal fees.

It was no small undertaking. Wiles had experience with fundraising, but overhauling the mechanics of a massive operation like Trump's was a different matter—and Trump had some serious issues. Chief among them: Few vendors wanted to work with him, or with the Republican Party for that matter.

Campaign Monitor, an email marketing platform, had been the primary distribution engine for Trump's fundraising emails but had suspended the Trump operation after January 6. And major donors, like Marriott, were no longer interested in giving to the GOP.

But issues with email lists and corporate snubs aside, Trump was still the star attraction for major fundraisers at Mar-a-Lago. Make America Great Again Action, a super PAC run by Corey Lewandowski, former Florida attorney general Pam Bondi, and Dave Bossie, held a fundraiser at Trump's New Jersey golf club at the end of May for which ticket prices started at $250,000. In the PAC's first two months it took in more than $3 million from major Republican donors like Don Ahern, a Nevada businessman who gave $1 million; Kelly Loeffler, the wealthy former Georgia senator who had lost her seat to Raphael Warnock in a runoff election; and MyPillow CEO Mike Lindell.

By the end of June, Trump and his political action committees had amassed a war chest of more than $100 million—an unprecedented amount of money (especially for a defeated ex-president) that rivaled the Republican National Committee and the GOP's House and Senate campaign committees. Much of that money was raised off Trump's false claims that the election was stolen, that he needed money to support the audits in Arizona and other states, and his promise to support MAGA candidates in the 2022 midterms. In a statement about his fundraising Trump thanked donors who "share my outrage and want me to continue to fight for the truth."

Trump's fundraising success in the first six months after being forced from office was a proof of concept that falsehoods about the election were now baked in and had become the new Republican "truth."

And it was very on-brand that Trump did not share the wealth. During that six-month period, none of the funds raised by Trump's PAC had gone to any of the audit efforts or boosting any of the candidates Trump had endorsed. Millions instead were spent on political advisers, events, travel, more fundraising outreach, and legal fees for attorneys who had defended Trump in his second impeachment trial. Trump was squirreling away money—and political capital in the form of endorsements—to put toward his next act.

"IT'S GREAT TO BE BACK," Donald Trump said with a grin to a packed room of North Carolina Republicans.

"God Bless the U.S.A.," by country star and conservative favorite Lee Greenwood, had just finished blasting over the speakers at the convention center in Greenville, and Trump paused onstage to look over the scene. Hundreds of die-hard Republican fans waved their phones, trying to catch a glimpse of the former president, and screamed, "I love you!"

Trump's political debut in the summer of 2021 wasn't a mega-rally at a stadium or arena, but a speech in front of just over a thousand Republicans at the annual North Carolina GOP convention.

Wiles and Trump's small group of advisers had planned out a

series of stops over the summer designed to reengage the ex-president with his base of supporters and set him up as kingmaker of the 2022 midterm elections.

They knew—as did Trump—that while he maintained an overwhelming majority of support among Republicans, he was, according to polls, still standing on shaky ground. More than 81 million people—many of them women and Republican-leaning suburban voters—had rejected Trump in the 2020 election. Following his behavior on January 6, top Republicans openly called for fresh leadership in the party.

It was an unprecedented and bizarre moment. The former president had lost his reelection bid and inspired a violent uprising at the U.S. Capitol, yet he maintained overwhelming support among Republicans and was building the foundation for a return to power. He was in a political limbo of his own making, a man at once formidable and cast aside by the general public. But inside the Greenville convention hall, Trump was still a dominating force.

Trump recognized that one of the best ways to assert that force in his post-presidency was to use his coveted political endorsement to promote or punish aspiring candidates. That night in Greenville, there was buzz among the press over whether he would announce his support for one of the three Republican primary candidates who came to the event in Greenville, or whether he would back his daughter-in-law and outspoken defender, Lara Trump, in the open race to replace Senator Richard Burr, one of the seven Republican senators who had voted to convict Trump.

For months there had been speculation about which of the Trump children would follow in his footsteps and co-opt the MAGA movement and Trump name to serve their own political ambitions—and Eric's wife, Lara Trump, who grew up in a middle-class family in Wilmington, North Carolina, and had recently signed on as a talking head at Fox News, seemed poised to jump in. During the 2020 campaign, Lara Trump hosted an in-house online program called *The Right View*. She shared her life on Instagram and built up a brand as a relatable suburban mom—who happened to be married to a Trump. That afternoon, she flew to North Carolina with Trump and invited her family to join her for the event.

Backstage, Trump shook hands with VIPs and met with the three Republican primary candidates, Representative Ted Budd, former governor Pat McCrory, and former representative Mark Walker, who were all eager to get Trump's backing, and Trump could smell blood in the water. In front of a sizable group of people, like a cat toying with its prey, Trump ribbed them about who might get his endorsement— that is, if his daughter-in-law decided not to run.

But he had already made up his mind. Right before walking on-stage, Trump quietly told Budd he had his support, and he made it official in his speech just minutes after his daughter-in-law confirmed she did not have plans to run for Senate.

The decision seemed to take even the die-hard group of Republicans in the room by surprise. Budd had the backing of the Club for Growth, an influential conservative antitax group, but he was polling behind his rivals and running against a former governor. But in the moment, none of that mattered to Trump, who wanted to make sure only the most MAGA made it into the House—but especially into the Senate, where he was less popular among Republicans and had often felt thwarted as president.

Trump's endorsement of Budd also seemed designed to humiliate McCrory, who looked stunned when Trump not only announced his support for Budd but poked at the former governor's record.

McCrory had been critical of Trump's stolen election claims, but Budd had propped up Trump's baseless allegations of voter fraud, objected to the certification of electoral votes on January 6, and, according to texts obtained by CNN, sent Mark Meadows, Trump's chief of staff, the conspiracy theory that Dominion Voting Systems was connected to billionaire liberal donor George Soros. Budd also made a trip to Mar-a-Lago earlier that spring.

Much of Trump's speech in North Carolina stuck to similar themes—claims of election fraud and his grievances over the inauguration of Joe Biden—and he found an audience eager and willing to soak it all in.

"It is coming out, things that happened in the recent election," Trump said. "Dead people voting, dead people. I'm talking about thousands and thousands of dead people, illegal aliens, Indians getting paid to vote in certain states."

"I'm not the one trying to undermine American democracy, I'm the one who's trying to save it," Trump said to cheers from the audience.

When Trump finished speaking, McCrory walked to the back of the room to give his two cents to the press. He was disappointed, he said, but didn't blame Trump, who he claimed had been ill-advised by "Washington insiders." He even suggested that Meadows, a fellow North Carolinian who was at the event, had influenced the decision against him. He was reluctant even to criticize Trump, who had just embarrassed him onstage. He told reporters that Trump had given a "good message."

WHEN IT CAME TO STAFF, there was one thing that mattered beyond anything else—loyalty. From the Trump Organization to the White House, Trump functioned like a mob boss and wanted to be surrounded only by people who demonstrated unfailing loyalty to both him and his immediate goals.

Loyalty was such a fixation for Trump that toward the end of his administration, his presidential personnel office, led by thirty-year-old John McEntee, had conducted "loyalty tests" with officials to root out people who leaked to the press or who weren't committed enough to Trump's agenda. And if Trump had won the presidency, he had planned to overhaul his cabinet and replace those deemed disloyal, those who would challenge Trump's agenda, or those he thought were working only for their own benefit.

Just as in his business career, that loyalty only went one way, and job security was nonexistent. The possibility that at any moment

Trump might decide to fire a senior administration official or cabinet official was very real. Trump was paranoid and believed there were people and forces constantly working to undermine him—the so-called "deep state"—that threatened not only his MAGA agenda but him personally.

Trump trusted few around him at the end of his presidency, and wanted to be certain that those around him were among the most loyal. Among those who initially joined Trump in Palm Beach were Margo Martin, the young and statuesque former White House press aide from Oklahoma, who moved down to help run press for Trump; Molly Michael, Trump's White House scheduler, who was a master of navigating Trump's requests and Rolodex; Will Russell, a special assistant who worked in advance at the White House; Nick Luna, Trump's former White House assistant, who moved down to Florida with his wife, Cassidy Dumbauld, an assistant to Jared Kushner.

For a brief time, Cassidy Hutchinson, who had worked as a right hand to Trump's chief of staff Mark Meadows in the White House, stayed on to work for Trump after the White House and had planned to move down to Palm Beach before some of Trump's staff complained directly to him about the prospect.

Part of Wiles's job was making sure the right team was in place to support Trump as he started getting more involved in the midterms, and that meant trimming the fat. Trump simply didn't need the kind of support staff that came with the job when he was in the White House, and Wiles encouraged some staffers who continued to float around to move along. They were young and ambitious, were starting families, and there simply wasn't a need for some of them while Trump mostly worked out of his golf clubs.

But Trump did still need a personal aide, someone who could handle his tedious daily demands and wasn't above being asked to pick up his briefcase or fetch him a Diet Coke.

Walt Nauta, Trump's military valet at the White House, occupied that role. A military valet was essentially a personal assistant for presidents, and Nauta came down to Palm Beach at the end of Trump's presidency to help get Trump settled. For the first sixty days of Trump's post-presidency, Nauta was in Palm Beach to help move Trump in—part of which included figuring out what to do with the mountains of boxes filled with papers and personal items that were shipped down from the White House and stacked at Mar-a-Lago.

Originally from Guam, Nauta was a member of the Navy, and in the White House he served as part of the presidential support detail as a military valet. Nauta was often found standing outside the doors to the Oval Office ready to assist with getting Trump his meals; he would carry luggage and jackets on trips, and at times would handle documents. He gained a reputation for staying out of the daily drama of the vipers' nest that was the West Wing, and he wasn't involved in policy or politics. His job was to make Trump's life easier.

Nauta was still on active duty with the Navy, and at the end of his tour in Palm Beach was called back to Washington, D.C. But not long after, he got a call from Wiles—Would he like to move down to Florida to work for Trump permanently? His absence had left a notable hole in the operation. Nauta understood Trump's personal rhythms better than anyone else, was loyal, and was not above any request from the former president. Nauta excitedly accepted the job and moved back down to Florida.

IF TRUMP BELIEVED PERSONNEL WAS policy in the White House, the same was true at Mar-a-Lago. As ever, the key to understanding his post-presidency was in the people he surrounded himself with once he got there.

Just as in the White House, there was a constant tension even within the small circle of advisers, aides, and former advisers at Mar-a-Lago, between the political professionals and the grifters who saw dollar signs next to the Trump name, the realists, and the "yes men" or fringe figures who were eager to get in Trump's ear to parrot back what he wanted to hear or to share some political fantasy.

In June 2021, Jason Miller, who had acted as an adviser and communications director for Trump, decided to step away to help run a new right-wing social media venture, Gettr. He had been in the center of the hurricane for months, solely responsible for juggling Trump and the onslaught of media emails and text messages from reporters, and had an opportunity to cash in and try his hand in the emerging conservative tech world.

With Miller gone, Trump needed someone to handle daily communications and the press. A few names were discussed, including Tim Murtaugh, the spokesperson for Trump's 2020 presidential campaign. But to the surprise of many working for Trump, it was announced that Liz Harrington would be joining the team as his new spokesperson.

The statement about her hiring made clear why Trump was eager to bring her on board. "Liz Harrington is a fighter," it read. "She was an important part of our receiving more votes than any incumbent President in U.S. history, far more than we received the first time we won."

Harrington had worked for Steve Bannon as the editor-in-chief of *WarRoom,* a website and podcast that became a hive for MAGA influencers, lawmakers, and figures from Trumpworld to appear and talk about 2020 election conspiracies, the COVID vaccine, or the latest story animating Trump's base. Harrington, with her short blond hair and talking points about the stolen election, became a fixture on the show. Before that, she had been a spokeswoman for the Republican National Committee, where she reliably echoed Trump's falsehoods about the 2020 election—and was repeatedly warned by RNC staff that she sometimes went too far. But she refused to tone it down, and so Harrington and the RNC parted ways.

Harrington wanted to work for Trump because she felt that he needed loyalists around him and that the RNC wasn't doing enough about the 2020 election. But she shared conspiracies about the election and January 6, and, according to aides, too often told Trump exactly what he wanted to hear.

She had been on the job for only a few weeks in July 2021 when she joined Trump for a meeting at Bedminster with the publisher and ghostwriter for a memoir Mark Meadows was working on, and Margo Martin, Trump's press aide, who had been sitting in on book interviews.

Meetings with authors took place with regularity in the spring and summer of 2021. Trump sat down for more than a dozen interviews with authors for books about his presidency.

At his Bedminster golf club in New Jersey, Trump was particularly fixated on a recent report that his handpicked chairman of the Joint Chiefs of Staff, Mark Milley, had stopped Trump from striking Iran in the final weeks of his presidency. "These are bad sick people," Trump said to the group, referring to Milley.

"That was your coup, against you," Harrington said in response. "Like when Milley is talking about, 'Oh you're going to try to do a coup.' No, they were trying to do that before you even were sworn in, trying to overthrow your election."

"With Milley—let me show you an example," Trump said. He then shuffled papers around to find the exact one he wanted to reference. "He said that I wanted to attack Iran, isn't it amazing? I have a big pile of papers, this thing just came up. Look—this was him. They presented me this—this is off the record but—they presented me this. This was him. This was the Defense Department and him. . . . I just found, isn't that amazing? This totally wins my case, you know. Except it is, like, highly confidential. Secret. This is secret information. Look, look at this," Trump said.

"Hillary would print that out all the time, you know. Her private emails," Harrington said.

"No, she'd send it to Anthony Weiner," Trump replied to laughs in the room in reference to the former Democratic congressman who was married to a top Clinton aide.

The conversation came from a recording that would be reported on two years later by CNN, as part of special counsel Jack Smith's indictment of Trump over the mishandling of classified information. And the papers Trump was shuffling around inside his golf club were alleged to be documents related to the Pentagon's plans to attack Iran.

"This is secret information," Trump said in the recording. "As president I could have declassified it. Now I can't, you know, but this is still a secret."

"Now we have a problem," Harrington replied, laughing.

Harrington, as it turned out, was exactly right. The episode would later become a major problem for Trump.

While Harrington remained as a spokesperson for Trump, just one month after she took on her new role, a decision was made to bring on someone else who could help run a tighter ship—both with Trump and the media.

IN JULY 2021, TAYLOR BUDOWICH found himself sitting across from Trump at his Bedminster club to interview for a job working as his spokesman and communications director. Thirty minutes later, he was hired.

Budowich wasn't a fixture on Bannon's *WarRoom* or on Fox News, but he was well known within Republican circles as a young and savvy media operator. A native Californian, he had been working in his home state with Ric Grenell, Trump's former acting director of national intelligence and U.S. ambassador to Germany, on Fix California, a political group aimed at registering voters and expanding school choice in the state.

Budowich got his start in politics working for a California-based group, Tea Party Express, when the Tea Party movement propelled a new wave of Republicans into Congress. Later, he worked for both Florida House speaker Richard Corcoran and Florida governor Ron DeSantis, and his first day on the job with DeSantis's campaign happened to be the same day Wiles started her work overhauling the then congressman's operation. His work in Florida introduced him to the Trump reelection campaign in 2020, where he worked closely with Donald Trump Jr. and his fiancée, Kimberly Guilfoyle.

Budowich was hired in summer 2021 in part because he had the trust of Trump's inner circle, which included Wiles, Trump Jr., and Grenell, whom Trump called to ask about hiring Budowich. But just as significantly, he wasn't part of the "crazies," as one aide put it, or the kind of people who tell Trump whatever they think he wants to hear at the moment.

There was a recognition among Trump aides that the former president was always going to be drawn toward fringe figures who encouraged his worst characteristics, whether it was to lash out at any perceived enemy or peddle unsubstantiated conspiracies because it fit a certain narrative. No matter how professional they tried to make Trump's operation, they couldn't always control who Trump was meeting with or calling, or what information would land in his lap.

Hiring Budowich and others with a firm grounding in reality, though, was a successful form of damage control. If they couldn't restrain Trump, at the very least they wouldn't encourage his worst impulses in ways that were politically—or even legally—damaging.

In addition to Wiles and Budowich, there was Dan Scavino, Trump's former golf caddie turned trusted confidant and adviser, who understood Trump better than anyone and had a finger on the MAGA movement. Trump particularly trusted Scavino for his willingness to offer an unvarnished opinion.

And for anything political in nature, Trump would turn to Brian Jack, the affable young operative from Georgia who had joined Trump's 2016 campaign as the national delegate director after working on the Ben Carson campaign and then served as Trump's deputy White House political director before his promotion around the 2018 midterms.

Almost every week that summer they would meet on a 10 A.M. call to map out the basic logistics for the former president. By all measures it was routine and unexciting—Trump's travel, his still limited media appearances, the latest lawmaker who planned to drop in. Brad Parscale would report on the number of emails that had been sent out. Andy Surabian, as well as Justin Clark and Bill Stepien, who had their own political consulting shop, would give a political update about primary races on the horizon and who had asked for a Trump endorsement.

What was remarkable about an otherwise unremarkable call in Trumpworld was the fact that it never seemed to leak to the press—and for the most part, there was little backbiting. There was always bad blood. Parscale and Stepien had open wounds from the 2020 campaign. And yet, for the first time, it wasn't making daily headlines.

"DO YOU MISS ME?" DONALD Trump said to cheers. "They miss me."

Trump was in Ohio for his first rally in almost six months. He had appeared at CPAC in February, given a speech in front of RNC donors at his club in April, and addressed the North Carolina GOP in early June, but his event in Ohio later that same month marked his official return to the rally settings that had become the signature of his movement—and served as a precursor to the riots on January 6.

The rally was meant to show the ten House Republican members who had voted for his impeachment that he and his base of supporters were out for blood.

Thousands of people sat in eight miles of traffic to make it into the dusty Lorain County Fairgrounds for a chance to see Trump. The surrounding area was packed with roadside vendors selling T-shirts and posters and flags and hats and just about any item of clothing the Trump name or a pro-Trump slogan could be emblazoned on.

WE THE PEOPLE ARE PISSED OFF, one popular rally T-shirt read.

Out of office and off social media, Trump was a diminished figure nationally, but his base still treated him like a rock star, and like the roving Deadhead fan base of the Grateful Dead, they followed him to Ohio. The "Front Row Joes," a group of Trump's most devoted fans, set up in a nearby parking lot over three days before the event began to secure the best spot near the stage. Others opened their tailgates and cracked open beers before going through the security mags required for entry.

The event was billed as a "Save America" rally in support of Max Miller, a young former White House aide who was running for Congress against Representative Anthony Gonzalez, the two-term congressman and former professional football player who was one of the ten Republicans to vote for Trump's second impeachment. It was also advertised as the "first of many appearances in support of candidates and causes that further the MAGA agenda and accomplishments of President Trump's administration." At the rally, Trump savaged Gonzalez with stories alleging the congressman requested to fly on Air Force One when he was president, only for him to turn around to vote for his impeachment.

Miller was one of the first candidates Trump endorsed. Hailing from a wealthy and influential family in northeast Ohio, he had worked on Trump's 2016 and 2020 campaigns and served as an advance man in the White House—a role with an outsize importance to the deeply image-conscious Trump, who loved his political rallies and events. In the White House, Miller was called the Music Man, according to his ex-girlfriend, White House press secretary Stephanie Grisham, because he put together the rally playlists and was sometimes called in to distract or calm Trump.

Trump's choice of Miller demonstrated the essential criteria for a Trump endorsement: Have a personal relationship with Trump, or back up Trump's false claims of a stolen election, or show an appetite for retribution to those who had been disloyal to Trump. Miller espoused Trump's "America First" principles and fitted neatly into each category.

"Come 2024, we're going to get him elected for the third time," Miller told the crowd.

They cheered, but the thousands of people sweating out in the hot sun were only there to hear from Trump, who rattled through a list of his greatest hits, and his litany of complaints about the Biden family and 2020.

"The subject matter is somewhat depressing," Trump said.

In a sign of just how much Trump's election lies had gripped his base, there was a palpable anger in the crowd—they believed Trump when he said the election was stolen and bought into the alternate reality Trump had created and that was on display at the rally.

As Trump mingled with VIPs backstage before the event, the crowd sat quietly to watch a PowerPoint presentation delivered by a Cincinnati-area math teacher who clicked through slides with charts and numbers meant to convince people that there was widespread election fraud.

Mike Lindell smiled and posed for selfies with fans in the crowd who called him a "hero."

Representative Marjorie Taylor Greene, the newly elected member of Congress from Georgia who expressed support for the conspiracy theories espoused by the fringe QAnon group, received a standing ovation when she came onstage and said the election was stolen by the "dirty, rotten Democrats."

"Let me ask you a question—who is president?" Greene said. "Trump! Trump! Trump!" the crowd chanted in response.

NOT LONG AFTER TRUMP HAD arrived in Palm Beach, a parade of Republicans made a pilgrimage down to Mar-a-Lago or requested an opportunity to kiss the ring and get an endorsement in their respective races. Trump's endorsement in the 2022 GOP primaries, they believed, would secure the vote of his steadfastly loyal and fanatical base of supporters.

Candidates and their well-paid advisers would fly in on private planes or cross-country flights to make their case for why he should pick them. Others would find ways to appear at events at Trump's club where they could bump into him or one of his aides. Even for Trump, who liked flattery and attention, the appeals were sometimes groveling and over the top.

There were lunches, dinners, meetings in his office at Mar-a-Lago, calls to Trump, and fundraisers strategically held at Trump properties to increase the likelihood that Trump might pop in during the hors d'oeuvres and give a short speech that might impress donors.

Before Trump left for Bedminster in the summer of 2021, over a dozen candidates including Arkansas gubernatorial candidate Sarah Huckabee Sanders, Senators Marco Rubio of Florida and Rand Paul of Kentucky, and Governors Ron DeSantis of Florida and Kristi Noem of South Dakota held fundraisers at Mar-a-Lago.

For the Noem fundraiser, $1,000 would get you into a cocktail party reception hosted by Trump Jr. and Guilfoyle, and a $4,000 contribution would get a private roundtable discussion and photo op in addition to the open bar at Trump's club.

And it wasn't just Mar-a-Lago—Bedminster also became a popular spot for Republicans to host their events. Representatives Elise Stefanik, Ronny Jackson, and Beth Van Duyne all held events at Trump's New Jersey club over the summer.

The efforts by Republicans to capture Trump's attention at times bordered on parody. As an example of just how feverish and competitive the Republican Senate candidates from Ohio were to vie for Trump's attention, in early 2021, according to *Politico*'s Alex Isenstadt, they all made a trip down to Palm Beach to attend a fundraiser at Trump's golf club for Max Miller—and try to get face time with Trump. After milling about the golf club with cocktails and hors d'oeuvres in hand, the four candidates were called to a back-room meeting. For fifteen minutes they sat around a table and tried to plead their case and attacked each other in an episode that was more akin to a dramatic reality TV reunion than a visit with an ex-president. No one left with Trump's endorsement.

There were other cases of candidates lining up an expensive fundraiser at a Trump property only to watch him pick someone else.

Lynda Blanchard, a Republican Senate candidate in Alabama, appeared confident that Trump would pick her in the race to replace retiring senator Richard Shelby. The wealthy Alabama businesswoman had donated nearly $1 million to political committees supporting Trump, and went on to serve as Trump's ambassador to

Slovenia—the home country of his wife, Melania Trump. And at a Mar-a-Lago fundraiser, Trump dropped by to say hello and to praise her diplomatic work.

But the Mar-a-Lago fundraiser was for naught. Trump was already leaning toward another candidate, Representative Mo Brooks, a longtime ally who spoke at the January 6 rally ahead of the Capitol riots. He was even overheard on Capitol Hill telling an unidentified person, "The president told me that when I do announce he would say good, strong, positive things about me."

Just a few weeks after the fundraiser, Trump announced his support for Blanchard's opponent, Brooks.

TRUMP'S ADVISERS UNDERSTOOD THAT THERE was a risk to the former president inserting himself into the 2022 election. If Trump-endorsed candidates lost en masse in the primaries, it could spell the end of his burgeoning 2024 ambitions. And they tried, as best they could, to put in place a system for endorsement requests.

Even if they could not control how Trump ultimately came to his decision on an endorsement, or who was able to get his ear at Mar-a-Lago, they were going to have some semblance of order.

A special inbox was set up for candidates to submit a formal request for an endorsement consideration. And Wiles asked Trump's other advisers to keep her posted on who they had political consulting contracts with, so it was clear among the immediate team of Trump advisers who was making money off different candidates.

The post-presidency process for advising Trump on the different candidates and races worked similarly to how things were done in the Trump White House.

For House races, Brian Jack, Trump's former White House political director, would walk him through races, district by district.

After leaving the White House, Jack spent the 2022 midterm election cycle running national political operations for soon-to-be-Speaker Kevin McCarthy, while also staying close to Trump's small team.

Jack and McCarthy first met the day after Trump's last State of the Union address in 2020 during a meeting with the president and his political team in the Yellow Oval Room of the White House. McCarthy had come to Trump asking him to endorse the House members who did not vote for impeachment—and reminded Trump that it was only right to return the favor after some of them stuck their necks out for the president. Trump got the message, and in the coming weeks, Trump would release batches of endorsements from his Twitter feed supporting almost all of the incumbent House candidates.

For the 2020 election, McCarthy and Senator Mitch McConnell would sometimes come to the White House for meetings with Trump to review potential endorsements with his team. In slideshows prepared by Jack, Trump would be shown a set of information, no matter the race: previous election results, race ratings, photos of the candidates, polling, and who of Trump's allies had already endorsed in the race. These were meant to be neutral, fact-based pages that Trump could review before making a decision—even if he was being worked on the side by whoever was advising a candidate.

The same kind of slideshows were presented to Trump by Jack, Wiles, and Stepien for the 2022 House races. If Trump didn't already have a relationship with a candidate, he would be shown options for a potential endorsement in meetings with his advisers, who tried their best to keep Trump on track. Donald Trump Jr., who had become popular with conservatives and the far right, also met with his father to encourage him to back certain candidates.

For Senate races, Rick Scott, the wealthy Republican senator from Florida who led the National Republican Senatorial Committee, would update Trump. Scott would fly in from Washington to sit on the patio with Trump at Mar-a-Lago and carefully flip through color-coded binders of Senate candidates, methodically pointing to each person's credentials, political dynamics, and internal polling. Scott didn't believe in getting involved in the primaries, but he knew he could not stop Trump from following suit. He also knew that flying down to Mar-a-Lago to say "Do not endorse someone" was a bad idea—it would either hurt their relationship or motivate Trump to endorse.

Trump considered Scott, unlike many of the political consultants and members of Congress who would try to give Trump their two cents on politics and policy, more like a peer. A wealthy former hospital executive turned governor and then senator, Scott was worth millions and never pressured Trump for financial backing—something Trump, never one to dole out money if he could avoid it, always liked.

Aides would often remark on how carefully Scott managed his relationship with Trump, which spanned more than two decades. Beyond being rich and teetotalers, they had little in common. Trump was brash, relished conflict, and liked to shoot from the hip. Scott was quiet and a devoted fan of Dale Carnegie's book *How to Win Friends and Influence People.* And although he had a ruthless side when it came to work and the Senate, he always made a point to write a thank-you note to anyone he spent time with.

When Scott was governor of Florida, Trump would call and complain about planes landing at Palm Beach airport because they flew over Mar-a-Lago. Scott would tell Trump he had no control over where the planes flew, but that didn't stop Trump from repeatedly demanding that Scott make the planes change course.

As chairman of the Senate Republican campaign arm, Scott would fly down to Palm Beach to give Trump personal updates on the races and once again listen to Trump's complaints. Scott and his aides had carefully studied how to communicate with Trump, including how best to present visuals to the ex-president. For example, they learned that Trump only liked to see graphs with a "hockey stick" trend line shooting sharply upward, so it became a running joke that any graphs or statistics were presented to show lines moving up to the right no matter what information was being shown.

At Mar-a-Lago, surrounded by members enjoying steak dinners, Scott would flip through his binder of candidates until Trump's attention was inevitably stolen by a phone call from Fox News host Sean Hannity or another friend of Trump's who just wanted to chat.

But Scott, like Trump's other advisers, was up against a man who bragged about going with his gut instinct on decisions and enjoyed holding court with candidates and advisers who were eager to flatter him. As much as Trump's team tried to bring order to the endorsement process, it was still at times arbitrary—Trump would be quick to endorse one candidate but hold off on getting involved in another race, for reasons that were sometimes unclear. And Trump was particularly consumed with making sure he stepped in to endorse in races where he felt crossed or betrayed by one of the candidates.

TRUMP ENDORSEMENTS WERE NOT ALWAYS about chemistry or Trump's gut instinct. They were sometimes simply about revenge.

Trump's earliest endorsements in 2021 were for people like Max Miller in Ohio and Representative Jody Hice, who was running for Georgia secretary of state against Brad Raffensperger, the incumbent who had refused to go along with Trump's request to "find 11,780 votes."

Trump and his advisers wanted all ten of those House Republicans to be pushed out or lose in the upcoming midterm primaries.

They had voted for Trump's impeachment because they believed the president incited insurrection on January 6, that he should face consequences for his actions, and further, that by impeaching Trump, the Republican Party might finally move in a new direction. But they were mistaken, and they faced punishment by their own party for having voted their conscience.

Over the following months, Trump and his team, led by Wiles, worked to recruit challengers for each of the ten members who had voted for impeachment.

But the top priority for Trump's team was finding the right person to take down Representative Liz Cheney, who had one of the most conservative records in the House conference, voting with Trump's position 93 percent of the time, but had become the most outspoken critic of Trump and his behavior on January 6, and the loudest voice calling for a change in the direction of the Republican Party.

"The President of the United States summoned this mob, assembled the mob, and lit the flame of this attack. Everything that followed was his doing. None of this would have happened without the President. The President could have immediately and forcefully intervened to stop the violence. He did not," Cheney said in a statement about her decision to impeach Trump. "There has never been a greater betrayal by a President of the United States of his office and his oath to the Constitution."

Overnight, Cheney had become the leader of the Never Trump movement and had attracted the support of disaffected Republicans and Democrats alike who agreed with her brutal assessments of the GOP, American democracy, and Trump's abuses of power.

House Republicans did their part to try to take down Cheney by stripping her conference chair title in retaliation for her criticisms of the party, Trump, and January 6. But Cheney pushed through with her personal mission to make sure Trump never returned to the Oval Office and that the GOP would finally face the music over the deadly riots on Capitol Hill and the belief—quickly spreading through the party—that the election was stolen. Less than two months later she was elevated by then Speaker Nancy Pelosi to join the Democratic-led January 6 investigation.

Cheney was well funded, propelled by her newfound popularity and media attention, and of course, she was part of a political dynasty in the state as the daughter of former vice president Dick Cheney, who for a decade represented Wyoming in Congress in the same at-large seat his daughter would later hold.

Trump and his allies believed defeating Cheney in her red Wyoming district was possible, but they needed to find the right candidate to take her on—and they could not miss. The race, they believed, was of existential importance to Trump. A loss by any MAGA candidate to Cheney could jeopardize Trump's entire political operation and his odds of a run in 2024.

Justin Clark and Andy Surabian were tasked with overseeing the Wyoming endorsement process and vetting potential Cheney challengers. Initially they met with each candidate over Zoom meetings, where they would ask for details about their policy positions, fundraising, and background. One of the early challengers to Cheney, Wyoming state senator Andy Bouchard, had already found himself embroiled in scandal after admitting he impregnated a fourteen-year-old girl, considered statutory rape in many places, and then married her when she was fifteen.

In late July, Trump scheduled meetings with Wyoming state representative Chuck Gray and attorney Darin Smith at his Bedminster golf club, but he was unimpressed with both. Trump was skeptical of polling they showed him in their separate meetings indicating that they were miles ahead of the other candidates. He was leaning toward Bo Biteman, a Wyoming state senator, who was backed by the Club for Growth, but he wasn't sold on any candidate yet.

As Trump and his advisers sat in his office in Bedminster, Surabian happened to bring up a separate race—the race for governor. A woman named Harriet Hageman reached out to Surabian asking to introduce herself.

Hageman was an attorney from Cheyenne and Republican National Committeewoman who unsuccessfully ran for Wyoming governor in 2018. But she was thinking about taking another shot at running against Republican governor Mark Gordon, and she had recently been encouraged to consider jumping into the race to challenge Cheney.

Surabian told Trump that Hageman had called to bring up the idea of her running against Cheney or the Wyoming governor.

As soon as Trump heard the name Gordon, though, his mind went elsewhere—to windmills. The Wyoming governor was a proponent of renewable energy in the state, in particular, wind farms. Trump loathed many things, but he reserved some of his most ardent vitriol for wind turbines, or windmills, as he called them, which he was known to rant at length about at rallies, often to the confusion of rallygoers.

His dislike of the renewable energy source originated in Scotland almost two decades earlier, when Trump built a golf resort on the northeast coast without realizing there were plans for an offshore wind farm near his course. Trump went to war with Scottish officials over the wind farm, which was built despite his protestations, and a personal, obsessive, anti-wind-turbine crusade was born.

Trump was intrigued. He asked his team to get in touch with Hageman to see if she wanted to primary the "windmill-loving governor." But Trump and his team soon recognized that she might be their best bet for taking on Cheney.

In July, Trump's former chief of staff, Mark Meadows, flew to Jackson, Wyoming, to have breakfast with Hageman and called up a Trump ally, Representative Jim Jordan of Ohio, to help him make the case. The next month, Hageman was on a plane to Bedminster to meet Trump, and soon, with the encouragement of staff and allies including Senator Cynthia Lummis, Trump gave her his support.

Over the course of August, a team of Trump allies that included Bill Stepien, Justin Clark, and former Trump campaign spokesman Tim Murtaugh mobilized to prepare a Hageman bid. Andrew Surabian, who worked closely with Donald Trump Jr., led a pro-Hageman PAC.

The effort by Trump and his team to find a Cheney challenger demonstrated how serious Trump was about taking revenge against the members who voted for his impeachment, but also how Trump's team—which had in the past been known for its petty drama and infighting—was actually functioning in a professional and coordinated way. Stepien, Clark, Nick Trainer, and Tim Murtaugh ran Hageman's campaign, while Surabian and Trump Jr. took charge of a super PAC supporting her.

They made sure that on the same day Hageman announced her candidacy, Trump gave his endorsement—to clear the field but also signal to Cheney backers he was going to quickly scramble resources into the race. And they did some work in advance to make sure that would happen.

Trump had been in touch with David McIntosh and the Club for Growth, and in the first real rift between Trump's team and the organization—the first of many to come in the midterms—the group finally encouraged Biteman, their preferred candidate, to stand down.

And after the other Wyoming candidates met with Trump in July, his advisers made a request of each of them as they walked them out of the meeting. "Will you commit to dropping out if Trump endorses someone else?" They all agreed.

Cheney and her team remained defiant—and had millions in the bank—but recognized it was going to be an uphill battle. The congresswoman—who had one of the most conservative records in Congress—was being singled out and vilified by her colleagues for speaking up about what she believed was her party's rejection of core principles, and Trump's team was hell-bent on making sure they destroyed her political future.

Only in America

HOW TO MAKE MONEY IN THE WORLD THAT MAGA MADE?

Donald Trump's business ventures were a sprawling web of things both tacky and grand. Over the years he had put his gold-plated name on five-star hotels, golf courses from Scotland to South Florida, wine, steaks, hats, and even water bottles. He was the ultimate marketer. Trump used his media savvy to sell how-to books and star in a reality TV show in which producers fashioned him into the character of a decisive and successful businessman who enjoyed firing people, a role that not only made him money but cross-promoted his businesses in the bargain.

The Obamas, Bushes, and Clintons all made millions in the years after they left the White House as authors and public speakers, and each stayed busy building presidential libraries and foundations. But upon retreating to Florida after his presidency, Trump took his own unique avenues for building his personal wealth and making a fortune off selling to his political base.

There would be a speaking tour with Bill O'Reilly—"The History Tour," with tickets starting at $100—a $75 photo book, MAGA merchandise, his social media brand, his NFT collection, and even a bar inside Trump Tower on Fifth Avenue named 45 Wine & Whiskey featuring cocktails called The Don, FLOTUS, Rose Garden, and a $45 offering called Forty Five, featuring an "Old Fashioned, Two All-American Beef Sliders with ketchup & Diet Coke."

Trump promised that the "History Tour" would be "fun, fun, fun for everyone who attends." He and O'Reilly would sit onstage and go back and forth over different topics such as the pandemic and January 6. With a "VIP Meet and Greet" package, which included photos with Trump and O'Reilly and a preshow reception, tickets could go for more than $8,500. Trump is reported to have made more than $3 million for his appearances with O'Reilly in Dallas, Houston, and Orlando.

And there was also the American Freedom Tour, which offered fans the chance to hear from Trump and a host of right-wing stars like Donald Trump Jr., former national security adviser turned conspiracy theorist Michael Flynn, and Dinesh D'Souza, the writer and filmmaker whose conviction for violating campaign finance laws had been erased by a Trump pardon. At these "conferences," Trump and his allies gave speeches, posed for photos with fans, and signed books, with tickets ranging from $9 to $3,995.

The events were lucrative even if ticket sales were sluggish. Trump promoted them by using his political action committee's email list, and at one point the National Republican Congressional Committee sent out a text to boost "History Tour" ticket sales. "Love Trump? Want to see him speak live? Enter now to win 2 tickets to Trump's tour with Bill O'Reilly. Link to enter expires in 1 hour," the text read.

But for Trump, the first and most important post-presidential business opportunity would have him building out his own media empire. Angry and bitter over his suspension from major social media platforms and frustrated with Fox News, Trump mused about creating a platform of his own.

The idea wasn't exactly new. Trump had signed the agreement with Wes Moss and Andy Litinsky in late January to create the partnership that would spawn Trump's Twitter alternative, Truth Social, and through the first half of 2021, Moss and Litinsky would work feverishly to build out the new company.

But Trump had long been obsessed with media stars, who were some of his closest confidants, and with the ups and downs of television ratings, which he tracked with weekly printouts while in the White House. Back in 2016, Trump's son-in-law Jared Kushner had discussions with a media executive about creating a Trump-branded television channel that could either capitalize on Trump's fans if he lost or help promote his agenda in the White House if he won, according to *The New York Times*. After Fox News called Arizona for Joe Biden on Election Night 2020, Trump considered building his own subscription-based digital streaming platform to compete with the right-wing cable giant.

While still in the White House, Trump had been approached by the right-wing website Parler about posting exclusively on its platform in exchange for a 40 percent stake in the company, an offer that did not get very far while he was still in office. But capitalizing on his persona had since the beginning of his career been his skill and his priority, and almost from the moment he left Washington, Trump had worked to restore his fortune and maintain his place in the public consciousness.

Litinsky and Moss had been competitors on *The Apprentice* in 2004, when Litinsky was a student at Harvard University and Moss was a wealth manager in Atlanta. Litinsky, better known as Andy Dean, went on to work with Trump on different production projects before hosting a radio show, and Moss returned to Georgia. But the two remained friends, and shortly after Trump lost the 2020 election they had hatched the idea for a media company that revolved around the former president and his brand of conservative culture.

After signing their deal with Trump, Litinksy and Moss had brought Will Wilkerson, an executive in conservative radio, on board to help run operations and get the idea off the ground. Creating a media company with Trump, they knew, was bound to be complicated—not only was there Trump to deal with, but his family, and advisers, both official and unofficial, who might want a piece of the pie. And they had big ideas for what Trump Media could be, from a social media app to a streaming service that offered shows they dreamed up—like a Tiger Woods golf special, a Paula Deen cooking show, maybe a political talk show with Lou Dobbs.

According to an extensive interview with Wilkerson and notes and documents related to the building of Trump Media, the group turned to investment banks to raise money, but so soon after January 6, many were skeptical of backing anything involving Trump. The risk of reputational harm was just too great for many investors to stomach. So the group started exploring the potential of SPACs, special purpose acquisition companies, which are shell companies that merge with private companies, essentially taking them public while avoiding the regulatory requirements that come with an initial public offering for two years. Rounds of cold-calling investors led them to Patrick Orlando, a financier based in Miami, who was interested in the project and had launched a SPAC called Benessere Capital Acquisition Corp. that had already raised $100 million.

To show Trump, Orlando, and potential investors that Trump Media Group was in fact a real project, and to demonstrate some progress so Trump wouldn't get cold feet, the group had met on February 22 at Mar-a-Lago.

More than a dozen people, including Dan Scavino, the conservative commentator Dan Bongino, Scott St. John, a top producer of game shows including *Deal or No Deal* and *America's Got Talent,* and Kraig Kitchin, the former head of Premiere Radio Networks, gathered in a tapestry-lined room at Mar-a-Lago to hear the presentation. The former president joined them after spending the morning playing golf with Jack Nicklaus, waltzing into the dining room wearing a polo and khakis and holding a photo of himself with the famous golfer that he had printed out to show off to the group.

"What do you think of all this?" Trump said to Bongino, who was seated next to him at the table as Moss and Litinksy sketched out the vision for Trump Media.

Bongino replied, "This is the greatest financial arbitrage of all time."

After the meeting, there was a breakout session between Moss, Litinsky, and Patrick Orlando, to iron out the bullet points. Orlando ordered rum. In the swirl around the partners, Mike Lindell walked out from the patio in Bermuda shorts and a Hawaiian shirt and engaged Dan Bongino about how he was avoiding going to Minnesota because lawyers for Dominion election systems were trying to serve him papers in their massive defamation lawsuit against him and multiple other MAGA defendants. This was a typical scene at Mar-a-Lago. And contrary to reports that Kevin McCarthy told colleagues on the Hill that he visited Trump in Palm Beach because the former president was depressed and not eating, the partners in the Trump Media Group observed a man who didn't seem to have missed a meal and showed no signs of being down.

To the partners, Trump seemed as voluble as ever. He would repeat himself a lot, saying the same five or six things. He was encyclopedic regarding his prior social media numbers—88 million on Twitter, a combined total of all social media of 134—but he generally seemed *pleasant*. They would come to understand that being charming and charismatic was how Trump drew you in, especially if he didn't know you. He charmed with funny Twitter stories, like the time when he was writing a tweet and the AutoCorrect on his phone changed "Melania" to "Melissa," and he almost sent out a tweet about "my beautiful wife, Melissa."

The team would become familiar with Trump's dark side as well. How he would use his wrath to get whatever he wanted. How, if people didn't bend to his whims, he would scorch the earth. The partners weren't naifs—they were aware of the prior four years and the revolving door of characters that had gone into and out of the White House, and the way they'd all been treated. So they knew they'd always be walking a fine line, but their view was that they were bringing him the potential of billions of dollars in new wealth, with zero exposure. Why would he turn on them?

Trump would call his new social media venture Truth Social, in part because he thought it was a good troll of the established media that had kept a running tally of the lies he had told during his presidency. Initially, the Trump Media team had been looking for a name with five letters, like "tweet." They considered names like "Xenon," "Trumpet," and "Vert," when Trump asked if the domain name Truth Social was available.

"You're not going to believe this," one of the Trump Media team members told him. "*Truth* is available and subject to you for the price of $2,300."

"Truth Social" may have been surprisingly easy to trademark, but TMG, or the Trump Media Group, they discovered, was already spoken for by an entity called Tiny Meat Gang, a comedy podcast. Litinsky and Moss solved that problem by morphing the name into Trump Media and Technology Group.

Through the spring of 2021, Litinsky, Moss, and a small team had worked to build a brand-new social media platform from the ground up. In early May, after having secured $2 million in financing, they returned to Mar-a-Lago for another meeting with Trump. As they snacked on crab cakes, sliders, and pigs in a blanket, they walked Trump through the next steps for the company—but the company's namesake, they found, was distracted by members buzzing by and daily social events—part of the spectacle that surrounded him at Mar-a-Lago.

A fundraiser for veterans was being held that night, and Lee Greenwood was performing. As his mind wandered, Trump reminisced about the time Chinese president Xi Jinping came to the club, and he warned him about Taiwan, and talked about the Taliban.

In order to make sure that they captured Trump's attention at the right time, Moss and Litinsky started paying two of Trump's aides at Mar-a-Lago. According to invoices, Will Russell and Dan Scavino, Trump's former caddy, were paid $15,000 and $20,000, respectively, as consultants. Among the things they consulted on was essentially monitoring Trump's mood, according to Wilkerson—giving their insight on Trump, determining the best time to call him, and relaying information on when he would be on the golf course.

Synchronizing schedules was crucial as the group worked to lock down investors and organize the business. There had already been signs that the company was on shaky ground. As the commercial potential of the venture became clear, and vultures began to circle, Litinsky, Moss, and Wilkerson had even adapted a theme song, "Whatever It Takes," by Imagine Dragons:

Falling too fast to prepare for this
Tripping in the world could be dangerous
Everybody circling, it's vulturous
Negative, nepotist

Having to balance so many competing interests, and stave off multiple competitors who were seemingly coming at Trump from all directions, they'd begun to feel embattled, and paranoid, and at a meeting with Orlando in April even became concerned that their financier might be wearing a wire, because he had started discussing the possibility of merging Trump Media not with Benessere Capital Acquisition Corp., but with a different SPAC that he planned to start, to be called Digital World. Paranoia was rampant in Trumpworld. But they believed the sudden discussion of a new SPAC could somehow be a setup, one which could get them in trouble with the Securities and Exchange Commission. There are strict financial rules that prevent pre-merger communications between a SPAC and a target company, and when Orlando filed a registration with the SEC for the new SPAC, he would claim in his filing that no one associated with Digital World had "initiated any substantive discussions, directly or indirectly, with any business combination target." Litinsky, Moss, and Wilkerson couldn't be sure that that was true. Was somebody setting them up?

A Friday in early June would become known as "meltdown day." The group was given a heads-up that Jason Miller, who continued working as an adviser and spokesman for Trump after he left the White House, had come to Trump with an offer to join his social media platform, Gettr (short for "getting together"), for millions of dollars and a stake in the company.

Just as Truth Social planned to do, Gettr would take aim at disaffected Trump supporters or right-wing social media users who were angry with Twitter for banishing Trump or who believed conservatives were being censored on mainstream apps. Gettr was backed by Chinese billionaire Guo Wengui, a friend of Steve Bannon's, who had gained notoriety in right-wing circles for casting himself as an anticommunist dissident.

Further complicating things—and despite having already signed an agreement to create Trump Media—Trump was also scheduled to meet with conservative commentator Candace Owens and billionaire right-wing donor and activist Rebekah Mercer about another social media app, Parler, at his Bedminster club.

Litinsky and Moss were livid. Trump was already showing himself to be an unreliable business partner—he was very nearly in breach of his agreement—and investors were concerned that he would make a side deal or flake entirely.

Trump stuck with his plans for Truth Social, although he would use Gettr for leverage in conversations about Trump Media. The overlapping pitches showed just how much money—and political influence—some investors saw in Trump's social media presence. Twitter had helped create Trump, but without the platform to shoot off his every thought, Trump felt he had lost significant cultural power.

"I need my voice back," Trump would say in meetings, over and over again.

On October 20, Trump announced his plans to create Truth Social by merging Trump Media and Technology Group and a SPAC called Digital World Acquisition Corp.

"We live in a world where the Taliban has a huge presence on Twitter, yet your favorite American President has been silenced. This is unacceptable," Trump said in a press release. "I am excited to send out my first TRUTH on TRUTH Social very soon. TMTG was founded with a mission to give a voice to all. I'm excited to soon begin sharing my thoughts on TRUTH Social and to fight back against Big Tech."

To run Truth Social, Trump recruited one of his staunchest allies in Congress, California representative Devin Nunes, who soon resigned his seat to take the job.

The same night Trump publicly announced Truth Social and his plans to take on Big Tech companies like Twitter and Facebook, he wanted to make a call to Apple CEO Tim Cook about the new app.

Litinsky prepared a script for him that went like this: "Hi Tim, it's your favorite President. I wanted to let you know that we are excited to have 'Truth Social' in the App Store. We are going to be an inclusive social network that doesn't discriminate against political ideology. We welcome all views, including liberals! Truth Social is like Twitter but we don't cancel conservatives, Christians, and libertarians. The good news, our moderation is great. We are using 'Hive'—they have the best artificial intelligence for moderation and you already know them . . . so we won't allow child porn or the sick stuff the Taliban does on Twitter that Twitter allows them to do. Tim, you are great. And who knows . . . maybe we will be having dinner in the White House again in a couple years. Take care."

Stock for Digital World Acquisition Corp. shot up like a rocket in what resembled the kind of frenzy that had greeted meme stocks like GameStop. Shares jumped from less than $10 to $45.50 by the end of the day after Trump announced the deal.

Trump called Litinsky from the golf course after the announcement to boast about the stock price, but also to make a request. Could Litinsky give a percentage of his equity to his wife, Melania? It was a strange question, especially as Trump already owned 90 percent of the company and might easily have given some of those shares to his wife. Instead he was asking his partner to transfer some of his own compensation to the former First Lady. It would be the first of several such overtures that got louder and louder, until Litinsky would be removed from his position with the company in March 2022. The entire project would become riddled with backstabbing and infighting. And up until the day Trump signed the merger agreements in October 2021, he was still threatening the team at Trump Media that he could jump ship to Gettr.

Wilkerson and others involved with Trump Media composed the first Truth Social post from their WeWork offices. "I am going to post, or rather compose, a Truth for the forty-fifth and soon to be forty-seventh president of these United States," Wilkerson said to the camera. At the moment, Trump had only eighty-two followers. Trump's first Truth Social post was added to his page: "Get Ready! Your favorite President will see you soon!"

And while the announcement built buzz, the rollout was less successful.

When Truth Social finally launched in February 2022, it was glitchy and full of bugs. The app had been made on preorder basis, meaning that instead of gradually scaling up in membership, it was dumped onto multiple email lists, creating a torrent of members all at once and forcing some vendors to abruptly stop anyone from signing up with Truth Social, as the company had reached its limit on users, creating a waiting list of more than a million prospective customers. This quickly became the butt of jokes—his new app, the gag went, was going the same way as his steaks and his vodka. For the next two years, it would be the only social media platform Trump would use, but it was not without serious business and legal issues.

Just one month later, the entire company went through an overhaul. Litinsky and Moss would be thrown off the board of directors of Trump Media and Technology Group. They were replaced with Nunes, Trump Jr., and Kash Patel, a Trump loyalist and former aide to Nunes and the secretary of defense, and top staffers were fired seemingly overnight. Wilkerson filed an SEC whistleblower complaint in which he alleged that the company was guilty of securities fraud, and shared his story with Drew Harwell at *The Washington Post*. He was then fired. Digital World—which had raised more than $300 million in its initial public offering in September 2021—would find itself in hot water, as SPACs are not allowed to hold serious merger discus-

Only in America | 135

sions before they go public, and the talks surrounding the formulation and early financing of the company had been anything but discreet or disciplined.

NO PRESIDENT IN THE MODERN era has not written, or participated in writing, his White House memoirs. Most recently, Barack and Michelle Obama had reportedly signed a $65 million contract for their memoirs. Given the peculiar presidency of Donald Trump, and its bizarre and historic ending, many New York publishing houses either had resolved not to seek the Trump memoirs or at least were conflicted about publishing a volume that might be less truthful and more self-justifying than a typical warts-and-all presidential memoir. Still, in 2021 there was ample speculation among publishers over who might try to get the rights to a post–White House Trump book.

Trump himself claimed he had been approached by two different book publishing houses about writing a book and had turned them down, although reporting found that none of the five major publishing houses had made any offers. The consensus was that helping Trump tell his story—and trying to do so in a factual way even as he continued to deny the results of the 2020 election—would likely just leave publishers sitting with a historically dubious book, deeply problematic from a PR standpoint, and a legal headache, especially given Trump's penchant for making false statements about other people.

"Two of the biggest and most prestigious publishing houses have made very substantial offers which I have rejected. That doesn't mean I won't accept them sometime in the future, as I have started writing the book," Trump said in a statement to *Politico*. "If my book will be the biggest of them all, and with 39 books written or being written about me, does anybody really believe that they are above making a lot of money? Some of the biggest sleezebags on earth run these companies. No morals, no nothing, just the bottom line."

Trump was annoyed that almost everyone around him—especially those he felt had betrayed him—was writing a book and making money off their experience serving in his administration. In early 2021, his former attorney general Bill Barr signed a book deal; so did former vice president Mike Pence, who signed a multi-million-dollar, two-book deal with Simon & Schuster to recount, in part, the events of January 6.

Over the summer, Trump and his associates saw an opening in the publishing space, specifically for "MAGA" voices. By October, Donald Trump Jr. and Sergio Gor, a former Rand Paul staffer turned Trump aide, had built their own publishing imprint, Winning Team Publishing, and signed on Trump and other conservatives. Their debut book, *Our Journey Together,* was a coffee-table book of photographs from Trump's presidency, annotated with Trump's own memories or scathing commentary on political enemies. Trump received a multi-million-dollar advance for the book, which was sold online and marketed at $74.99, or $229.99 for a signed copy. Trump also used his own massive fundraising list and big screens at rallies to sell the book to his political supporters.

Gor worked with Trump to publish a second book, *Letters to Trump,* a collection of the former president's correspondence with celebrities and lawmakers over the course of several decades. Priced at $100, the coffee-table book included letters from Oprah Winfrey, Diana, Princess of Wales, and Arnold Palmer, as well as Presidents Richard Nixon, George H. W. Bush, George W. Bush, and Barack Obama. There were also his famous "love letters" to North Korean dictator Kim Jong Un, which shed light on one of the more bizarre moments from Trump's presidency.

"Your excellency Mr. President," Kim began in a letter dated July 30, 2018, "I express my deep appreciation to Your Excellency for having a firm faith in the excellent relations established between us during the first summit and exerting yourself to honor the promise made in that historic day."

The letter went on to say, "I feel pleased to have formed good ties with such a powerful and preeminent statesman as Your Excellency, though there is a sense of regret for the lack of anticipated declaration on the termination of war."

In a separate letter, dated January 8, 2019, Trump wrote, "Dear Chairman Kim, I heard it was your birthday and I wanted to wish you a happy day. You will have many great years of celebration and success. Your country will soon be on a historic and prosperous path."

Trump wrote alongside the letter, "I was also given credit for calming down a very serious situation. When I met with Barack Obama before assuming the Presidency, he told me North Korea is the biggest problem the United States and the world has. I believe they would have gone to war with him had I not become President. Under my watch, there was no war—not even close."

The letters showed just how much Trump used flattery to win over everyone from celebrities to the leader of a hermit kingdom. Trump would often show off his correspondence with Kim to people visiting him in the Oval Office. In his post-presidency, they made it into an expensive book that was sold on the official Trump store.

"I talked to him a lot. I got to know him very well. He was very smart," Trump told reporters on a call ahead of the book's release. "Very cunning, very streetwise. And we spoke a lot. Actually, we spoke a lot. And I think we had really, you know, a great relationship," Trump said. "I don't know if you remember when we started that relationship was very, very nasty. Very tough."

GIVEN HIS PENCHANT FOR THE game and the many courses he owns, perhaps it's not surprising that the final piece of Trump's strategy to capitalize on his MAGA persona involved golf. And interestingly, the Saudis.

In the summer of 2022, he would ink a deal with the controversial new professional golf league that had been founded by the Saudis and financed by the Saudi sovereign wealth fund—LIV Golf. As the first LIV tournament at Bedminster got under way, chants of "Four More Years!" and "Let's Go Brandon!" broke out among the crowd of spectators at the sight of Trump, who smiled in his signature red cap from the patio overlooking the sixteenth tee.

It was the first LIV golf tournament at a Trump club and only the second LIV event in the United States, and the attention was less on the players than on the political spectacle surrounding the ex-president. Flanking Trump was the king of Fox News, Tucker Carlson, and the brash, controversial congresswoman from Georgia, Marjorie Taylor Greene.

By most standards, that tournament wasn't a huge success—tickets did not sell out and crowds were sparse. But Trump was pleased. Top golfers were once again at his courses, and he was able to give a middle finger to the Professional Golf Association.

One of the biggest personal blows to Trump in the aftermath of January 6 was the decision by the PGA to pull its annual championship tournament from Trump's Bedminster club, scheduled for May 2022, and the R&A's announcement that the organization planned to avoid hosting its annual British Open championship at Trump's Turnberry golf course in Scotland for the "foreseeable future."

The public rejection by two of the most important entities in the game of Trump and his courses, some of which are considered among the best internationally, had Trump seething.

Bedminster was scheduled to host the 2022 PGA Championship back in 2014, years before Trump won the presidency, and in 2017 hosted the United States Women's Open. And he was still upset over the PGA's decision to move its Grand Slam of Golf from Trump's Los Angeles golf club in 2015.

Even in the White House, Trump fretted over bringing the British Open back to one of his golf properties in Scotland. According to *The New York Times*, he even asked then ambassador to the United Kingdom Woody Johnson to float the idea to British officials, who told him they had absolutely zero control over where a golf tournament is played. In a press conference, Trump denied making the request.

Golf was an important, if not essential, part of Trump's life. He played almost daily, loved to compete with his friends, played in his club's annual tournaments and in pro-am events, and closely followed the PGA Tour, as he counted some professional players as his friends and golf partners. And as president, he gave four professional golfers—Tiger Woods, Annika Sorenstam, Gary Player, and Babe Didrikson Zaharias—the Presidential Medal of Freedom.

He was more or less a scratch golfer according to his alleged handicap, although he also had such a thirst to win that he was known at his club for kicking his ball or taking "gimme" putts, according to sportswriter Rick Reilly. His frequent club championship wins sparked gossip at his club by members who thought he cheated or rigged the game to come in first each time.

In October 2021, Greg Norman, the famous Australian golf champion who was known for his independent streak, announced his plans to create a brand-new alternative to the PGA. The group, LIV Golf Investments, was backed by the investment arm of Saudi Arabia's government, the Public Investment Fund, and was the culmination of a decades-long effort by Norman to create a PGA rival. But critics saw the new golf tour as an attempt by the Saudi government to whitewash its human rights record.

Soon Norman and the Trump Organization were in discussion about potentially hosting one of the tournaments. For the Trumps, the partnership made perfect sense. Trump was personally frustrated by the PGA and the R&A's rejection and attracted by the opportunity for retaliation. Trump and his golf courses were eager to get back into the professional circuit, and Trump had known Norman for years. Trump Bedminster would go on to host one of the tour's first North American events.

LIV Golf was advertised as "golf but louder," aiming to attract a fan base that was young and hip, not stereotypical old country club members. It attracted a star-studded roster of PGA talent signing contracts that in some cases reached over $100 million, but also plenty of controversy.

Trump was less concerned about the controversy. For him, it was simple. He hated the PGA and saw an opportunity to make money, get free advertising for his courses, and once again have top golfers compete at his clubs.

"I think LIV has been a great thing for Saudi Arabia, for the image of Saudi Arabia," Trump told *The Wall Street Journal.* "The publicity they've gotten is worth billions."

And when pro golfers who joined LIV were suspended from participating in PGA Tour events, Trump went on Truth Social to fan the controversy between the two tours and encourage golfers to sign up.

"All of those golfers that remain 'loyal' to the very disloyal PGA, in all of its different forms, will pay a big price when the inevitable MERGER with LIV comes, and you get nothing but a big 'thank you' from PGA officials who are making Millions of Dollars a year," Trump said on Truth Social. "If you don't take the money now, you will get nothing after the merger takes place, and only say how smart the original signees were."

But the partnership raised questions about Trump and his family's personal connections to the Saudis just a few years ahead of a presidential election.

Jared Kushner, Trump's son-in-law, landed a massive $2 billion investment for his newly formed private equity firm Affinity Partners from the kingdom's Public Investment Fund just half a year after leaving the White House.

There was also a more personal element. In the days leading up to the first LIV golf tournament at Bedminster, the families of 9/11 victims protested the event over Saudi Arabia's connections to the terrorist attacks, writing to Trump to express their "deep pain and anger" over his hosting the Saudi-connected event at his club and requesting a meeting with the ex-president to express their concerns. An aide to Trump called in response to express that 9/11 was "near and dear" to Trump—a message that rang hollow to some of the 9/11 families who protested the tournament.

"I don't know much about the 9/11 families, I don't know what is the relationship to this, and their very strong feelings, and I can understand their feelings," Trump told *The Wall Street Journal.* "I can't really comment on that because I don't know exactly what they're saying, and what they're saying who did what."

Saturday Night's Alright for Fighting

DONALD TRUMP WAS SITTING WITH HIS POLITICAL TEAM REVIEWING EN-
dorsements one by one for the midterms at Mar-a-Lago in December
2021 when a news story distracted him.

Trump and his team had been sitting in his office going over polling and the latest news story from each race. They would discuss the
candidates and dynamics of a race, and if Trump made up his mind
about an endorsement that afternoon, his team would get the Republican candidate on the phone for a quick phone message from Trump
offering a "terrific endorsement."

But as they ticked through their list of candidates, Trump stopped
the process to read aloud from a news article about Representative
Mo Brooks of Alabama distancing himself from Trump's claims
about the 2020 election—and was not happy. Daily, Trump's aides
would print out news stories of interest to him—about Trump, his
family, business, or important news events—and give him a collection
to read through. But after reading about Brooks, Trump demanded
his team get the Alabama congressman on the phone. Immediately.
He was reaching the end of his rope with Brooks.

Trump's endorsement of Brooks in the spring of 2021 was one of his first significant political moves of the midterm election, and signaled the kind of Republican he planned to back. Brooks had a right-wing record in Congress, led efforts in the House to challenge the 2020 electoral votes, and was a speaker at the January 6 rally that served as a precursor to the violent attack on Capitol Hill. He had been steadfastly loyal to Trump and Trump repaid him by backing him in the Senate race.

But Brooks had started pushing for Republicans to work on beefing up voting laws for future elections instead of focusing on 2020, and he disagreed with the insistence by Trump and his allies that lawmakers could somehow reverse the results of the 2020 election and that Trump could be reinstated as president.

"Mo, this isn't good, Mo," Trump said, tightly clenching the news story in his hand.

"What do you mean, sir?" Brooks replied.

"I'm reading a story right now, Mo, and I gotta say, it's not good. It's bad."

"What do you mean?"

"Let me read it to you," Trump said, as he shared the story with Brooks.

"That's not true! I never said we shouldn't talk about the election."

"It's in there, Mo, you're telling me you didn't say this? It's right here."

"It's not true!" Brooks was adamant and wouldn't back down from Trump's interrogation over a news story that happened to be printed out and shared with the ex-president.

"Mo," Trump said, "you've been running a bad campaign, you know when it went wrong. You were up fifty points with my endorsement and you said 'we need to look forward instead of backwards' and you got booed, Mo. And the people of Alabama never forgot that. You're crashing. You've got to get your shit together, Mo."

Trump, now agitated, continued to go through the list of races including the contentious Ohio Senate contest. Of all the races, the

Ohio Senate race received the most attention from Trump's aides—many of whom had direct connections to one of the Republican candidates in the crowded field.

"J.D. Vance . . . I like J.D. but they tell me he is dead as a dog," Trump mused out loud. "He has said some nasty stuff in these Club for Growth ads that they tell me is killing him. Is that right? What do you say to that, is he getting killed?" Trump said, turning to one of his political advisers and explaining that polling he had seen showed Josh Mandel, the eager young Republican from Ohio, was up significantly in polling.

Trump's advisers jumped in. While Vance was behind in polling by the conservative antitax group Club for Growth, which had backed Mandel, there was still potential for Vance, who wasn't as far behind in other polls. But Trump wanted to hear from the head of the Club, David McIntosh, and ordered his aides to put him on the line.

For years, Trump and McIntosh had a close and mutually beneficial relationship. McIntosh would fly with Trump aboard Air Force One and, later, travel to Mar-a-Lago for private meetings with Trump. Although they weren't always ideologically aligned, McIntosh's influential Club for Growth eventually worked with Trump to shape races, with the ex-president giving his endorsement in exchange for millions in campaign ads.

McIntosh assured Trump that Mandel was the right pick and remained up in the polls. But Trump was skeptical. Perhaps more than with any other race, Trump was under pressure to make an endorsement in order to whittle down the crowded field in a must-win state for Republicans. He was close to making an endorsement of Mandel, but still had his reservations. In the meantime, he seemed to relish the backbends the candidates were doing to prove their allegiance to him.

Vance, unlike Brooks, was once critical of Trump. The *Hillbilly Elegy* author and venture capitalist once called himself a "Never Trump guy" and called Trump "cultural heroin," an "idiot," "noxious," and "reprehensible." But he had since changed his tune and was now, backed by billionaire Peter Thiel, unapologetically "America

First." Trump liked Vance's media savvy, but he also found converting onetime critics irresistible.

Over the next several months in the spring of 2022, Vance would go on to win Trump's endorsement, despite his previous Trump-bashing, while Brooks would have his endorsement taken away over his weak campaign and statements about the election.

Brooks said he and Trump would occasionally talk on the phone about the election, but in February 2022, he received a call from Trump that would end their relationship. Trump called him up and told him he needed to publicly advocate for the rescission of the 2020 presidential election, the forcible removal of President Joe Biden from the White House and the holding of a special presidential election. Brooks told Trump the one word he hates to hear—no—and flatly stated that it would violate the Constitution. It was the last time they spoke. The next month, Trump revoked his endorsement of Brooks. Brooks learned about it in the news.

Vance and Brooks had opposite trajectories in the 2022 midterms. Vance went from critic to ally. He skillfully maneuvered Trumpworld relationships and the media to win Trump over, even if his newfound embrace of Trump and Trumpism made some conservatives suspicious. Brooks went from sycophant to potential witness in the January 6 investigation. He had stumbled in the polls and backed away from Trump's claims about the election—two cardinal sins in the eyes of the former president.

LEADING CANDIDATES IN THE OHIO Senate race worked to win over the former president with expressions of their loyalty. That dynamic captured just how much Ohio and the state's Republican Party had changed since Senator Rob Portman, the mild-mannered moderate, ran for reelection. The state that voted for former president Barack Obama and former governor John Kasich, who would later endorse Joe Biden, was now thoroughly red, populist, and MAGA.

At the beginning of July, Vance joined the chaotic seven-person primary and his rivals were immediately out to draw blood. Vance had come under scrutiny by Trump and his challengers for his past comments about the ex-president, including an appearance on PBS's *Charlie Rose*, where he stated, "I'm a Never Trump guy, I never liked him." His comments were quickly turned into advertisements by his rivals.

Trump was drawn to Vance's story—a young man from Appalachia who pulled himself out of poverty to become a Marine and graduate from Harvard Law School—and how telegenic he was. But Vance had never run for office, and Trump was leery of backing anyone who had harshly criticized him in the past. Still, he wasn't sold on any of the other candidates, either, even as they paraded through his club.

Jane Timken, the former Ohio GOP chair Trump endorsed in 2017, tried to get Trump's attention and support, but he became skeptical of her after she seemed to support Representative Anthony Gonzalez, the Ohio congressman who had voted to impeach Trump. Mike Gibbons, an investment banker who largely self-funded his campaign, didn't need Trump's support to raise money, but he still failed to elicit much love from the ex-president. Josh Mandel, the baby-faced former state treasurer, was backed by the influential and conservative Club for Growth, but there were questions about his bona fides. Pre-Trump, Mandel was a moderate, but he quickly pivoted to becoming a right-wing warrior—a move that reflected the realities of the electorate and the party not only in Ohio but across the country.

Two months before the primary, the race narrowed to Mandel and Vance. Vance faced a barrage of outside polling indicating he wouldn't perform as well in the general election as his rivals. But the core of their argument wasn't about differences of policy—it was about fealty to Trump.

But Trump, who watched Republican opinion of him change like the wind, seemed unmoved by the criticisms. And he noted the backing that Vance, a relative outsider to Ohio politics, did have—Fox

News host Tucker Carlson, Charlie Kirk, and Donald Trump Jr. were among his supporters.

Trump's son took an immediate interest in Vance. Andy Surabian mentioned to him that he was working on Vance's super PAC. "I read *Hillbilly Elegy* and I really fucking like that guy," Trump Jr. replied. But he remembered the harsh criticisms Vance had had for his dad in 2016. "I fuckin' loved that book and I never really understood how he didn't understand" Trump. "Is he on our team now?"

Surabian said yes, and he proceeded to put Trump Jr. and Vance on a three-way call. "How didn't you understand Trump back in 2016?" Trump Jr. asked Vance. By the time they hung up the phone, Trump Jr. had said he wanted to help.

But Vance's first meeting with Trump was actually arranged by billionaire venture capitalist and Republican megadonor Peter Thiel. Thiel was a mentor to Vance; he had backed his venture capital firm and in recent years had become a kingmaker for MAGA-aligned Republicans like Vance. He was particularly focused on a handful of races he was pouring millions into, and he flew down to Palm Beach to personally make sure the introduction of Vance to Trump went smoothly.

"You weren't a big fan of me in 2016," Trump said with a smile. "I like you but you said some really nasty things about me."

Trump was particularly fixated on Vance's looks. Every time Trump saw Vance on Fox News, he would remark, "This J.D., he really looks the part . . . he looks like a senator . . . very handsome man."

With so many allies and advisers involved in the Ohio Senate race, Trump remained torn over which candidate to support. Mandel was backed by the Club for Growth; Vance was backed by Thiel, Carlson, and his son; Timken had the support of two longtime Trump hands, Corey Lewandowski and Dave Bossie; and then there was Mike Gibbons, who had recently been shooting up in the polls. Trump considered sitting out of the race entirely until the debates.

———

IN MID-MARCH 2022, VANCE, TIMKEN, Mandel, and Gibbons squared off in the first Senate GOP debate—and it turned ugly, with the two leading candidates, Gibbons and Mandel, nearly breaking into a fistfight onstage. But their awkward encounter turned into a golden opportunity for Vance, who snagged a positive headline in *Breitbart:* CHAOS IN OHIO GOP SENATE DEBATE: GIBBONS, MANDEL IN HEATED ALTERCATION AS VANCE BERATES THEM FOR CONDUCT UNBECOMING.

The first debate was so lively that Trump requested the link to the livestream to watch the second. His takeaway was that Vance won.

Vance got lucky with Trump in other ways. He was invited to play golf with a Trump friend at the Trump golf club in West Palm Beach, where the ex-president would play and dine on a daily basis in the winter and spring. Vance's only issue was that he wasn't a strong golfer.

On the day of his invitation, Vance played in the foursome in front of Trump, who watched as Vance teed off each hole. Vance, to his relief, later told acquaintances it was his best ever round of golf. After the round, Trump was eating lunch in the clubhouse when Vance walked in.

"Are you the *Hillbilly Elegy* guy?" a woman asked Vance as he entered the room. Trump watched as the Ohio Senate candidate proceeded to shake hands and take photos with club members. He turned to Chris Ruddy, the CEO of Newsmax and a longtime Mar-a-Lago member, and said, "Do you know the great J.D. Vance? I hope Newsmax is helping him."

As Vance was about to leave, Trump called him over for a photo together.

"Do you mind if I post that?" Vance asked. "I wouldn't do that," Trump said. "But you are one handsome son of a bitch."

One criterion with outsized importance to Trump was physical looks and being telegenic, two things he would frequently tell people he liked in Vance.

Up until the last minute, Trump remained on the fence about who to support. Club for Growth donors were calling him to support

Mandel. Vance's team asked for influential conservative commentators to nudge Trump toward Vance, including Jack Posobiec, Dan Bongino, Maria Bartiromo, and Mollie Hemingway.

To try to seal the deal, Vance called then Fox News anchor Tucker Carlson, asking him to put in a good word. Although Trump and Carlson weren't speaking as regularly in Trump's post-presidency, he had the kind of voice that Trump would listen to.

Perhaps it was too good a guess. Carlson made his case for Vance in a call with Trump, who proceeded to put him on FaceTime for two hours in the middle of his golf game.

A Trump adviser told Vance that he should make a call himself, and be smart about how he talked to the ex-president. Sucking up to Trump was a fine art—he liked flattery but wouldn't respect someone if they went too far, and Trump had found some of the other candidates' compliments obnoxious. So late one evening in April, when Trump was alone in his residence at Mar-a-Lago, he received a call from Vance.

Trump told Vance that he was going to be "very happy."

The next day, Donald Trump Jr., Surabian, and Trump's aides breathed a sigh of relief when he finally sent out an endorsement.

"Like some others, J.D. Vance may have said some not so great things about me in the past, but he gets it now, and I have seen that in spades," Trump said. "I've studied this race closely and I think J.D. is the most likely to take out the weak, but dangerous, Democrat opponent."

Trump's decision to back Vance was in part because of his relationship with his son, who had been one of Vance's most loyal backers, and the megadonor Thiel, who had dumped millions into backing pro-Trump candidates, but it was a torpedo to Trump's relationship with the Club for Growth and David McIntosh, who had supported Mandel and hoped Trump would stay out of the race entirely.

In retaliation, the Club for Growth financed a series of ads in support of Mandel that attacked Trump and his endorsement of Vance, and highlighted Vance's past criticism of Trump. The ex-president had long expected that the Club and McIntosh—like much of the GOP—would follow his lead and coalesce behind his chosen candidate. He was furious when they did not.

The same day that an advertisement aired highlighting Vance's criticism of Trump, the ex-president asked an assistant to send McIntosh a message from him. It read, "Go fuck yourself."

FOR TRUMP, WINNING THE SENATE seat left by Senator Pat Toomey in Pennsylvania was personal. Trump lost Pennsylvania in 2020 after winning the state in 2016, and Toomey, who consistently voted with Trump in the Senate and authored Trump's signature tax bill, was one of seven Senate Republicans who voted to impeach Trump.

With loyalty top of mind, Trump decided to back a U.S. veteran and MAGA acolyte named Sean Parnell in September 2021.

Parnell, a former Army Ranger who served in Afghanistan and received the Purple Heart, earned the support of Trump in part because of his friendship with Donald Trump Jr. But less than three months later, he called Trump to say he planned to drop out of the race after ugly details about his divorce and custody battle went public. Parnell's wife, Laurie Snell, testified in court that Parnell had abused her and their kids and shared ugly text messages in which he called her names. Parnell denied the accusations of abuse.

Trump, furious about the avalanche of headlines coming out of the state, blamed his son for encouraging him to make the endorsement.

The other candidates in the race—Jeff Bartos, a real estate developer, and Carla Sands, Trump's former ambassador to Denmark—trailed Parnell in the polls and left the door open for more high-profile candidates.

JUST ONE WEEK AFTER PARNELL'S news, Dr. Mehmet Oz, a heart surgeon and celebrity physician who hosted a daytime talk show, announced he was entering the race. Oz was famous for dispensing at times controversial medical advice and untested, unproven remedies. His decision to run and pour millions of his own money into the race, he said, was spurred by the COVID-19 pandemic and harmful advice given by "elites." But little was known about his political leanings.

Oz's entry was joined by David McCormick, former chief executive of Bridgewater Associates, the world's largest hedge fund, a few months later. McCormick had a made-for-the-Senate pedigree, with a degree from West Point, experience as an Army Ranger, a Ph.D. from Princeton, service in the Bush administration, and success in finance. But there were criticisms of his business ties to China and, as with Oz, whether he was even a resident of the state. Both men primarily lived in residences outside Pennsylvania.

Parnell's ugly custody battle laid bare concerns from top Republican officials about the vigor of Trump's vetting process and whether he was backing people who might not be able to win in a general election. Trump was hesitant at first to get behind another disappointment—but that didn't stop people around him from pushing their favorite candidate in front of Trump.

Both McCormick and Oz found support in a cast of former Trump White House aides and personalities. McCormick, whose wife, Dina Powell, was an influential adviser in the early Trump White House years, had the support of figures like Hope Hicks, Kellyanne Conway, and Sarah Huckabee Sanders.

But it was Oz who had the most powerful backers: Fox News host Sean Hannity, hotel magnate Steve Wynn, and Trump's wife, Melania Trump.

When McCormick learned Trump was close to endorsing Oz, he flew down to Mar-a-Lago to make a last-minute pitch: Stay out of the primary.

Sitting across from Trump in his office at Mar-a-Lago, McCormick said that he should let the voters decide. But Trump had made up his mind. Trump called in his assistant Molly Michael, McCormick later shared in a book, and she proceeded to cue up a video on the television screen across from Trump's desk.

McCormick sat with Trump as he played a video of an interview he had done shortly after January 6. In the video, McCormick said Trump bore some of the responsibility for the political divisiveness in the country, and he appreciated Biden's message of bringing the country together. Neither message, he wrote, went over well with Trump.

"You know you can't win unless you say the election was stolen," Trump told McCormick. He endorsed Oz three days later.

THERE WAS ONE RACE IN particular during the 2022 midterms in which Republican officials feared Trump was poised to make a terrible decision: the Missouri Senate race.

One of the lead candidates was Eric Greitens, the former governor of Missouri, a Rhodes scholar and Navy SEAL who had resigned from office after his hairdresser and mistress accused him of blackmail and sexual assault. The accusations were sordid and horrific: Greitens was accused of being sexually abusive with the hairdresser, taping her hands and blindfolding her before snapping a photo of her that he threatened to use as blackmail. The ugly details were shared not just in Missouri news but in national papers and tabloids.

The allegations, which Greitens denied, were a political nightmare—one which grew worse in early 2022, after Greitens's ex-wife accused him of physical abuse against her and their young son. But among those working to boost Greitens was none other than Kimberly Guilfoyle, who was being paid as an adviser to the candidate and tried to say Greitens was being unfairly targeted by establishment Republicans. Boris Epshteyn and Rudy Giuliani also supported Greitens, and he was a regular on Steve Bannon's *War-Room* podcast.

Running against Greitens were Eric Schmitt, the Missouri attorney general, and Representative Vicky Hartzler, who had the support of Senator Josh Hawley.

Guilfoyle was determined to get Trump's endorsement for Greitens. She traveled to Trump's Bedminster club, where an LIV golf tournament was being held, and tried to lobby for the disgraced former governor whenever she had a moment with Trump. At the same time, top Republican officials were dead set on making sure that that did not happen.

SO WITH JUST 24 HOURS until polling places opened in the Missouri primary on August 2, a particularly unhinged episode in the 2022 midterm races ensued.

On Monday morning before the Missouri primary, Trump announced on social media he planned to make an endorsement. But what was left unsaid is that he had not yet made up his mind on who he would support.

Trump was meeting with RNC chairwoman Ronna McDaniel that day to go over the midterm elections at Trump's Bedminster club, but she was particularly concerned about the Missouri race and that an endorsement of Greitens, with all his personal baggage, would likely mean an expensive and needlessly dramatic general election race.

Trump told McDaniel he was still figuring out which candidate he wanted to support, and as he often did, Trump called up friends and allies to get their take. One call went out to Senator Josh Hawley, the young Republican senator from Missouri, who was no fan of Greitens and emphasized to Trump that he was down in the polls. Not long after he hung up the phone with Hawley, Guilfoyle joined the meeting with McDaniel and tried to make the case that Trump should endorse Greitens because he was up in the polls.

"If he is going to win, then why does he need the president's endorsement?" McDaniel asked out loud.

It didn't take long for word to get back to Washington that Trump was actually serious about Greitens and might risk giving Democrats a seat Republicans had held since 1987.

With so much pressure to endorse Eric Greitens or Eric Schmitt, an idea was jokingly raised to Trump: Why not endorse both men?

Trump was skeptical at first—he wanted to check if both Greitens and Schmitt's first names were spelled the same. Just in case he changed his mind yet again, two separate statements were prepared for Schmitt and Greitens. But finally, he drafted a statement for a bizarre dual endorsement:

"I trust the Great People of Missouri, on this one, to make up their own minds, much as they did when they gave me landslide victories in the 2016 and 2020 Elections, and I am therefore proud to announce that ERIC has my Complete and Total Endorsement!"

Before the statement was blasted out to the world, Trump called for Margo Martin, one of his assistants, to print it out and bring it to his desk.

"Get me Eric's phone number," Trump asked.

"Which Eric?" his aides replied.

"Both," Trump said.

Trump then proceeded to call both Greitens and Schmitt separately.

"I'm putting out a statement, I think you'll really like it, you're doing a great job so go out and win," Trump said, without mentioning that the statement would not specify which Eric—Greitens or Schmitt—he had endorsed.

The double endorsement was seen as both genius and stupid. Trump, his aides said, thought it was one of the cleverest things he had ever done.

IF TRUMP HAD WAFFLED OVER who to support in the Missouri Senate primary, there was never a doubt that the ex-president would back the ex-NFL star.

In September 2021, Trump officially endorsed Herschel Walker, a superstar, larger-than-life figure in Georgia sports and culture. Walker was the star running back on the University of Georgia football team that won the national championship in 1980 and he went on to win the Heisman Trophy in 1982. He was also friends with Trump.

Trump was the owner of the now defunct United States Football League's New Jersey Generals in the early 1980s when Walker was just starting out his professional career. The twelve-season NFL star would go on to appear on Trump's *Celebrity Apprentice* reality TV show, where Trump pronounced, as he was cut from an episode, "You know how much I like you. I love you. I love you. I am not a gay man, and I love you, Herschel. Herschel, you're fired."

And over the years, Trump's and Walker's families remained close. Walker would visit the Trumps at their mansion in Greenwich, Connecticut, and would take Trump's kids on trips with his family. "I don't know if you all know this," Walker once recounted, "but I've known Donald before he became The Donald. As a matter of fact, Little Ivanka and Little Donald, they were with me for a week for five years during the summer. I was the one to take [them to] every amusement park, Disney World, Sea World, and every place they went. I kept them for a week."

Walker remained loyal to Trump through his 2016 presidential election, when he came to Trump's defense over accusations that he was a racist. And later, as Trump tried to overturn his loss in 2020, Walker tweeted his support. As Walker was considering a run against Senator Raphael Warnock in the midterm elections, and GOP consultants and Republican officials began discussing who might be a front-runner, Trump jumped in to give an early boost to his friend.

"Wouldn't it be fantastic if the legendary Herschel Walker ran for the United States Senate in Georgia?" Trump said in an email sent to his supporters. "He would be unstoppable, just like he was when he played for the Georgia Bulldogs, and in the NFL. He is also a GREAT person. Run Herschel, run!"

Seeking retribution and lining up Trump loyalists to run against his political enemies was a top priority for Trump and his team after he narrowly lost Georgia to Biden in 2020. Trump was under investigation by Fulton County prosecutors over whether he illegally influenced the election when he tried—and failed—to pressure Governor Brian Kemp to rig the results in his favor.

In his quest to seek revenge and send a message politically, Trump endorsed Representative Jody Hice, the firebrand state representative who objected to the inclusion of Georgia's votes in Biden's favor on January 6, to run against Secretary of State Brad Raffensperger. Raffensperger had certified Biden's win after several recounts and harassment by Trump supporters.

Trump also encouraged Georgia senator David Perdue to mount a bid against the popular Governor Kemp, the Republican he blamed—more than anyone else—for his loss in the state.

Trump saw the election of Walker—a loyal friend who supported his election claims—as key to his efforts to weaken the "establishment Republican" leadership in Georgia. But Walker's stardom in the state of Georgia blinded Trump to some glaring—and ominous—signs for his candidacy.

Just one month before Trump's endorsement, the AP reported on Walker's history of struggling with his mental health and multiple personality disorder, and court documents outlining accusations that he'd threatened to kill his ex-wife.

Among top Republicans in Georgia, there were also whispers about even more issues for Walker—among them, that he'd paid for multiple abortions. The claims would fly in the face of the Christian pro-family platform Walker later touted on the campaign trail. And it would become an even bigger problem once a bombshell on abortion rights in America hit in the spring of 2022.

But Trump downplayed Walker's growing list of personal issues, according to an interview with Maggie Haberman for her book *Confidence Man: The Making of Donald Trump and the Breaking of America.* "Twenty years ago would've been a bigger problem. I don't think it's a problem today," he said.

A POLITICAL BOMBSHELL WENT OFF in early May 2022 when two re-porters at *Politico*, Josh Gerstein and Alexander Ward, broke the news that the Supreme Court planned to overturn the landmark abortion case *Roe v. Wade*.

Within a day, the nearly one-hundred-page draft opinion written by Justice Samuel Alito was confirmed to be accurate by the Supreme Court, and both Republicans and Democrats alike braced for the his-toric fight that would play out in the midterm elections just months away.

For conservatives, the end of *Roe v. Wade* marked the culmination of a decades-long fight to end federal abortion rights and let states decide whether—and how—to impose restrictions.

As antiabortion groups and Republicans celebrated the decision, Trump—the president who put three conservative justices on the court who would later go on to overturn *Roe*—remained publicly si-lent.

But behind the scenes, he was telling aides and friends that he was worried Republicans didn't "know how to talk about" abortion and it could end up costing them suburban women in the midterm elec-tions. Some of his advisers thought Trump should get out in front of the decision to emphasize—particularly to the sometimes Trump-skeptical religious conservatives—that he should get credit.

Trump had been almost superstitious with how he talked about abortion after fumbling the issue in the past. He would often demur when asked about abortion or *Roe*, and shortly after the draft came out, he focused publicly on the leak and not on the contents of the leak.

"Nobody knows what exactly it represents, if that's going to be it," Trump said when asked about the decision at Mar-a-Lago soon after the *Politico* scoop. "I think the one thing that really is so horrible is the leaking . . . for the court and for the country."

But among some at the top of the Republican Party, there was a serious understanding about the political impact the decision would have. At the RNC, Ronna McDaniel turned to her chief of staff, Richard Walters, after the draft leaked. "We just lost the Senate," she said. She had been watching the issue unfold from her home state of Michigan, where a ballot measure adopting abortion rights into the state constitution was going to be voted on in the midterms.

It wasn't just McDaniel. Republican groups like the NRSC recognized the challenge their candidates would face over the news. The NRSC held focus groups on abortion, and workshopped messaging for GOP candidates that encouraged them to paint Democratic positions on abortion as "extreme." The RNC released a memo to Republican candidates advising them on how to talk about abortion. Kellyanne Conway, Trump's former White House counselor and a Republican pollster, helped advise the party on the issue. But instead of leaning into the issue, and putting their Democratic opponents on the spot over how far into a pregnancy they would allow an abortion, many candidates shied away from it entirely.

Once, as McDaniel and Conway were in the car on their way to the airport coming from an event, they called up Oz in Pennsylvania to warn him that he needed to get out in front of the issue of abortion. He replied that his consultants were telling him the race was about the economy.

On multiple occasions, Trump advised candidates behind closed doors that they should be careful how they talked about the issue on the campaign trail. He recommended that they embrace exceptions in cases of rape, incest, or risk to the life of the mother.

Trump approached Tudor Dixon, a young conservative media personality who was running for governor of Michigan against Democrat Gretchen Whitmer, about how she was discussing abortion. After Dixon lost, she detailed a private conversation she had with Trump where he warned her that her position went too far and would be unacceptable to some of the electorate. Dixon supported a total ban on abortions except in life-threatening emergencies, and said she would not support abortion even in the case of rape.

As Trump complained that Republicans were too extreme on abortion—an issue he liked to brag helped put him in the White House—the party could not figure out how to thread the needle on an issue that would become a linchpin of the 2022 midterms. Even as Trump's own aides boasted of a "red wave" coming in those elections, Trump privately remained skeptical because of the way Republicans were handling abortion.

"He did not see it," said an adviser. "And he didn't see it in large measure because of the abortion decision."

Pinball Wizard

EVER SINCE ANNOUNCING HIS PRESIDENTIAL CAMPAIGN IN 2015, DONALD Trump had managed a feat of political engineering unprecedented in American history. He had projected a persona onto the national psyche that had him at once being both the biggest aggressor and the most aggrieved party, the most successful and resilient son that America had ever produced and also history's greatest victim. Depending on the day or the audience, no one had ever done more with his advantages, and no one had ever been treated so unfairly. No one had more to brag about, no one had worked the system so effectively, and no one had had so many things rigged against him. The only conceivable explanation for Trump's losing at anything would be that the outcome had been rigged. During his presidency, lawful investigations into his administration were always dishonestly initiated and the facts alleged were invariably "hoaxes." In his first year in office, he had taken the occasion of a commencement address at the Coast Guard Academy to declare to the graduating cadets and their families, "No politician in history, and I say this with great surety, has been treated worse or more unfairly." Perhaps overlooked in that statement were the assassinations of four of his predecessors.

Or perhaps not. As his criminal and civil legal peril increased during his time in exile—with steadily advancing federal and state investigations into things that he had done before, during, and after his term in office—he would present himself as a martyr for his supporters, with the most fervent comparing him to Christ. And it is from a position of grandiose victimhood as those investigations closed in on him in the summer and fall of 2022 that Trump would again fully find his voice and forge his future. More than ever, he would become his own rallying cry. *I am suffering for you* would become his gospel.

Somehow, impossibly, the more prosecutors investigated him, the more finely honed his sense of persecution became, the stronger he got. And the stronger he got, the more conditioned his acolytes in Congress and in the chattering classes became to the belief that there could be no such thing as a valid investigation into anything that Donald Trump had ever done. All would be put down to the "criminalization of politics" and be dismissed as "political prosecution." It was not Trump's actions after the election in 2020 that threatened American democracy, went this line of thinking; it was the pursuit of justice for those actions that was the real threat.

And then, in the summer of 2022, came a profound turning point. Trump would claim many firsts in the history of American post-presidencies, and this would be among them: He would be the first former president to have his residence raided by federal agents, in search of classified documents so sensitive that carelessness with them could jeopardize the security of the country.

Trump was at his office on the twenty-sixth floor of Trump Tower in New York on the morning of August 8, 2022, when he received a call from his son Eric, who had just gotten off the phone with staff at Mar-a-Lago. FBI agents were at the club with a search warrant, he said. A political—and legal—bombshell was about to detonate.

By 10 A.M., thirty or so federal agents had descended on Trump's private club in Palm Beach. They didn't wear jackets or hats emblazoned with "FBI" and they didn't carry weapons. Instead the agents dressed in T-shirts and nondescript khaki cargo pants. They would have looked out of place if it had been social season in Palm Beach. But it was late in the summer, when wealthy families and Mar-a-Lago members decamp to their yachts and summer homes in Nantucket and the Hamptons. Their goal was to come and go quietly.

Trump and his family had been spending the summer, as they typically did, at his Bedminster country club in New Jersey. On Sunday nights, Trump would sometimes travel into New York City to take meetings at Trump Tower on Monday and return to his club on Tuesday. No one was at his Palm Beach club except for some security and staff attending the upkeep of his massive seaside property. But just a few hours before federal agents arrived, they gave a heads-up to the Secret Service stationed at Trump's Florida home.

FBI agents drove up to the tall stucco walls of Mar-a-Lago in black SUVs and fanned out across Trump's property. Over the course of the next eight hours, they searched Trump's bedroom, closets, office, and a first-floor storage room for classified government documents that contained some of the most sensitive secrets in the world. And while their goal was to quietly move through the property and not make a scene, they sparked one of the most dramatic chapters of Trump's post-presidency.

The execution of the search warrant was the culmination of a process that had begun the year before, as personnel from the National Archives had sought to recover an unknown number of documents that had improperly been sent to Mar-a-Lago at the end of the Trump presidency and remained in Trump's possession.

Eight months before the search, in January 2022, the counsel for the National Archives had notified the Department of Justice that classified documents had been found in the boxes it had recovered, and that there was reason to believe that not all the documents had been recovered. In May, the Justice Department had issued a subpoena for all classified materials still in Trump's possession, and in June, the head of the DOJ counterintelligence division, Jay Bratt, had personally gone to Palm Beach to recover the documents himself, and had been assured by attorney and Trump ally Christina Bobb, who

had been designated Custodian of Records in response to the subpoena, that a diligent search had been conducted and that all documents had been returned.

Now, in August, Susie Wiles had just spent the weekend with
Trump in Dallas, where he had spoken at CPAC—and teased a 2024
announcement—and had decided to stay in Texas to visit with family
when her phone rang. It was Evan Corcoran, one of Trump's attorneys, who called to say there were FBI agents searching through
Trump's Florida property. Minutes after Corcoran called Wiles, the
two of them got Eric Trump on the phone with a dozen other advisers to make a plan for how to handle the fallout from the search. *What
do we say? What can we say? What is off-limits to say?*

Whatever the line was going to be, Trump wanted his allies to immediately blanket the airwaves in his defense. But first they needed to
get a lawyer on the physical premises at Mar-a-Lago to monitor what
was going on and answer questions from the agents. None of Trump's
regular lawyers were in Palm Beach, and his aides were scattered
across the country. Christina Bobb happened to be in the area, and
she raced over to Mar-a-Lago about an hour after the search began.
But by the time she got there, federal agents had fanned out through
the property looking for classified material buried amid Trump's
pack-rat piles of documents stacked in boxes throughout the property.
She announced that she was there as legal representation for Trump,
asked to see the warrant, and then was instructed to stand outside
Mar-a-Lago in the sweltering Florida heat as she described the scene
unfolding to aides on the phone. Lindsey Halligan, another young
lawyer who was working for Trump, drove up from Fort Lauderdale
to meet Bobb at the property.

That day, Trump and his son were able to watch on a live feed as
agents moved throughout the mansion, despite the request by those
agents that all security cameras inside the property be turned off.
Trump erupted in rage when he found out later from an aide that
Melania Trump's closet had been among the areas agents searched.

At 6:18 P.M., when the search finally wrapped, Bobb signed two "receipts of property" listing the items the FBI had hauled away in a Ryder van from Trump's office and storage area in thirty-three boxes. Layered between magazines and even clothing were eighteen documents marked as top secret, fifty-four marked as secret, thirty-one marked as confidential, and forty-eight empty folders with CLASSIFIED written across the top. There were other odds and ends: an Executive Grant of Clemency for Trump ally Roger Stone, and a document containing sensitive information about the president of France.

As the FBI team was packing up to leave, Peter Schorsch, a deeply wired former Florida GOP operative and publisher of the online news blog *Florida Politics,* received a phone call from an old friend wanting to catch up. After a few minutes of small talk about work, his friend, who wasn't a member at Mar-a-Lago but had connections in Florida politics and law enforcement, casually mentioned in "true Seinfeld, yada-yada-yada-fashion" that FBI agents were currently at Mar-a-Lago. Schorsch was shocked. After a quick Google search he saw that nothing had been reported about any FBI presence at Trump's club.

Schorsch then called a person close to Trump to confirm.

"Hey—is it true the FBI is at your place?"

"They just left," they replied matter-of-factly.

Another Trump adviser asked Schorsch to wait five minutes before breaking the news, as they were about to put out an official statement. But not wanting to be scooped by Trump's team, he decided to reach out to a few other reporters about the news. Five minutes later, Schorsch tweeted out the news.

"Scoop—The Federal Bureau of Investigation @FBI today executed a search warrant at Mar-a-Lago, two sources confirm to @ Fla_Pol. 'They just left,' one source said. Not sure what the search warrant was about. TBH, Im not a strong enough reporter to hunt this down, but its real," Schorsch tweeted at 6:36 P.M.

Newsrooms raced to match Schorsch, and thirty minutes later,

Trump's team informed the former president's allies that Trump was about to release a statement. What he released was angry and defiant, exaggerated and aggrieved, and it set off a political firestorm.

These are dark times for our Nation, as my beautiful home, Mar-A-Lago in Palm Beach, Florida, is currently under siege, raided, and occupied by a large group of FBI agents. Nothing like this has ever happened to a President of the United States before. After working and cooperating with the relevant Government agencies, this unannounced raid on my home was not necessary or appropriate. It is prosecutorial misconduct, the weaponization of the Justice System, and an attack by Radical Left Democrats who desperately don't want me to run for President in 2024, especially based on recent polls, and who will likewise do anything to stop Republicans and Conservatives in the upcoming Midterm Elections. Such an assault could only take place in broken, Third-World Countries. Sadly, America has now become one of those Countries, corrupt at a level not seen before. They even broke into my safe! What is the difference between this and Watergate, where operatives broke into the Democrat National Committee? Here, in reverse, Democrats broke into the home of the 45th President of the United States.

The political persecution of President Donald J. Trump has been going on for years, with the now fully debunked Russia, Russia, Russia Scam, Impeachment Hoax #1, Impeachment Hoax #2, and so much more, it just never ends. It is political targeting at the highest level!

Hillary Clinton was allowed to delete and acid wash 33,000 E-mails AFTER they were subpoenaed by Congress. Absolutely nothing has happened to hold her accountable. She even took antique furniture, and other items from the White House.

I stood up to America's bureaucratic corruption, I restored power to the people, and truly delivered for our Country, like we have never seen before. The establishment hated it. Now, as they watch my endorsed candidates win big victories, and see my dominance in all polls, they are trying to stop me, and the Republican Party, once more. The lawlessness, political persecution, and Witch Hunt must be exposed and stopped.

I will continue to fight for the Great American People!

As the sun set in Palm Beach, local police positioned themselves outside Mar-a-Lago in front of the club entrance, bathing the outside of the mansion in a dramatic crime scene glow with flashing blue and red lights. Trump sympathizers set up camp along Southern Boulevard to protest, and news anchors lined up along the water across from the club to give minute-by-minute updates.

That night Trump made clear he wanted his team—anyone—on TV immediately to defend him. Not all of the interviews were particularly effective. Bobb and Trump's lawyers stumbled through television appearances that once would have gotten them fired. But Trump, who was typically hypercritical of anyone who went on television to talk about him, notably didn't mind, according to aides.

Trump allies in the press saw the end of the republic.

Marc Levin called the search "the worst attack on this republic in modern history, period."

"This is going to absolutely enrage the country, especially the Republican base, a base that is clearly behind the ex-president," Fox News host Jesse Watters said as news of the search broke. "I think everyone is very emotional about this raid."

On the air, Dan Bongino called it "some third-world bullshit right here."

Sean Hannity channeled Trump's outrage, calling the search "a dark day in history," and tried to characterize the FBI's actions as part of a grand conspiracy against Trump associates by the federal government, making comparisons to Hunter Biden. "This would have never happened to a Democrat," Hannity said.

"Sean, this didn't come from the little local FBI field office in

Palm Beach, Florida. You know who this came from. This came from one place and one building, and that is the White House in Washington, D.C.," Eric Trump said.

"To have thirty FBI agents—actually more than that—descend on Mar-a-Lago, give absolutely no notice, go through the gates, start ransacking an office, ransacking a closet, they broke into a safe. He didn't even have anything in the safe," Eric claimed. "I mean, give me a break. And this is coming from, what, the National Archives?

"My father always kept press clippings, newspaper articles, pictures, notes from us," he went on. "He had boxes. He moved out of the White House. He's very collaborative. If you want to search for anything, come right ahead. It was an open-door policy, and all of a sudden thirty agents descend upon Mar-a-Lago?" Trump's son went on to describe a lawyer who had been working on the documents case as "totally shocked."

"He goes, 'I have such an amazing relationship with these people and all of a sudden, on no notice, they send twenty cars and thirty agents?'" Eric Trump said.

But for all of their assertions that the lawyers had a great relationship with the National Archives and that Trump had been cooperating, the National Archives had hit a breaking point. They believed Trump was sitting on state secrets that could endanger sources and betray allies. Not only that—the collection of documents they were concerned Trump had was sitting unprotected at a country club, where well-connected members and guests or even an intruder could easily obtain access to top secret information.

The search of Mar-a-Lago that Monday in August was the dramatic culmination of an exasperated push by the National Archives to get the documents back from Trump, and Trump's resistance, grounded in his mistaken belief that as a former president he had the right to possess all the government documents he wished to possess, despite the federal law spelling out precisely how documents and records that pertained to official White House business be handled.

The Presidential Records Act was passed by Congress following a years-long struggle between Congress and former president Richard Nixon over his effort to maintain control over the White House documents and tapes that revealed the details of the Watergate break-in. Ultimately, the law made clear that presidential files belong not to the individual holding the office but to the people of the United States, and it set up a mechanism for transferring documents to the National Archives when a president leaves office.

In January 2022, a contractor with the National Archives, or NARA, traveled to Palm Beach to collect fifteen boxes that contained an assortment of letters, gifts, and documents subject to the Presidential Records Act, including some that NARA would describe as "classified national security information." The news was scooped by Jacqueline Alemany, Josh Dawsey, Tom Hamburger, and Ashley Parker at *The Washington Post*.

After reviewing what NARA discovered, the FBI opened an investigation to figure out how many documents with classified markings had been packed up and shipped down to Mar-a-Lago, and where and under what conditions they were being stored.

By May, federal prosecutors had begun a grand jury investigation and issued a subpoena to obtain "any and all documents or writings in the custody or control of Donald J. Trump" with CONFIDENTIAL, CLASSIFIED, or TOP SECRET markings, and they requested interviews with some of the people who had worked in the White House in the final days of the Trump administration and played a role in boxing up documents.

Trump was receiving conflicting advice on what to do. Tom Fitton, the head of the conservative activist group Judicial Watch, had reached out to Trump that spring according to CNN, telling him the records belong to him and he should hold on to the documents. And Boris Epshteyn, who had joined Trump's team as a legal adviser in April 2022, gave Trump the similarly imprudent advice that the former president should push back on government requests to return the documents—which is just what Trump wanted to hear.

It was Epshteyn's combination of unfailing loyalty and combativeness that endeared him to Trump. He had started in Trumpworld as a reliable attack-dog media surrogate in 2016 before briefly serving on the White House communications team, then reemerging as a strategic adviser in 2020. But those close to Trump say the door back into the inner sanctum opened for Epshteyn shortly after Election Night in 2020. In the days after the election, he crisscrossed the country as the campaign filed lawsuits contesting the results, spending long stretches in Arizona.

"After the 2020 election, when essentially everyone dropped off the face of the earth after Election Day, he was still there," said a former Trump campaign official. "He was still there, he was still working, he was still trying to do what Trump wanted in spite of everyone leaving." Epshteyn appeared beside fellow Trump lawyers, including Rudy Giuliani, Sidney Powell, and others, at the Republican National Committee as they made claims about voting machines and election fraud that would be widely debunked. He coordinated with Steve Bannon, Bernie Kerik, and others on efforts to challenge the certification of the election on January 6.

His endeavors as a 2020 election dead-ender might have earned Trump's loyalty, but reviews from other Trump lawyers were decidedly mixed, with former White House attorney Eric Herschmann calling Epshteyn "an idiot." In an email between Herschmann and two members of the legal team representing Trump in both the documents case and the federal investigation of his efforts to overturn the election, Herschmann wrote, "When I questioned Boris's legal experience to work on challenging a presidential election since he appeared to have none—challenges that resulted in multiple court failures—he boasted that he was 'just having fun.'"

In the documents case, though, the National Archives was not playing around, and with each request they made, there was a growing anxiety among some of Trump's aides about where the investigation would lead. The agency seemed exhausted by attempts to work with the former president on returning documents, and on May 10,

Debra Steidel Wall, the acting archivist of the United States, wrote to Trump attorney Evan Corcoran:

> As you are no doubt aware, NARA had ongoing communications with the former President's representatives throughout 2021 about what appeared to be missing Presidential records, which resulted in the transfer of 15 boxes of records to NARA in January 2022. In its initial review of materials within those boxes, NARA identified items marked as classified national security information, up to the level of Top Secret and including Sensitive Compartmented Information and Special Access Program materials.
>
> It has now been four weeks since we first informed you of our intent to provide the FBI access to the boxes so that it and others in the Intelligence Community can conduct their reviews.
>
> Notwithstanding the urgency conveyed by the Department of Justice and the reasonable extension afforded to the former President, your April 29 letter asks for additional time for you to review the materials in the boxes "in order to ascertain whether any specific document is subject to privilege," and then to consult with the former President "so that he may personally make any decision to assert a claim of constitutionally based privilege."

In June 2022—just one month after that letter was sent to Trump's lawyers—federal agents made their first visit to Mar-a-Lago. Jay Bratt, chief of the Justice Department's counterintelligence and export control section, made the trip to Florida with three FBI agents to collect more documents and see the storage areas where Trump had been keeping some of the boxes he took from the White House.

Bratt and his team were greeted upon arriving at Mar-a-Lago by Corcoran, who had done his own search through the boxes for classi-

fied material before the agents arrived at the club, and Christina
Bobb, a fixture on the far-right One America News Network, who
had also joined the Save America PAC that March.

They took the agents to a basement storage room beneath the
dining room of Mar-a-Lago, where Trump's attorneys claimed everything taken from the White House was being stored. But they did not
allow the agents to look through the boxes themselves.

Before they left, Trump had briefly met with Bratt's team. "I appreciate what you're doing," Trump told the agents as he stood on the
steps at the front entrance of his club. "Anything you need, let us
know."

After his visit, Bratt sent a letter to Trump's lawyers asking that
they put a stronger lock on the storage room where documents were
being kept. "We ask that the room at Mar-a-Lago where the documents had been stored be secured and that all the boxes that were
moved from the White House to Mar-a-Lago (along with any other
items in that room) be preserved in that room in their current condi-
tion until further notice," Bratt wrote.

That day, Bratt's team walked away with a single Redweld enve-
lope, double-wrapped in tape, containing a folder with thirty-eight
classified documents and a statement signed by Bobb that read:

> Based upon the information that has been provided to me, I
> am authorized to certify, on behalf of the Office of Donald J.
> Trump, the following: a. A diligent search was conducted of
> the boxes that were moved from the White House to Florida;
> b. This search was conducted after receipt of the subpoena, in
> order to locate any and all documesnts that are responsive to
> the subpoena; c. Any and all responsive documents accompany
> this certification; and d. No copy, written notation, or reproduc-
> tion of any kind was retained as to any responsive Document.
>
> I swear or affirm that the above statements are true and
> correct to the best of my knowledge.

It was an untrue claim, and Bobb would likely come to regret ever signing that statement.

Just weeks later, the government was tipped off that there were even more classified documents at Trump's club, and a subpoena was issued to the Trump Organization for surveillance footage from Mar-a-Lago security cameras for a sixty-day period. They had reason to believe that boxes had been shuffled around the club and moved from the storage room they had inspected.

On August 5, the FBI obtained a search warrant from a federal magistrate judge in West Palm Beach granting permission to survey all of Mar-a-Lago, including Trump's office, private quarters, and any room where documents might be stored.

Federal agents would later write that after their search on August 8, they found "twice as many documents with classification markings as [were produced by] the 'diligent search' that the former President's counsel and other representatives had weeks to perform," adding that it called into "serious question" the attestation made by Bobb and the cooperation of Trump's lawyers.

Some senior Trump aides thought Trump should have just given the boxes back at the National Archives's first request, but they never expected that the former president's intransigence would culminate in the dramatic events of August 8. For other Trump staff at Mar-a-Lago, the boxes were seen as a giant mess, a chore that the former president had kept putting off.

"I'll clean them out, I'll clean them out," Trump would promise aides, who thought maybe he would eventually get around to sorting through the documents and wouldn't really be able to get on to whatever he might choose to do next until he did.

And while Trump's attorneys acknowledged that the National Archives personnel might have been fully within their rights under the law to do what they did to recover vital documents, they still complained bitterly about the way the Archives had handled the case from the beginning.

NARA "started demanding these boxes, 'you must give them to us.' Yeah, Trump is resistant, understandable, because they didn't make a gentle approach," said a former member of Trump's legal team. "If you go to Trump and say, 'Mr. President, this is the procedure and this is how we'd like to handle this.' And you explain everything to him and say, 'Yeah, this is the normal procedure. This is what the law requires.' You know what he does? He says, 'Go ahead.'"

"But if you go to Trump and say, 'I want your stuff,' what does he say? 'Screw you.'"

Trump was known for holding on to papers and mementos he wanted to show off to friends, something he continued as president. He would show off correspondence from Kim Jong Un to visitors to the Oval Office. He was also known to rip up and shred papers while president—something that would create a headache for staff who would then have to meticulously try to piece together and preserve the papers, as required by law.

And Trump had strange views on how he could declassify documents. In 2019, for example, Trump was fascinated by a satellite image of an Iranian space facility accident he was shown during a presidential briefing and tweeted it out to his millions of followers. Experts said the image likely came from a classified satellite or drone.

"We had a photo and I released it, which I have the absolute right to do," Trump said when asked about the image.

Basically, Trump believed he could wave his hand like a magic wand and broadly declassify documents, according to aides. Kash Patel, who was a senior official in the Defense Department, claimed Trump declassified a set of documents before he left the White House.

"Trump declassified whole sets of materials in anticipation of leaving government that he thought the American public should have the right to read themselves," Patel said in an interview with *Breitbart*.

For those around Trump, the search was seen as a kind of Rorschach test: It was either a terrible development that demonstrated the mounting legal problems Trump and his team faced, or it was a political gift right before the midterm elections and as Trump was preparing to launch a 2024 campaign. Epshteyn told a member of Trump's legal team that the former president's polls would go up 10 points—a prediction that would prove somewhat accurate but also horrified and disgusted the Trump attorney. Other aides to Trump described getting texts that read "Trump just won."

Trump's political fortunes aside, the implications of the search were gravely serious. Trump was under investigation for alleged crimes under the Espionage Act and violations of the Presidential Records Act, which requires the preservation of memos, letters, notes and other written communications related to a president's official duties. It was soon reported that nuclear secrets were among the documents.

Trump's team would keep tabs on who was—and who wasn't—sufficiently defending him. Trump and his allies also kicked up some outrageous conspiracy theories about what had just happened. Some of the ideas shared included the belief that the FBI had planted evidence or recording devices, or that the entire search was carefully planned for that day because it was the same day Nixon resigned in 1974.

"You often say there are no conspiracies, and there are also no coincidences, the fact that this raid on Trump's private residence happened on August 8, 2022, the anniversary of President Nixon's announcement he would resign effective the next day, was absolutely not a coincidence. There are no coincidences when it comes to the deep state. They know exactly what they're doing," Monica Crowley, a former top official in the Trump Treasury Department, said on Bannon's *WarRoom* podcast.

Epshteyn echoed Crowley. "No conspiracies but no coincidences, I think they're scared that Trump is going to do what we expect, which is announce a run for president in 2024. They're doing all they can to pull out all the stops," Epshteyn said.

The night of the raid, Trump held a tele-rally for Sarah Palin, the former governor of Alaska who was running for a congressional seat.

"Another day in paradise," he said as he got on the call. "This is a strange day—you probably all read about it, but very important."

———

THE NEXT DAY, TRUMP AND his team tried to make sense of what had happened.

Molly Michael, a longtime assistant to Trump, went to Mar-a-Lago to clean up the mess, and she relayed news back to Trump and his team on the state of his office and living quarters.

Trump's political team moved quickly to turn the former president's fight with the FBI into multiple fundraising pleas from his political action committee. "They are trying to stop the Republican Party and me once more," one Save America email read. "The lawlessness, political persecution, and Witch Hunt, must be exposed and stopped."

Trump traveled back to Bedminster from Manhattan for a dinner with the Republican Study Committee at his golf club. Sitting around a table in the wood-paneled dining room, Trump became animated describing what the agents had searched through—his safe, his wife's closet, and his son Barron's room.

Trump was "fired up" and determined to get into the presidential race sooner rather than later, according to Indiana representative Jim Banks, the chair of the Republican Study Committee and one of the dozen Republican lawmakers who had dinner with Trump.

On August 11, a few days after the search, Trump's attorneys got on the phone with Bratt and wanted to relay a message to Attorney General Merrick Garland on behalf of the former president. It was as ominous as it was unusual.

"President Trump wants the Attorney General to know that he has been hearing from people all over the country about the raid. If there is one word to describe their mood it is 'angry.' The heat is building up. The pressure is building up. Whatever I can do to take the heat down, to bring the pressure down, let us know," the message to Garland read.

A few hours later, Garland held a press conference at which he announced he personally approved the search warrant for Mar-a-Lago and planned to unseal it to the public.

He didn't acknowledge Trump's message in his statement but came to the defense of the law enforcement and FBI agents who bore the brunt of criticism from Trump and his allies that week: "I will not stand by silently when their integrity is unfairly attacked."

In the following weeks, Trump played golf in the mornings with friends, ate dinner on the patio at night, and hosted fundraisers for Republican candidates at his club. He projected a sense of normalcy to those around him, which helped reinforce the belief that the search on his property would be wind at his back for a 2024 announcement. Shortly before the raid, Trump had started telling people close to him he had decided to run.

The public boost he got from his supporters encouraged him. Polling showed him with a double-digit lead over any of his potential GOP rivals, including Florida governor Ron DeSantis. And while the public showed support for the investigation continuing, Trump saw his support within the Republican Party spike. Some of his supporters on the far right had started calling for civil war over the search. Senator Rick Scott likened the FBI to the "gestapo." Representative Marjorie Taylor Greene wrote on her Facebook page that the search of Trump's property is the "type of things that happen in countries during civil war."

The raid on Mar-a-Lago was an escalation event, and a harbinger of things to come. By the end of the year, a cascading series of criminal and civil investigations from Atlanta to Washington to New York City would begin to gather steam. By November 2022, the attorney general would appoint a lone special counsel to investigate Trump's handling of the classified documents he had failed to return as well as his role in the attack on the U.S. Capitol on January 6 and his larger effort to remain in power despite losing the 2020 election. A career prosecutor named Jack Smith, severe and monklike, would lead both investigations.

On a parallel track, prosecutors in Fulton County, Georgia, had also opened a criminal inquiry into Trump's sprawling conspiracy to reverse the 2020 election results in the state, efforts that had included the seizure of voting machines in rural Coffee County; the high-profile character assassination of several Black election workers in Atlanta, which resulted in myriad death threats, forcing them into hiding; and Trump's astonishing attack on the Republican secretary of state, Brad Raffensperger, which culminated in the now infamous phone call on which he demanded that Raffensperger "find 11,780 votes" and then told him that failing to do so would be a crime.

In New York City, Manhattan district attorney Alvin Bragg—after having shut down a criminal investigation into a long pattern of business fraud by Trump and the Trump Organization upon taking office in early 2022, which had resulted in two of his prosecutors resigning in anger—had by that fall decided to revive the long-abandoned investigation into hush money that Trump had paid to a porn star just before the 2016 election in violation of state election laws.

That same year in Albany, New York, Attorney General Letitia James had taken up where Bragg's prosecutors had left off, filing a sweeping civil suit against Trump, his two grown sons, and the Trump Organization, alleging that Trump's businesses had committed fraud on a systematic basis, routinely overvaluing its properties in order to improperly secure operating capital.

As the legal bills piled up for the different investigations, Trump and others in his orbit asked the Republican National Committee to help pay for it all. The RNC had paid for Trump's legal bills when Trump was president and was being investigated for alleged connections to Russia. McDaniel decided she would bring the request to the RNC's executive committee for a vote. Neither she nor her co-chair, Tommy Hicks, voted. But the committee agreed to pay the lawyers who were defending Trump in the New York investigation, because in that case, James campaigned on "shining a bright light into every dark corner of his real estate dealings."

In Trumpworld, all investigations were illegitimate and it was the prosecutors who were the criminals. Jack Smith was "a deranged person who wants to hurt people." Letitia James was a "racist." Alvin Bragg was also a "racist," and "an animal" who was "doing the work of Anarchists and the Devil." Trump's torrent of abuse would become so severe that the judge in the case would ultimately decide to impose a gag order, to stop Trump from attacking jurors, court staff, prosecutors, and their families.

As these simultaneous investigations closed in on Trump, the whole world awakened to the stark possibility that the former president might achieve yet another first: being the first former president to be criminally indicted.

Trump's allies in official Washington, while perhaps not hurling the same invective as their party leader, were right in sync with him when it came to the illegitimacy of all investigations, and every allegation. Regarding the prospect that Trump could be indicted for mishandling classified documents, Lindsey Graham of South Carolina, himself a former military prosecutor, said that there would be "riots in the streets" were that to happen.

Memory

DONALD TRUMP DEMANDED LOYALTY BUT AT TIMES DID NOT INSPIRE IT. IN part, that is because one was loyal at one's peril, as with Trump, loyalty was seldom reciprocal. Another important reason that so many high-level appointments went so badly in the Trump White House is that he had chosen officials who had long professional careers behind them, with portfolios of real accomplishment and reputations to protect, who understood well that in the American system, loyalty to the president who appointed you is always subordinate to loyalty to the Constitution and the law.

In fact, in many instances, it was loyalty to the oaths they had taken—sweetened by post–White House book deals and the platform to settle scores—that compelled Trump officials turned critics. Former national security adviser John Bolton had been one of the first out of the gate, offering his brutal assessment of Trump's foreign policy and antidemocratic tendencies in the summer of 2020, when Trump was still in office.

Once Trump decamped to Palm Beach, his critics seemed to multiply, and they found an audience eager to hear the shocking story of the rogue president and his reckless behavior in the White House—

such as the accounts by General Mark Milley, the former chairman of the Joint Chiefs of Staff, of his efforts to block the president from striking Iran and sparking war, or former attorney general Bill Barr's account of his rapidly devolving relationship with the former president over Trump's election delusion.

Barr's book, *One Damn Thing After Another*, would come out in the spring of 2022. In it, he would write that "Trump cared only about one thing: himself. Country and principle took second place. . . . Donald Trump has shown he has neither the temperament nor persuasive powers to provide the kind of positive leadership that is needed."

Scribes who find their muse in the most powerful boss in history are nothing new. And former cabinet secretaries and presidential aides who think they have something important to say have produced a full library of books over the life of the American democracy, ranging from perhaps the first "White House memoir," *Inside the White House in War Times*, by Lincoln's personal secretary, William Osborn Stoddard (an essential history published twenty-five years after Lincoln's assassination), to the brilliant self-justification of Henry Kissinger's *White House Years* to the bombshell counternarrative of David Stockman's *The Triumph of Politics: Why the Reagan Revolution Failed* (which came out in 1986, just when the revolution was starting to sputter) to the deft distancing maneuver of George Stephanopoulos's *All Too Human*. The larger category of these books runs the gamut from consequential to trivial, essential to disposable.

The books that have come out of the Trump White House are in a category all their own. While there were some fawning firsthand accounts of Trump, never before have so many books sounded alarms about an executive branch run amok and a president untethered to norms or even to reality, reported instances of disloyalty and potential criminality, and issued dire warnings about his possible return to the presidency.

Each and every one of these books infuriated Trump. Feeling betrayed, and unable ever to let anything go unremarked, he called his fourth and last chief of staff Mark Meadows's description of his more-serious-than-previously-reported bout with COVID—from Meadows's book, *The Chief's Chief*—"fake news."

But he reserved a special ire for Barr, whom he had not long before called "a man of unbelievable credibility and courage," and responded to an interview Barr did with NBC News's Lester Holt with a three-page letter bashing the former attorney general, which read in part: "Bill Barr cares more about being accepted by the corrupt Washington Media and Elite than serving the American people. He was slow, lethargic, and I realized early on that he never had what it takes to make a great Attorney General."

He was particularly apoplectic over an account from an apostate former staffer that wasn't even a memoir at all. In no fewer than four books—Michael Bender's *Frankly, We Did Win This Election*, Jonathan Karl's *Tired of Winning*, Michael S. Schmidt's *Donald Trump v. the United States*, and Jim Sciutto's *The Return of Great Powers*—Trump's second chief of staff, John Kelly, described, among many other things, Trump's utter ignorance about the rise of European fascism and his corresponding penchant for saying nice things about Adolf Hitler. "Well, Hitler did a lot of good things," he told Kelly, according to Bender. Trump denied making the comments.

And then there were the jaw-dropping accounts of his behavior behind the scenes that would be curated and published by the House Select Committee's investigation into the January 6 attack on the U.S. Capitol.

For more than a year after getting under way in late July 2021, the committee had interviewed a thousand witnesses and collected evidence to establish exactly what had transpired on January 6 and the events—and Trump's psychology—leading up to the attack. And the committee sought to answer what exactly Trump was doing in the West Wing as violence bubbled over and hundreds of his supporters bloodied and beat police officers, broke into the Capitol, and disrupted the certification of Joe Biden's 2020 election.

Their goals were twofold: to create a definitive historical record of what happened on January 6, and to gather evidence for potential prosecutions.

Using subpoena powers, the committee requested the testimony of a broad swath of former aides from the White House and campaign, Trump allies and confidants.

Trump instructed some of his former aides to simply ignore the subpoenas from the House committee, including Mark Meadows, Dan Scavino, Kash Patel, and Steve Bannon. Trump's lawyers argued that the committee was asking for documents and correspondence that were covered by executive privilege. His push to prevent certain people from testifying demonstrated just how rattled Trump was by the prospect of those closest to him being questioned by committee investigators, and it put his allies in severe legal jeopardy.

Some of those who were subpoenaed by the committee saw the whole exercise as an amusing badge of honor. They had custom made navy blue caps with SUBPOENAED proudly embroidered across the front; Caroline Wren, a Republican fundraiser who helped bring in money for the "Save America" rally on January 6, wore one at CPAC in February 2022 and at Trump events.

But as much as Trump's allies tried to downplay and belittle the committee's work, they were unprepared for the shocking testimony that played out live on TV in the summer of 2022.

The committee turned congressional hearings—what are typically sleepy public affairs events—into high-stakes, high-tension television drama. To pull it off, the committee brought on James Goldston, the former president of ABC News, to sort through the hours upon hours of recorded testimony and footage and edit them into compelling visual storytelling.

On June 9, 2022, the first prime-time hearing of the committee opened with a two-hour presentation on the extremes Trump went to in order to keep himself in office, the horrors that unfolded on the steps of the Capitol, and how Trump had been told over and over again that his claims of widespread voter fraud and a stolen election were false. The production was masterfully produced television; it featured a parade of high-level Trump advisers distancing, dissembling, and attacking their former boss, as well as the gripping testimony of Capitol Hill cops who were the last line of defense on January 6.

Caroline Edwards, a Capitol Police officer, emotionally described what she witnessed as a "war scene," with officers on the ground "throwing up" and "slipping on people's blood."

"It was carnage. It was chaos," she recalled, as video played of a vicious crowd breaking through windows and scaling the walls of the Capitol.

Jason Miller described being in the Oval Office with Trump and staff from the campaign, and "at some point in the conversation, Matt Oczkowski, who was the lead data person, was brought on, and I remember he delivered to the President, in pretty blunt terms, that he was going to lose."

And in video testimony, Bill Barr delivered the coup de grâce: "I made it clear I did not agree with the idea of saying the election was stolen and putting out this stuff, which I told the president was bullshit," he said. "And I didn't want to be a part of it."

Vice Chair Liz Cheney explained the hearings were specifically designed to explain Trump's "sophisticated seven-point plan" to overturn the 2020 election and prevent the peaceful transfer of power. According to the committee, "President Trump engaged in a massive effort to spread false and fraudulent information to the American public claiming the 2020 election was stolen from him," "President Trump summoned and assembled a violent mob in Washington and directed them to march on the US Capitol," and "As the violence was under way, President Trump ignored multiple pleas for assistance and failed to take immediate action to stop the violence and instruct his supporters to leave the Capitol."

"You will see that Donald Trump and his advisers knew that he had in fact lost the election," Cheney said. "But despite this, President Trump engaged in a massive effort to spread false and fraudulent information to convince huge portions of the U.S. population that fraud had stolen the election."

Not only was the committee's presentation riveting television but, most galling to Trump, it was also a ratings bonanza, with at least twenty million viewers, most of whom stayed for the entire broadcast. Trump and his allies were flat-footed in their public defense; just twenty-four hours before the first hearing, they had not formalized any plans for countering the witness testimony, because they didn't even know who would be scheduled to speak. Matt Schlapp, the chairman of the American Conservative Union, got his organization to set up a website to "fact check" the hearings as they happened.

But it was surprising to aides on the January 6 committee—and even people close to Trump—that his team wasn't doing more to go on defense. There was a sense among Trump's team that the public opinion "cake is baked." Trump paid attention to the hearings, and he would watch clips, read some of the transcripts, and follow the headlines after he finished with his daily rounds of golf at his Bedminster club.

He projected nonchalance, but Trump was irritated by the fact that he had zero political allies on the committee to defend him and cross-examine witnesses. For that, he blamed House Minority Leader Kevin McCarthy.

After Speaker Nancy Pelosi barred two of Trump's staunchest allies in the House, Jim Jordan of Ohio and Jim Banks of Indiana, from serving on the panel, McCarthy boycotted, withholding any Republican participation in the committee. Without bipartisan support, Pelosi created a select committee on January 6 and appointed Cheney of Wyoming and Adam Kinzinger of Illinois to serve as the two Republican representatives, even though most of their conference had turned on them and Republicans believed, however foolishly, that sitting out would make the hearings appear to the public as partisan and one-sided.

Trump viewed it as a serious mistake and complained to aides and even guests at Bedminster that he didn't have his people defending him or cross-examining the witnesses.

"We have nobody on that panel who can fight back!" Trump said in a radio interview. "Republicans should be ashamed of themselves."

And so Trump took his defense into his own hands. Onstage at the Faith and Freedom Coalition's annual gathering in Nashville ten days after the prime-time hearing, Trump went on a long rant about the January 6 committee, which he dubbed the "unselect" committee. He assailed it as a "sham" and accused lawmakers of unfairly editing interviews to fit a narrative, making a point of attacking the two Republicans on the committee.

"The committee is taking the testimony of witnesses who defended me for eight hours, chopping it up, and truncating sound bites to make it sound like what they said was absolutely terrible," Trump said. "Meanwhile, the committee refuses to play any of the tape of people saying the good things, the things that we want to hear. It's a one-way street. It's a rigged deal."

But on a more personal level, he was angry to see some of those closest to him give stinging testimony about how they knew his claims of a stolen election were false. His own daughter Ivanka voluntarily appeared before the committee and said in recorded testimony that she believed Barr when he said he had found no signs of fraud.

"Ivanka Trump was not involved in looking at, or studying, Election results. She had long since checked out and was, in my opinion, only trying to be respectful to Bill Barr and his position as Attorney General (he sucked!)," Trump wrote on Truth Social after clips of her April 2022 testimony aired.

But no testimony irritated Trump and his circles more than the account delivered by former White House aide Cassidy Hutchinson.

Hutchinson did not set out to be a lightning rod for Trumpworld after she was first subpoenaed by the committee. But over the course of her interviews, it became clear to Cheney and the committee that her proximity to power at the end of the Trump White House made her a unique and important witness.

Hutchinson had served as chief of staff Mark Meadows's assistant in the White House, working so closely with Meadows that aides thought of her as an extension of him. She traveled by his side, including on Air Force One, and Meadows empowered her to send texts, answer calls, and even give orders on his behalf. Her influence was at times a point of contention among staff in the White House who derisively called her "Chief Cassidy" behind her back.

She had formed strong contacts with Republican members on Capitol Hill from her previous job in the White House Legislative Affairs office, and when she went to work under Meadows when he became chief of staff, members would directly text or call Hutchinson to get a line to him and the White House.

But in the final days of the Trump White House, she had a front row seat to the chaos, when few people were around, her boss was ushering in a rotating cast of fringe characters to the Oval Office, and most notably, she had insight into the mysterious hours between the "Save America" rally at the White House Ellipse and the violence on Capitol Hill when Trump was unaccounted for.

Hutchinson briefly worked for Trump after he left the White House, and had planned to move down to Florida to continue to work for him, but Trump decided against bringing her to Palm Beach on the objection of some of the other young aides who were going to work for him at Mar-a-Lago and did not want her to be part of the team.

When federal agents delivered a subpoena to Hutchinson in early 2022, she was unemployed, and she turned to Trump's leadership PAC, Save America, for help in paying the hefty legal fees, and hired Stefan Passantino, Trump's former White House ethics lawyer, as her representation. But she became concerned that her lawyer, who was being paid by Trump's PAC, was actually sharing information about her testimony with the other witnesses and people close to Trump.

"It wasn't just that I had Stefan sitting next to me; it was almost like I felt like I had Trump looking over my shoulder," Hutchinson said during one of her interviews with the committee. "Because I knew in some fashion it would get back to him if I said anything he would find disloyal. And the prospect of that genuinely scared me."

Hutchinson's experience with the January 6 committee and with her former White House colleagues over the course of the spring and summer of 2022 showcased how loyalty was rewarded and betrayal punished by Trump and those close to him. As Hutchinson explained in her testimony, she was given reassurances that if she protected the former president she would be taken care of and set up with job prospects, and she was reminded every step of the way that people were watching.

At one point Hutchinson was approached about working with Jason Miller at Gettr, according to her book. She was introduced to a conservative firm, Red Curve, for a job. And Pam Bondi, the former attorney general of Florida who started working for Trump's PAC, texted Hutchinson to tell her that she was the topic of conversation at a dinner with Trump.

Hutchinson testified to the committee, "Pam texted me that night and said something to the effect of: 'Susie, Matt Schlapp, and I had dinner with POTUS at Mar-a-Lago tonight. Call Matt next week. He has a job for you that we all think you'd be great at—that you all—we all think you would be great in. You are the best. Keep up the good work. Love and miss you.'"

The night before her second deposition with the committee, Hutchinson recounted receiving a message from Ben Williamson, a former Trump White House aide who worked for Meadows.

"He said something to the effect of: 'Well, Mark wants me to let you know that he knows you're loyal and he knows you'll do the right thing tomorrow and that you're going to protect him and the boss. You know, he knows that we're all on the same team and we're all a family. Do well,'" Hutchinson testified.

And she was made aware that Trump was paying attention. After parts of her interviews became public in April when the committee filed a brief in response to Meadows suing the House over its subpoena of him, Passantino told Hutchinson that Trump wasn't upset about what he read.

"I would have heard if he was mad about anything discussed in yours, but it's just a good reminder that the boss does read transcripts," Hutchinson testified that Passantino told her. "And we want to make sure that, like, whatever he's reading isn't going to put you in a bad situation." He added that Trump had, however, read Miller's testimony and he was "really ticked off."

But Hutchinson testified that she finally decided she was tired of feeling "frustrated" and "disgusted" with herself for not being completely forthcoming with the committee. She said she met with Alyssa Farah Griffin, who also worked for Meadows in the White House, and had cooperated with the committee and agreed to act as a back channel.

On the night before her fourth deposition with the committee she received an ominous phone call. A person, the caller said, "let me know you have your deposition tomorrow. He wants me to let you know he's thinking about you. He knows you're loyal. And you're going to do the right thing when you go in for your deposition."

It was like a warning from a mob boss. And the committee, concerned that Hutchinson's testimony might leak and that someone in Trumpworld was clearly trying to intimidate their witnesses, decided to make Hutchinson their star surprise witness the next week.

On June 28, wearing a simple white blazer she'd picked out from Zara the day before, Hutchinson sat at the hearing room table and gave a shocking overview of Trump's behavior around January 6 and painted a portrait of a president who was belligerent and even mentally unstable.

Over the course of two hours, Hutchinson said she was told by one of Trump's top security officials, Tony Ornato, that Trump wanted to go to the Capitol after the "Save America" rally on the Ellipse and became irate when he was told they would be heading back to the White House in his presidential vehicle, "the Beast." Hutchinson claimed Ornato told her that Trump had lunged for the steering wheel of the car and had to be held back by Robert Engel, the head of his Secret Service detail.

"The president said something to the effect of, 'I am the fucking president. Take me up to the Capitol now,'" Hutchinson said.

And in the most damning statement of her testimony, Hutchinson said Ornato told her that Trump was informed that some of the rally-goers had weapons.

"I don't effing care that they have weapons; they're not here to hurt me. Take the effing mags away. Let my people in. They can march to the Capitol from here. Let the people in. Take the effing mags away," Hutchinson testified that she heard Trump say.

She related that Trump was so upset after Barr told the Associated Press in an interview that he found no evidence of widespread fraud in the 2020 election that the president threw his plate of food at the wall, leaving "ketchup dripping down the wall and a shattered porcelain plate on the floor."

Hutchinson's testimony was explosive. And Trump furiously responded to Hutchinson on Truth Social and tried to cast her testimony as revenge for his not keeping her on staff in Florida after he left the White House.

"I hardly know who this person, Cassidy Hutchinson, is, other than I heard very negative things about her (a total phony and 'leaker'), and when she requested to go with certain others of the team to Florida after my having served a full term in office, I personally turned her request down," Trump wrote. "Why did she want to go with us if she felt we were so terrible? I understand that she was very upset and angry that I didn't want her to go, or be a member of the team. She is bad news!"

Trump said the account of his lunging at the steering wheel of the Beast was "sick" and "fraudulent." "Wouldn't even have been possible to do such a ridiculous thing," Trump wrote. "There is no cross examination of this so-called witness. This is a Kangaroo Court!!"

He gave an interview to Newsmax where he called Hutchinson a "social climber" and smeared her for living in a "fantasy land." Trump's allies worked to discredit her online.

Save America PAC released an angry twelve-page rebuttal from Trump slamming the January 6 committee as a "smoke and mirrors show" and perpetuating falsehoods about the election, including allegations made in the debunked Dinesh D'Souza documentary about ballot harvesting in the 2020 election.

The committee stood by Hutchinson's testimony as Trump and his allies worked to discredit her. They pointed to the fact that the Secret Service disputed her account about a physical altercation inside the Beast—which of course was seized on by Trump allies—but they did not deny that Trump wanted to go to the Capitol after the "Save America" rally.

While there were questions about some details of her testimony after the fact, Hutchinson described a presidency in complete chaos. Trump was concerned that the hearings over the summer would impact his standing with Republicans ahead of any presidential announcement. Critics believed that the testimony presented was so damning—so embarrassing—they could finally break through.

Trump did not like the optics of not having any Republican defenders on the committee, but he paid close attention to national polling, which showed little to no impact on his approval rating.

Trump and his allies thought the committee waited too long—more than a year—after January 6 to break through and that the economy and gas prices on average as high as $5 meant more to the average person than what was transpiring on TV.

Once more, Trump appeared to benefit from a combination of blind dedication from his supporters—the same group he mused would back him even if he were to stand in the middle of Manhattan's Fifth Avenue and "shoot somebody"—and timing.

AS THE SUN SET OVER the craggy peaks of the Teton Range in Jackson, Wyoming, Liz Cheney stood at a simple wooden lectern to concede her congressional race to Harriett Hageman.

Cheney had anticipated losing for months. She had lagged in the polls against Hageman. Described as a "workhorse" by staff on the January 6 committee, Cheney poured her energy and attention into what would become her legacy-defining work—partly because she knew her fate in the primary, but also because she was facing death threats and campaigning could be a security risk. All because she stood up to Trump.

Just two years prior, in 2020, Cheney had won her primary with more than 73 percent of the vote. In 2022, the woman who was once one of the most powerful people in Congress and the heir to the Cheney political dynasty started by her father, former vice president Dick Cheney, secured only 28.9 percent of the vote, making it the second-worst finish for a House incumbent in sixty years.

Trump and his team viewed Cheney's loss as the defining victory of his midterm crusade against those who crossed him. Of the ten Republicans who had cast a vote to impeach Trump from office on charges he incited a riot, Cheney's defeat was the fourth and final win for Trump. Four other lawmakers decided not to run for reelection, while just two, Representatives Dan Newhouse and David Valadao, advanced past their primaries and went on to keep their seats.

"This is a wonderful result for America, and a complete rebuke of the Unselect Committee of political Hacks and Thugs," Trump declared on Truth Social. "Liz Cheney should be ashamed of herself, the way she acted, and her spiteful, sanctimonious words and actions towards others. Now she can finally disappear into the depths of political oblivion where, I am sure, she will be much happier than she is right now."

Except that Cheney had no plans to ride off into the sunset.

She used her concession speech to issue a warning—and to vow she would continue her fight against Trump and all that she believed he stood for.

"Our nation is barreling, once again, towards crisis, lawlessness, and violence. No American should support election deniers for any position of genuine responsibility, where their refusal to follow the rule of law will corrupt our future," Cheney said. The survival of democracy in America, she warned, is "not guaranteed."

It was not lost on those watching her speech that it felt more like a presidential announcement than like someone bowing out of a race. It was carefully staged with the help of James Goldston, the former ABC News executive who produced the January 6 committee hearings, against the dramatic backdrop of the Wyoming landscape. Her speech was perfectly timed, although not on purpose, so that the shadows settled in behind her as she vowed to take on Trump.

"We must be very clear-eyed about the threat we face and about what is required to defeat it. I have said since January 6, that I will do whatever it takes to make sure Donald Trump is never again anywhere near the Oval Office," Cheney said. "This is a fight for all of us together."

Tom Petty's "I Won't Back Down" played as she walked from the podium.

The next day, Cheney's team converted her campaign committee and the nearly $7 million in funding it had held back on using in the race into a leadership PAC called "The Great Task," a nod to Abraham Lincoln's Gettysburg Address. Her new mission, she said on the *Today* show, was to do "whatever it takes to keep Donald Trump out of the Oval Office." And she didn't rule out running for president herself.

While Cheney had been charting out life beyond Congress, Trump's team poured their resources into the race as part of their effort to purge anyone not loyal to Trump from the party. Trump held a rally for Hageman in the spring and spent over $1 million on her race. And he personally called the governor of Wyoming and state lawmakers to encourage them to change the state's election laws and pass a bill that would prevent crossover voting in a primary election, with the goal of preventing Democrats and independents from registering as Republicans to help Cheney.

But even after all their personal meddling in the election, they were surprised by how little of a fight Cheney put up.

Her last campaign ads did not mention Hageman at all. Instead, it was focused on preserving the Constitution, pushing back against the "big lie," and Trump. In lieu of a campaign tour ahead of the primary, Cheney flew out to California weeks before the vote to deliver a searing rebuke of Trump and the Republican Party at the Ronald Reagan Presidential Library.

"We are confronting a domestic threat that we have never faced before—and that is a former President who is attempting to unravel the foundations of our constitutional Republic," said Cheney. "And he is aided by Republican leaders and elected officials who have made themselves willing hostages to this dangerous and irrational man."

"Republicans," Cheney said, "cannot both be loyal to Donald Trump and loyal to the Constitution."

Start Me Up

TRUMP WAS GOING TO RUN FOR PRESIDENT IN 2024. THAT MUCH WAS CERtain, according to his advisers.

But what always remained unclear to his team throughout the summer of 2022 was when—and how—he would make his announcement.

Trump wanted to get into the race as early as August 2021, after the Afghanistan withdrawal he thought was botched by President Joe Biden, according to his advisers who said his mindset about running in 2024 changed that day.

Trump went from wanting to be a candidate to right the wrong he felt had been done to him, according to one adviser, to wanting to be president because he thought the country had been disgraced and he would do a better job. "It was as clear and quick as that." Trump would watch Biden on TV and grouse that he wished the election was sooner.

In spring 2022, there was discussion of Trump's forming an exploratory committee, or, as the Federal Election Commission calls it, "testing the waters." Essentially it would allow Trump to raise money without officially becoming a candidate. Trump formed an exploratory committee in 1999 when he was considering running as a Reform Party candidate, and then again in 2015 when he decided to run on the Republican ticket.

But this time, the idea never got far. T-shirts were made and sent to Trump's team that read WE WANT TRUMP—2024 EXPLORATORY COMMITTEE. Trump never saw the shirts. When the idea of an exploratory committee was brought up, Trump knocked it down immediately.

"What the fuck do I need to explore? I was president," Trump said in response to the idea. An exploratory committee, Trump and his team decided, wasn't needed—Trump was the most recognizable person in the country—but they also thought it might suggest to the public that he wasn't serious about running. And he was.

People around Trump were split on when he should announce. There were some, like Steve Bannon and Charlie Kirk, who urged Trump to announce early to galvanize the base and start putting together a 2024 operation. Others warned him that jumping into the race before the midterms would make him the scapegoat for the results.

There were rumors that he planned to announce his candidacy as early as July 4 as a way to draw maximum attention and clear the field of other Republicans considering a run for the presidency. But speculating whether Trump would do any particular thing proved, again, to be an impossible task; the date came and went.

Trump told *New York* magazine's Olivia Nuzzi around the same time that he had made up his mind about running for president. The only question left for him was whether any announcement would occur before or after the midterm elections in November.

"I just think that there are certain assets to before," he told Nuzzi. "Let people know. I think a lot of people would not even run if I did that because, if you look at the polls, they don't even register. Most of these people. And I think that you would actually have a backlash against them if they ran. People want me to run."

Over the summer, Trump had been quietly taking the temperature of some of his wealthiest donors across the country in places like

Nashville, Houston, and Las Vegas with his leadership PAC, Save America. The stated goal of the intimate salon dinners was to give an update on the midterms and Trump's endorsement record—but it also provided Trump's top donors the chance to pick his brain about a 2024 run and dish out their own feedback.

Trump had sensed there were GOP understudies eagerly waiting in the wings.

He and his team had been keeping a close eye on the shadow campaign for president that was well under way. Some of Trump's former cabinet members, like Vice President Mike Pence, former secretary of state Mike Pompeo, and former U.N. ambassador Nikki Haley, made visits, along with prominent Republican senators, to the early voting states of Iowa and New Hampshire. And behind closed doors, they held meetings with party donors, like Trump's former education secretary Betsy DeVos, who were interested in hearing from a Trump alternative.

And of course, they were watching Ron DeSantis like a hawk. The Florida governor rose to national prominence during the pandemic, and had been trying to fashion himself as Trump Lite, or the former president without the personal messiness. DeSantis attracted some of Trump's top donors—like Home Depot founder Bernie Marcus and Las Vegas casino mogul and Trump friend Phil Ruffin— who collectively shelled out millions for his reelection campaign. In private, Trump quizzed his advisers and wealthy friends about what they thought of DeSantis, and whether they thought he would actually launch a bid against him.

Publicly, Trump brushed aside any suggestion that he saw DeSantis as a rival. But as he watched DeSantis's numbers tick up in the polls over the summer, and some of his deep-pocketed Palm Beach peers pull out their checkbooks and write "Ron DeSantis for President" on the Payable To line, he became more prickly about the prospect of the man whom he'd endorsed and whose campaign he'd resuscitated turning on him.

Trump's potential rivals smelled blood in the water. A majority of

Americans, according to polling that summer, did not want Trump to run for reelection. The search of his Mar-a-Lago home demonstrated just how serious the FBI was about their investigation into his handling of classified documents. In hearing after hearing, the House committee investigating the January 6 attack painted a portrait of a president who was not only out of control but a threat to the Constitution. Federal prosecutors were investigating the scheme to send fake electors to Congress to certify the Electoral College vote. Trump was legally and politically vulnerable.

But Trump saw his set of circumstances differently. He turned the search of Mar-a-Lago into a kind of mythic event in which he once again was the righteous hero unfairly targeted by his enemies. He saw wall-to-wall news coverage, a chorus of prominent Republicans coming to his defense, and an explosion of online donations. But also the very real chance he could face criminal charges. Trump was more eager than ever to get into the race—and soon.

BEFORE THE MAR-A-LAGO SEARCH, TRUMP had privately told people close to him that he was going to run. But around Labor Day, he made it clear to Susie Wiles and others on his team that they needed to have a plan in place for whenever he decided to pull the trigger.

He did so in a roundabout way. Trump never gathered all of his donors and advisers in one room to tell them he was running. There was no polling or focus groups. He just decided he was going to do it and had been letting his advisers, like Wiles, Taylor Budowich, and Brian Jack, privately know he was committed to running in 2024 and they needed to have a team ready to go.

And this time, Trump made clear to them, it was going to be different. Trump wanted his team to be small and scrappy—reminiscent of his 2016 campaign—because, he would tell people, that was when he won.

Trump told Wiles to go out and find someone tough to help run his operation. He trusted Wiles and she had been a respected leader of the team, but he wanted someone else who could balance her out and rule with an iron fist. And of course there was an obvious benefit in Trumpworld to not being the lone person with a target on your back.

Jeff Roe, the political consultant who ran Virginia governor Glenn Youngkin's successful gubernatorial campaign, met with Trump in December 2021. The meeting had been pitched as a way to smooth over his relationship with Trump after Youngkin's campaign very carefully tiptoed around involving the former president and Trump did not feel he got enough credit for Youngkin's win in the state.

Youngkin, according to Trump advisers, was gracious after his win, calling Trump to thank him for his support and writing him a letter. But Roe called Wiles and asked if he could personally set the record straight with Trump. Except, according to Trump advisers, he didn't just come to set the record straight; he came to ask for a job. Trump, while skeptical, was momentarily interested, but it didn't last long—Trump was warned by some candidates that Roe, who famously liked to fly around on a private jet, would spend all of his money.

But in the spring of 2022, at a loss for who a good, "tough" partner on the campaign would be, Wiles called on Trump's pollster, Tony Fabrizio, for any recommendations.

"I want you to meet my friend Chris," Fabrizio said, referring to Chris LaCivita.

LaCivita had more than three decades of political experience and was a longtime fixture of national Republican politics. But he was most famously known in GOP circles as the unrepentant architect of the infamous "Swift Boat Veterans for Truth" campaign that helped sink Democratic presidential nominee John Kerry in 2004. A Marine veteran who served in the Gulf War, he worked for the National Republican Senatorial Committee and the Congressional Leadership Fund, a Republican super PAC.

He also helped head off rumblings of a contested convention at the 2016 RNC, smoothing the way for Trump's first coronation as the

Republican presidential nominee. He had helped establish the Preserve America super PAC, and in 2022 he was running Wisconsin senator Ron Johnson's reelection campaign. He was different from Trump in just about every way. He liked drinking bourbon and smoking cigars and spending hours out in the wilderness hunting. Once, he was on the phone with a reporter about a campaign while he was out shooting, and killed a bird midinterview.

If there was one thing he had in common with Trump, it was that he shared an ethos with the former president of being "unpredictable": "If you become predictable in politics, you become irrelevant," he told the *Richmond Times-Dispatch* in 2011.

Wiles and LaCivita had never met before, although each knew of the other by reputation, but over the course of a few dinners in Fort Lauderdale, she became convinced he was the right person for the job and arranged for a dinner with Trump at Mar-a-Lago.

"Mr. President," Wiles said, introducing him to Trump, "Chris made the Swift Boat ad."

"Everybody says they made the Swift Boat ad, you're full of shit," Trump replied. Over dinner out on the patio of Trump's Palm Beach club, as Trump DJed for his guests, they talked about the midterms and the possibility of LaCivita's joining Trump's team. But both Trump and LaCivita were uncertain it was the right fit.

"If that is who you really want," Trump told Wiles a few days later, "I guess it's okay."

So on June 24, 2022, Wiles invited LaCivita to Bedminster for another meeting with Trump.

As LaCivita sat across from Trump's desk at his club, his phone buzzed with news. The Supreme Court had announced the *Dobbs* decision.

"Mr. President, you just did what a lot of people have never been able to do," LaCivita said. "You overturned *Roe v. Wade.*"

Wiles told Trump that they would need to make a decision soon. LaCivita was working on Senate races, and although he wouldn't need to come on board officially until November, Trump had to hire him or else they quickly needed to figure out an alternative. In September, LaCivita was invited back for one more meeting with Trump, except this time, Wiles knew, and didn't tell LaCivita out of fear he might turn it down, that Trump was going to offer him a job. LaCivita accepted.

In September, Wiles convened a group of more than a dozen Trump advisers and allies at Trump National Golf Club in West Palm Beach to hammer out the logistics of an announcement they knew could come at any time. It was not inconceivable that the former president could suddenly decide he was going to make his decision official to the world and post about it on social media without telling any of them. They needed to be prepared to turn on an entire presidential operation when that moment inevitably came.

From midmorning until around dinnertime, Wiles and a group that included LaCivita, Trump's pollster John McLaughlin, Brad Parscale, communications adviser Steven Cheung, Taylor Budowich, Alex Pfeiffer, and lawyers went over the official hoops they would need to jump through immediately after any announcement and any branding. Trump, who was at the club for lunch, stopped by to say hello to the group for a few minutes.

Around the same time, Budowich, who had been Trump's communications director, launched Make America Great Again Inc., or MAGA Inc., a super PAC that would dump millions into the final stretch of the midterm races and also give Trump a boost as his official super PAC whenever he jumped into the race. But it would also serve as an initial landing spot for Trump's 2024 presidential campaign.

AS TRUMP'S TEAM WAS STARTING to carve out a 2024 campaign operation, some of the former president's preferred candidates for the November midterm election were embroiled in embarrassing personal scandals and political faux pas that had party leaders questioning Trump's instincts for endorsements and concerned that they faced an uphill battle in the general election simply because of who Trump decided to support in the Republican primary.

Doug Mastriano, Trump's pick for governor in Pennsylvania, was struggling out on the campaign trail. His crowds were small. He was being significantly outspent by Democrats supporting Josh Shapiro. The Republican Governors Association was not spending money on his campaign, which they viewed as a lost cause as he trailed in the polls by double digits. And privately, Trump had come to regret his decision to endorse Mastriano. Privately, Trump was especially frustrated by Mastriano's position on abortion—no exceptions, including when the life of the mother is at risk—which he thought was extreme.

Dr. Mehmet Oz was also trailing in polls in the Senate race against John Fetterman in Pennsylvania. Trump had picked Oz in part because he viewed celebrity as key to political viability, and liked the idea of a cardiologist turned reality TV star in the U.S. Senate. But Oz stumbled throughout the general election, first by disappearing for most of the summer and staying off the campaign trail, giving an opening to Lt. Gov. John Fetterman. Fetterman suffered a stroke in spring 2022 that left him struggling to communicate, but he was still able to hammer Oz as an elite from New Jersey—where Oz had a home—who was out of touch with Pennsylvanians and did things like call a veggie platter "crudités."

But there was no race that caused more national Republican heartburn than the Georgia Senate race. Roger Sollenberger from *The Daily Beast* churned out a series of scoops over the summer and fall about Republican candidate Herschel Walker, including that he secretly fathered a child and paid for a girlfriend to have an abortion, and finally, just days before the runoff election, a report on domestic violence allegations from Walker's ex-girlfriend. The scandals flew in the face of Walker's persona as a pro-family candidate who railed against deadbeat fathers and called for a ban on abortion.

And they created a media frenzy at the worst possible moment, just weeks before the midterm election, as Walker and Democratic senator Raphael Warnock were tied neck and neck. Walker's son,

Christian, who had a large following on social media as a conservative influencer, disavowed his father's Senate bid and behavior in a string of viral tweets. But Republicans, including Trump, stood by Walker.

Trump said Walker was being "slandered and maligned" by Democrats and the media. "Herschel has properly denied the charges against him, and I have no doubt he is correct," Trump said. "They are trying to destroy a man who has true greatness in his future, just as he had athletic greatness in his past."

THE JITTERS ABOUT SOME OF Trump's star endorsements came as the Republican Party was expecting a so-called "red wave" on Election Night, driven by voter concerns about the economy and disappointment with President Joe Biden. Partisan polls fed a political narrative—particularly in right-wing media—that Republicans were bound to have sweeping wins in November, and it was a narrative Trump fed himself in interviews and social media posts, even if he privately had his doubts, concerned that Republicans were going to fumble because of *Dobbs*. There were two hurdles for Trump's 2024 comeback: the results of the midterm elections, and his most likely rival, Florida governor Ron DeSantis.

And during a rally in Latrobe, Pennsylvania, on November 5, Trump tried out a nickname he had been workshopping for DeSantis with friends and aides. Trump felt DeSantis had been disloyal to him, and he especially did not like an ad DeSantis had just released that morning called "So God Made a Fighter."

In the black-and-white ad, a take on the famous "So God Made a Farmer" speech that turned into a well-recognized commercial for Ram Trucks, DeSantis is never mentioned. But God was invoked ten times over images of the Florida governor.

"And on the eighth day," a voice in the ad narrated, "God looked down on his planned paradise and said: 'I need a protector.' So God made a fighter."

Trump thought the ad was arrogant and added it to his irritations about the Florida governor. The list was growing.

First there was the fact that Trump felt that DeSantis did not give him enough credit for helping him win in the 2018 Florida GOP primary, when Trump gave DeSantis his endorsement. It lifted the little-known congressman from relative obscurity and led him to a win over one of the biggest and most well-funded Republican names in the state.

Trump thought DeSantis was trying to mimic him with his hand gestures and populist style. He didn't like that DeSantis criticized the COVID vaccines developed during his administration. And it did not go unnoticed that during DeSantis's only debate against his Democratic rival for governor, DeSantis dramatically sidestepped a question about his 2024 ambitions.

His annoyance with DeSantis finally bubbled over with the ad, and even though he was hundreds of miles from Florida, Trump could not resist the opportunity to take a swing at the governor as a screen behind him showed poll numbers for Trump and his potential 2024 rivals, including DeSantis.

"We're winning big in the Republican Party for the nomination like nobody's ever seen before," Trump said, referencing polls that were placed on a glowing screen behind him. "There it is, Trump at 71 percent, Ron DeSanctimonious at 10 percent."

Trump had almost let the nickname for DeSantis slip at an earlier event, according to aides, who said Trump started to say "DeSanctimonious" before catching himself. He was "proud" of the moniker he produced, too, according to aides. Throughout his short political career, Trump took pride in assigning insulting nicknames to his political rivals: "Crooked Hillary," "Little Marco," "Pocahontas" for Elizabeth Warren, "Little Rocket Man" for North Korean dictator Kim Jong Un.

He thought of himself as a political "genius" for pinpointing what the public didn't like about someone and flipping it into a disparaging label. But with days to go until the midterm election, the insult made waves among the Republican donor class who thought it was a low and unnecessary blow to DeSantis. But it wasn't the only slight. For a rally the next day in Miami, Trump and his team had notably—and intentionally—not invited DeSantis, whose team decided instead to hold a rival event on the opposite side of the state.

TRUMP ARRIVED IN MIAMI EAGER to continue his fight against DeSantis. By the fall, Trump understood DeSantis was going to announce a run against him for president and he wanted to get out in front of it and fast. At his rally for Senator Marco Rubio, he was ready to take another swipe at DeSantis and was adamant that he should not give his potential 2024 rival an endorsement, or even an acknowledgment, onstage.

Trump's advisers just wanted him to offer support for DeSantis and move along in his speech. State party leaders had shown up to support Rubio and Trump, and many of them were also close to the governor. It was one thing to throw out an insult at a potential 2024 rival at a rally in Pennsylvania, but another to attack him on his home turf and in an area of the state, and with a Hispanic audience, that the Republican Party had invested heavily in. The last thing they wanted to come out of the rally was yet another story about Trump picking a fight with the popular governor, who was on a glide path to a second term.

Ahead of the rally, Trump was holding a meeting at a secure building near the Miami-Dade County Fair & Exposition grounds with his team, who were pleading with him to hold his fire. But Trump wasn't taking anyone's advice.

Wiles was with Trump and knew that Roger Stone, the Florida-based Republican consultant and Trump ally, planned to attend the rally with his wife. Wiles and Stone had known each other for decades, from when they both worked for Jack Kemp. And she understood that if there was anyone who would understand the current political microclimate they found themselves in on the southern coast

204 TRUMP IN EXILE

of Florida, and if there was anyone Trump would listen to, it would be Stone.

Stone was a longtime Republican consultant and self-proclaimed political "dirty trickster" who was credited in many ways with pioneering modern political mudslinging. He went on to work for Richard Nixon—whose face is tattooed across his back—after the White House, campaigned for Ronald Reagan, and with his friend Paul Manafort and the political consultant Charlie Black, built a powerful D.C. lobbying firm. Stone encouraged Trump to run for president in the late 1980s, and he stayed close to Trump through his presidency when their relationship paid off.

As one of Trump's final acts as president, he pardoned Stone, who was convicted of obstructing a congressional investigation into Trump's campaign and its potential ties to Russia and was sentenced to forty months in prison by a federal court.

"Are you here?" Wiles asked Stone. "Can you come and see the president for a minute?" "Sure," Stone said. A golf cart was sent to get him and drive him the short distance to where Trump and his team waited in a secure holding place.

"What's up?" Stone asked Wiles when he arrived.

"Do you think that in his remarks, he should endorse Ron DeSantis?" Wiles asked.

"Yes," he replied.

"Well," Wiles replied, "he's refusing to do it. Would you go in and talk to him?"

Stone, who had been skeptical of DeSantis's rise, agreed to go in and explain to Trump that he should not snub the incumbent Republican governor of his home state right before the election.

Trump stood inside a waiting room with a paper in his hand and asked Stone, "Have you seen this shit?"

"No, what is it?" Stone said.

"This is what they want me to say about Ron DeSantis," Trump said.

"Well, the larger question is should you endorse DeSantis. And the answer is yes," Stone said.

"You hate DeSantis," Trump said.

"Yes, I do too," Stone said. "I have my own reasons. But, you're the head of the party. He's going to win. It would be notable if you didn't endorse him. I'm not saying you have to bury him in accolades," Stone told Trump, "But just make it a pro forma endorsement. Heap praise on Marco Rubio and then say, go vote for DeSantis."

Trump replied, "I hate it."

"I hate it too but I think you should do it," Stone said.

Trump stood with his arms crossed and begrudgingly agreed. "All right, all right, I'll do it."

At the rally, beneath blue Miami skies, Trump decided to play it nice.

"You're going to reelect the wonderful, the great, friend of mine Marco Rubio to the United States Senate," Trump said. And without any flourishes he added, "and you are going to reelect Ron DeSantis as your governor."

IN THE DAYS LEADING UP to the midterm elections on November 8, Trump worked to keep the spotlight on himself even as he campaigned for candidates across the country.

At a rally in Iowa, Trump told his supporters, "I will very, very probably do it again . . . Get ready." Then during his speech in Miami, Trump said that he would be holding a "big, big rally" in Ohio, the day before the election. "Stay tuned."

The speculation and media buzz about the possibility of Trump's announcing another run for president reached a crescendo on Monday as Trump was bound for Vandalia, Ohio, for his very last midterm rally—this time to support J.D. Vance.

It was unclear—even to some on Trump's own team—whether

Trump, who liked to suspensefully dangle news to the press as if he was doing PR for a reality TV show, was trying to gin up media attention for Vance's rally or if he was actually serious and planned to make his announcement the day before the midterm election.

"To all the press texting & calling me: Trump should announce tonight," close Trump ally Representative Matt Gaetz tweeted. "His candidates won the primaries. Biden's central message was the 'ULTRA MAGA' scare. And we are going to win BIGLY! Trump deserves all the credit for this wave election & announcing tonight he will seize it."

Trump had been warned for months that any announcement before the midterms would mean that he would absorb any blame for results. But Trump didn't seem to care either way. And on his private "Trump Force One" plane to Ohio, he had to be talked out of the idea by family and advisers as they flew from Florida to Ohio.

There had been multiple voices in Trump's head convincing him that he should announce a run. Jason Miller, Steve Bannon, and Charlie Kirk, the young conservative commentator, had made their cases publicly and privately to Trump that he should announce a 2024 run early.

During a private dinner with Trump at Bedminster, in August before the Mar-a-Lago search, Miller told Trump he needed to jump in before the midterms. "Why?" Trump asked. "You need to galvanize the GOP and get everyone together. Look, if you don't, my concern is that you're going to wake up post-November and DeSantis is going to be ahead of you in the polls," Miller explained.

It ticked off Trump, who didn't like hearing that DeSantis could ever be ahead of him in polling.

"The Paul Ryans, the Karl Roves, the *National Review* set, they're going to try and rally everyone around DeSantis. He's about to win in Florida by huge numbers and they're going to say it's time to turn the page," Miller said.

They all told Trump that he was going to get blamed or praised for the midterms no matter what the results were, so why not go ahead and get in now?

Trump's idea of making an impromptu presidential announcement at a rally for a top Senate candidate set off a scramble among his own team and party leaders to get him to hold off. It was, as one aide described it, a "painful" fight with Trump the entire flight to Ohio and one that they desperately needed to win. Ronna McDaniel, who had gotten a whiff of the situation, got on the phone asking Trump to hold off. Trump wasn't persuaded.

But it was Donald Trump Jr., who was traveling with his father to Ohio for the last rally of the midterms, who ended up convincing him to wait. Now, Trump Jr. said, was not the time for a big 2024 announcement.

Trump Jr. had learned over the years to pick his battles with his father. It was Trump Jr. who told his dad for over a year that he needed to stop talking about the COVID vaccines and instead target vaccine mandates, because he knew Trump's base was skeptical of the vaccines. But Trump Jr., according to people close to him, also understood that if you were constantly in Trump's ear, you risked getting tuned out.

But at this moment, he thought it was important to step in. Trump agreed and decided to push his announcement to the following week, after his daughter Tiffany's wedding at Mar-a-Lago.

"I'm going to be making a very big announcement on Tuesday, November 15, at Mar-a-Lago," Trump said on the eve of the wedding, adding he wanted "nothing to detract from the importance of tomorrow."

Nessun Dorma

ON ELECTION NIGHT 2022, A HURRICANE FORMING OFF THE EASTERN coast of Florida pelted Mar-a-Lago with heavy winds and rain as it swirled closer to the coast. Inside Trump's tropical retreat, a tempest of a different kind was brewing.

For weeks, Trump and his team had been calling on his supporters to help him deliver the "red wave" Republican strategists had been predicting, which would serve as a launching pad for his comeback and 2024 campaign. The political conditions seemed ripe for a GOP sweep. Inflation was at a forty-year high. President Joe Biden's approval rating was dismal.

And a series of partisan polls only seemed to confirm what Republicans had been saying: The Supreme Court's decision to overturn *Roe v. Wade* had come too early in the summer, gas prices fell too late, and concerns about inflation would push voters out in droves to deliver a decisive win for House Republicans and even deliver enough Senate seats for Republicans to regain the majority there.

Trump and his team were primed to make a victory lap on Tuesday night after investing heavily in shaping the next Congress to his liking. Trump had endorsed more than 330 candidates, held thirty rallies, and made appearances at dozens of fundraisers. And to celebrate all their work they invited donors, political allies, grassroots leaders, and Mar-a-Lago members to enjoy a hot buffet, hors d'oeuvres and cocktails in the main ballroom of his club, where television screens were set up at the front of the room to watch the results.

The ornate gold and ivory room with glittering chandeliers was set up for Trump to deliver a speech, with red, white, and blue lights and a podium flanked by American flags. Loudspeakers piped out Trump's campaign soundtrack along with Election Night coverage from Martha MacCallum and Bret Baier on Fox News.

Trump spent the early evening with his advisers up in his office and walked downstairs to the ballroom around 6:30 P.M., where he made a beeline for the media.

"Interesting evening," Trump said matter-of-factly to a group of reporters gathered in the back of the room. Some reporters left early because the hurricane threatened to keep them in Palm Beach an extra day. Meanwhile, Trump's invited guests milled around the room and watched results from their tables. "We have some races that are hot and heavy," he said, "and we're all watching them here."

Earlier in the day, Trump ventured to his polling place in Palm Beach County and cast a ballot for DeSantis. But he also fired an early warning shot at the Florida governor. DeSantis, Trump said, would "hurt himself badly" if he ran for the White House in two years. Then he ominously added that he planned to share "things about [DeSantis] that won't be very flattering."

Trump had already started spinning the election results earlier on Tuesday. He said he wouldn't take any blame if Republicans lost, and fed into baseless claims of fraud being pushed by Republicans in some areas of the country like Phoenix. And he had preemptively padded his record by backing races where a Republican was all but guaranteed to win.

"Well, I think if they win, I should get all the credit. And if they lose, I should not be blamed at all, okay, but it'll probably be just the opposite," Trump told Markie Martin of NewsNation (the older sister of Trump aide Margo Martin) in a rare sit-down interview earlier in the day.

"Usually what would happen is, when they do well, I won't be given any credit, and if they do badly, they will blame everything on me," Trump said. "So I'm prepared for anything, but we'll defend ourselves, I think we had a lot to do with it. We had a lot to do with the success of what's going to happen."

The former president disappeared for a few hours to eat dinner and huddle with his advisers, who presented him with the latest tranche of results. But when Trump reappeared, the mood in the room had shifted. It became more and more clear Republicans were not, in fact, going to have a strong night and that Trump would—as had long been predicted—take the blame.

He was happy they notched wins in some of the marquee Senate races. When he stood onstage around ten o'clock that night, he ticked through a list of successes: J.D. Vance won in Ohio. Ted Budd won in North Carolina. Eric Schmitt won in Missouri. And Katie Britt, as expected, won in Alabama. He talked about the rain at the rally for Marco Rubio a few days before, and the crowds for Vance in Ohio.

"The numbers have been amazing so far," Trump said. He said there was some doubt they would be successful in the general election, but that they overall had a great night. "We are eighty wins and three losses," Trump said. "Enjoy the food and everything this evening."

Trump made no mention of DeSantis and the Florida governor's 20-point win over Democratic challenger Charlie Crist, which was already receiving a fawning reception from conservative media. But as DeSantis's victory speech was played on televisions around the room, the crowds mostly shrugged and continued their conversations.

As the night wore on, a disappointing portrait of Trump's midterm endorsements emerged.

Republicans were down a seat in the Senate. Herschel Walker's race in Georgia was heading to an expensive runoff election. Doug Mastriano, the controversial gubernatorial candidate in Pennsylvania, lost without even much of a whimper. Don Bolduc lost his Senate race in New Hampshire. And other Trump-backed contenders fell early, too, including House candidates J.R. Majewski in Ohio, Karoline Leavitt in New Hampshire, and Yesli Vega in Virginia. Trump and his team thought Adam Laxalt would win in Nevada, but he lost too.

The disappointment was fanned by polling that had predicted a banner night for Republicans and losses in some of the biggest, most expensive races. Trump told aides he had expected wins in the House but recognized that some of his Senate candidates were not as strong as he hoped.

In particular, Trump had shared his doubts to advisers about Pennsylvania, where Democrat John Fetterman defeated Mehmet Oz. Millions of dollars had poured into the state—it was the most expensive race in the country—but even with concerns about Fetterman's health after he suffered a stroke, Oz at times seemed uninterested in campaigning.

Trump spent most of his evening sitting up at a table at the front corner of the room with Susie Wiles, Dan Scavino, Boris Epshteyn, and Citizens United president Dave Bossie, a longtime adviser.

As the results rolled in, Trump started pressing his advisers on what was going wrong in some of the biggest races.

Trump called Brian Jack, who was with Kevin McCarthy at a watch party inside the Westin hotel ballroom in D.C. along with GOP staffers, lobbyists, Republican National Committee chairwoman Ronna McDaniel, and Minnesota representative Tom Emmer, who ran the House GOP's campaign arm. They watched together as their hopes for a historic red wave were dashed.

Trump wanted a general update on where the races stood, and he was increasingly concerned that Republicans might not even take back the House. A year before, McCarthy and top Republicans had predicted that the GOP might pick up more than sixty seats—a sea change that would have nearly matched 2012's Tea Party wave, where Republicans swept into power with sixty-three new House seats.

Trump was at least outwardly, and in the eyesight of the press, upbeat according to people who encountered him at Mar-a-Lago throughout the night. But he was worried. They might lose the Senate and House. And as they watched Fox News he started to get annoyed and irritated by the coverage of DeSantis, who was dubbed the party's golden boy overnight.

Aides ushered reporters out of the room shortly after midnight as the wind picked up outside and Trump mingled with some of the stragglers who stayed late to watch the results before retiring himself.

"174 wins and 9 losses. A GREAT EVENING, and the Fake News Media, together with their partner in crime, the Democrats, are doing everything possible to play it down. Amazing job by some really fantastic candidates!" Trump declared in his last post of the evening on Truth Social.

Ultimately, Republicans won the House by a narrow margin. Considering the economic climate and broad dissatisfaction with Biden, though, there was criticism that Trump had pushed too many candidates simply on the grounds that they supported his lies about the 2020 election, or that some of the candidates Trump anointed in the primaries could have had easier races if they had not taken positions that were outside the mainstream, particularly on the issue of abortion.

A ballot issue vote in Kansas in August previewed the influence abortion would have on the midterm elections, when voters turned out to keep abortion rights enshrined in the state's constitution. Trump, aides said, warned some candidates to soften their position. And Trump privately conceded to his advisers that the issue of abortion was going to be more of a problem for Republicans than they had imagined.

And then there was the issue of democracy. It was the first election since the January 6 attack on the Capitol, and Trump had made the midterm election largely about himself and his designs to run again in 2024. Biden centered his midterm message around the threat that Trump and his MAGA acolytes posed to democracy. Weeks before the midterms, Biden stood in front of Independence

Hall in Philadelphia to make a speech on the "battle for the soul of the nation."

"Donald Trump and the MAGA Republicans represent an extremism that threatens the very foundations of our republic," Biden said.

IT WAS THE WORST PERFORMANCE by an out-of-power party in decades. Historically, the party of a first-term incumbent faced serious losses, like during President Barack Obama's first term in 2010, when Republicans gained 63 seats in the House, or President Bill Clinton's first term in 1994, when Republicans won 54 House seats. But the narrow win by Republicans in 2022 with an unpopular president showed just how unattractive the GOP argument was to voters.

Trump woke up the next morning to gloomy skies and rain pelting down on his mansion, and even more ominous headlines. DeSantis's victory—albeit against a weak candidate in a state that Democrats had largely abandoned in the midterms—was being hailed by pundits and op-ed pages as a "blowout" that served as the precursor to a 2024 run.

And by any measure it was a blowout. DeSantis won his race by the largest margin in 40 years. He won 62 of Florida's 67 counties. He won a majority of the Hispanic vote and he was the first Republican candidate for governor since 2022 to win Miami-Dade County.

Trump's favorite tabloid, the *New York Post*, declared DeSantis and his win "DeFUTURE." *The New York Times*, Trump's other favorite paper, prominently featured a photo of DeSantis in front of an American flag and a front page story that debunked right-wing disinformation—some of it pushed by Trump—about voting issues in swing states.

Overnight, the center of the Republican universe seemed to shift from Palm Beach to Tallahassee, where DeSantis hinted at his presidential ambitions and his allies excitedly discussed the governor's next steps.

Cheers of "Two more years!" broke out among the governor's

supporters at his victory speech in Tampa—a nod to his running for president in 2024.

Some top Republicans encouraged DeSantis to jump into the race fast—lest he miss out on a window to displace Trump while he was politically vulnerable.

Back in Palm Beach, widespread disappointment and the prospect of a Senate runoff race in Georgia in early December led some of Trump's aides to propose he postpone his 2024 announcement, which was scheduled to take place at Mar-a-Lago the next week.

Jason Miller, who had encouraged Trump to get into the race early over the summer, was now among those telling the former president to hold off until after the runoff in Georgia, which was already causing some heartburn among Republicans who recalled Trump's half-hearted effort in the early 2021 Georgia Senate elections, when Trump barely lifted a finger in the state and some of his supporters simply chose to stay home after listening to his ranting about fraud.

Senator Lindsey Graham, a close confidant and ally of Trump's, told the former president he should wait until the 2022 races had all officially been called and after the Georgia runoff.

This time, Republicans in Georgia hoped Trump would stay out of the way entirely.

Trump himself wondered to aides whether they had a point and he should consider a delay. But that was an afterthought to what consumed him in the moment, which was the avalanche of blame from Republicans.

The Wednesday after the midterm election was one of Trump's lowest political moments since January 6, when he watched as party leaders quickly cast him aside. He groused to his advisers and friends about Mastriano's loss and the bad advice he received from Sean Hannity and Melania Trump to endorse Oz, especially when many of the advisers around him weren't enthusiastic about the celebrity physician. Trump had rallied for both candidates just days before the midterms. And he complained that he wasn't getting credit for any of the Republican wins—just the big Senate and governor losses.

Trump denied he was ever upset about the blame game for the midterms. The day after, he found other distractions, and according to one of his advisers had a phone call with the rapper Kanye West, who he had been trying to set up a dinner with.

Republicans were openly questioning whether Trump should continue as the leader of the party after such an underwhelming performance where it appeared Republicans would lose the Senate and only narrowly win the House in a year where they should have swept.

"For those many people that are being fed the fake narrative from the corrupt media that I am Angry about the Midterms, don't believe it," Trump wrote on Truth Social. "I am not at all angry, did a great job (I wasn't the one running!), and am very busy looking into the future. Remember, I am a 'Stable Genius.'"

For all the public hand-wringing, Trump still found support among his hard-core base of supporters—and even some on Capitol Hill. Representative Elise Stefanik, the GOP conference chair who replaced Liz Cheney after her 2021 ouster from leadership, endorsed Trump just days after the midterm elections, making her the highest-ranking Republican leader to back the former president. The young congresswoman wanted to be seen as prescient and loyal ahead of Trump's announcement.

Trump understood that his own political fate was tied up with the results of the night, and he was determined to change the narrative as his future was once again called into question. But according to aides, he felt he had done what he could do and planned to forge ahead with an announcement, telling Fox News, "We had tremendous success—why would anything change?"

FOR MONTHS, TRUMP'S AIDES HAD been sketching out the campaign and working to organize an operation they could launch immediately whenever Trump decided to announce.

After forcing a scramble in the sky on the way to the Vance rally and then teasing an announcement the following week, Trump had finally made up his mind to announce a 2024 run and gave his team less than a week's notice to make it happen.

Lawyers had to create a joint fundraising committee for Trump's campaign, Wiles and LaCivita had to make hiring decisions, and they had to plan a huge event at Mar-a-Lago.

Taylor Budowich, who had been running communications for Trump, was the CEO of the Make America Great Again super PAC and could not legally interface with Wiles and the campaign, so Jason Miller, who was still at Gettr, came on and helped Steven Cheung run communications.

Sandwiched in between—and dictating some of their scheduling—was the opulent wedding of Tiffany Trump to Michael Boulos at Trump's Mar-a-Lago club, a black-tie affair with pastel floral arches and, reportedly, a million-dollar budget.

Trump's early announcement seemed motivated, in part, by the legal peril he found himself in. Jumping into the 2024 race could potentially shield him from the investigations he was facing over his conduct on January 6 and underscored his complaints—which turned into rallying cries for his base—that he was unjustly targeted and a victim of political persecution. Running could potentially put a pause on or at least slow down the investigations, and if the investigations ramped up while he ran for office, then they fit his narrative. A self-fulfilling prophecy.

But his determination to make an announcement early was also based on his own belief, bolstered by his allies, that jumping in now would clear the field and prevent Republican rivals—in particular DeSantis—from deciding to run. Trump would suck up all the energy and attention around the 2024 race, and dare Republicans to defy him and face his wrath.

A shadow campaign for president had already begun, with potential 2024 GOP candidates like Mike Pence, Tim Scott and Nikki Haley flocking to early voting states, setting up political action committees, writing books, and courting donors.

Calls for a fresh face to take up the Republican mantle from

Trump only grew louder in the aftermath of the GOP's anemic midterms, with DeSantis and Virginia governor Glenn Youngkin getting the most buzz.

So it was both unsurprising and shocking when Trump viciously lashed out at DeSantis and Youngkin in the days after the election.

"Young Kin (now that's an interesting take. Sounds Chinese, doesn't it?) in Virginia couldn't have won without me," Trump wrote on Truth Social. "I Endorsed him, did a very big Trump Rally for him telephonically, got MAGA to Vote for him—or he couldn't have come close to winning. But he knows that, and admits it. Besides, having a hard time with the Dems in Virginia—But he'll get it done!"

Not only was Youngkin newly christened as a potential 2024 contender, but his lieutenant governor—Winsome Earle-Sears, who in 2020 had served as co-chair of Black Americans to Re-elect the President—had recently taken a swipe at Trump over the party's midterm results. John Fredericks, a radio host who worked on Trump's presidential campaigns, suggested she spoke out against Trump at the direction of Youngkin.

"What we saw was, even though he wasn't on the ballot, he was, because he stepped in and endorsed candidates," Earle-Sears told *The Washington Post*. "And yet, it turns out that those he did not endorse on the same ticket did better than the ones he did endorse. That gives you a clue that the voters want to move on. And a true leader knows when they have become a liability to the mission."

Trump was most upset about the uptick in praise for and interest in DeSantis, though, blasting him for being "disloyal" and accusing him of being cute about his presidential ambitions. The statement was stunning for its vitriol and savagery.

Trump rambled on for paragraphs about DeSantis:

NewsCorp, which is Fox, the Wall Street Journal, and the no longer great New York Post (bring back Col!), is all in for Governor Ron DeSanctimonious, an average REPUBLICAN Governor with great Public Relations, who didn't have to close up his State, but did, unlike other Republican Governors, whose overall numbers for a Republican, were just average—middle of the pack—including COVID, and who has the advantage of SUNSHINE, where people from badly run States up North would go no matter who the Governor was, just like I did!

Ron came to me in desperate shape in 2017—he was politically dead, losing in a landslide to a very good Agriculture Commissioner, Adam Putnam, who was loaded up with cash and great poll numbers. Ron had low approval, bad polls, and no money, but he said that if I would Endorse him, he could win. I didn't know Adam so I said, "Let's give it a shot, Ron." When I Endorsed him, it was as though, to use a bad term, a nuclear weapon went off. Years later, they were the exact words that Adam Putnam used in describing Ron's Endorsement. He said, "I went from having it made, with no competition, to immediately getting absolutely clobbered after your Endorsement." I then got Ron by the "Star" of the Democrat Party, Andrew Gillum . . . , by having two massive Rallies with tens of thousands of people at each one. I also fixed his campaign, which had completely fallen apart. I was all in for Ron, and he beat Gillum, but after the Race, when votes were being stolen by the corrupt Election process in Broward County, and Ron was going down ten thousand votes a day, along with now-Senator Rick Scott, I sent in the FBI and the U.S. Attorneys, and the ballot theft immediately ended, just prior to them running out of the votes necessary to win. I stopped his Election from being stolen . . . And now, Ron DeSanctimonious is playing games! The Fake News asks him if he's going to run if President Trump runs, and he says, "I'm only focused on the Governor's race, I'm not looking into the future." Well, in terms of loyalty and class, that's really not the right answer.

This is just like 2015 and 2016, a Media Assault (Collusion!), when Fox News fought me to the end until I won, and then they couldn't have been nicer or more supportive. The

Wall Street Journal loved Low Energy Jeb Bush, and a succession of other people as they rapidly disappeared from sight, finally falling in line with me after I easily knocked them out, one by one. We're in exactly the same position now. They will keep coming after us, MAGA, but ultimately, we will win. Put America First and, MAKE AMERICA GREAT AGAIN!

Neither Trump nor DeSantis had announced a presidential bid, but the 2024 rivalry was born, and Republican operatives and donors started to fall in line. DeSantis's own advisers were torn over whether the Florida governor should get into the race quickly, to blunt any gains by Trump, or wait it out and let the former president self-destruct with his angry posts and propensity to shoot himself in the foot.

Trump's advisers considered holding a rally in a battleground state, but Trump wanted to make his announcement in the best place he knew: Mar-a-Lago. And for Trump's advisers, it worked for his brand. He had come down Trump Tower's golden escalator in 2015 to announce his presidential run. This time, it would be announced from Mar-a-Lago.

The grand ballroom of his club had just hosted his midterm watch party, and he ordered his team to put together an announcement party with a stage and lectern and to invite some of his biggest supporters. They also discussed the possibility of Sean Hannity's setting up a small studio off to the side of the stage, where he could do his show live. But according to one adviser, they pulled the plug at the last minute.

Since DeSantis's victory on Tuesday night, the network and its anchors had become enamored with the Florida governor, and the media empire controlled by Rupert Murdoch cast the midterm elections as an opportunity to move on from Trump and Trumpism. It was an abrupt breakup between Trump and his most important media ally.

Splashed across the front page of the *New York Post* after the midterms was a depiction of Trump as Humpty Dumpty, wobbling on a brick wall, with the headline "TRUMPTY DUMPTY: Don (who couldn't build a great wall) had a great fall—can all the GOP's men put the party back together again?" The *Post*'s political analyst, John Podhoretz, wrote he had two words for why the red wave was a "red trickle"—Donald Trump.

Fox News host Laura Ingraham said, without mentioning Trump by name, that the next 2024 GOP candidate should not be fixated on "score settling," saying, "If the voters conclude that you're putting your own ego or your own grudges ahead of what's good for the country, they're going to look elsewhere."

The Wall Street Journal's banner editorial the day after the midterms read TRUMP IS THE REPUBLICAN PARTY'S BIGGEST LOSER. And the Monday before Trump's announcement, the *Journal* published a scathing takedown of the former president, warning voters that while Trump had many conservative wins in the White House—the Abraham Accords, energy security, judicial nominations—"his character flaws—narcissism, lack of self-control, abusive treatment of advisers, his puerile vendettas—interfere with that success."

"Last week's elections showed that clinging to 2020 election denial, as Mr. Trump has, is a loser's game. Republicans who took this line to win his endorsement nearly all lost. The country showed it wants to move on, but Mr. Trump refuses—perhaps because he can't admit to himself that he was a loser. Mr. Trump will carry all of that baggage and more into a 2024 race," the editorial board wrote.

Meanwhile, DeSantis and Youngkin were depicted as the drama-free alternatives to Trump.

None of it went unnoticed by Trump and his team. Trump blasted Fox News after Election Night for their criticisms of him.

"Despite having picked so many winners, I have to put up with the Fake News. For me, Fox News was always gone, even in 2015–16 when I began my 'journey,' but now they're really gone. Such an opportunity for another media outlet to make an absolute fortune, and do good for America. Let's see what happens?" Trump wrote on Truth Social.

"If CNN were smart, they'd open up a Conservative network, only have me on, and it would be the most successful network in History. Fox only made it because of me," he posted.

While Trump and Murdoch never had a cozy relationship, they had a symbiotic one. Trump understood the importance of using the network to reach his base of supporters who loyally tuned in each day, and Murdoch understood political star power. That's also why Murdoch was suddenly interested in DeSantis.

The Club for Growth, a conservative antitax organization, piled on to the doubts with a memo released the night before Trump's announcement showing Trump trailing DeSantis by double digits in one-on-one matchups in the critical early voting states of Iowa and New Hampshire, and Trump behind DeSantis in Florida. David McIntosh, who was once a staunch ally of Trump, suggested he would do more harm than good by announcing before the Georgia runoff and that the influential group might back DeSantis in the primary.

It was from a position of weakness—the conservative media ecosystem eagerly pushing Trump away, the former president fuming over his rivals and fretting about his legal fate—that Trump decided to make his announcement for president.

Trump's aides were just glad he agreed to put it off until after the midterms. They had already fought him on announcing before Election Day and didn't have the capital to tell him he should wait any longer.

Trump's team arranged for him to make the announcement in the exact same Mar-a-Lago ballroom where he held his election watch party the week before. His speechwriters, Vince Haley and Ross Worthington, had to quickly draw up an announcement speech and Trump worked with his team to review and revise it in his office in the hours before he took the stage.

Trump's advisers told him the speech was an opportunity for him to "reset" after the midterms, and in order to get maximum attention he had to keep the speech shorter than his typical rally speeches in which he could ramble on for almost two hours. But they also told him this wasn't a speech where he should fixate on 2020 and the last presidential election. His campaign, Trump was told, could not just be about the past.

As guests arrived at Mar-a-Lago for Trump's speech, a plane flew above the club with a sky banner reading YOU LOST AGAIN DONALD! #DESANTIS2024. Trump's team invited a mix of club members, donors, top grassroots supporters, lawmakers, and aides to the event. But notably, no sitting senator or Republican governor traveled to Palm Beach for the event. Instead the VIPs included outgoing representative Madison Cawthorn, who lost his Republican primary in North Carolina, MyPillow CEO Mike Lindell, Kash Patel, Sebastian Gorka, Roger Stone, Blake Marnell, the former Right Side Broadcasting reporter turned political activist also known as "Brick Suit Man," and Truth Social CEO Devin Nunes.

Steve Bannon was not at the announcement, but he called someone from his team to ask who was there.

"Tell me what the crowd is like," he said. "Is Maggie [Haberman] there? Is [Robert] Costa there?" And he kept naming top reporters, who were not in the room. "Who are the VIPs?" From camera livestreams in the room he spotted "Brick Suit Man" in the VIP section.

Standing along the front row for Trump's announcement were his top advisers, including Jason Miller, who was still working as the CEO of Gettr but also helping run communications for Trump; Steven Cheung, who would step into the role of communications director; Chris LaCivita and Susie Wiles, who had agreed to work in tandem leading the campaign; and Justin Caporale, Alex Pfeiffer, Kimberly Guilfoyle, Eric and Lara Trump, Barron Trump, and Jared Kushner.

Conspicuously missing were Donald Trump Jr. and Ivanka Trump. Trump's son tried to get back to Florida but was stuck on a hunting trip along with Trump aide Sergio Gor, but Trump's daughter Ivanka, who had served as a senior adviser in the White House, was resolved to wash her hands of politics, spend more time with her young family, and resume her pre–White House life that included running in her old high-society social circle.

She posted to Instagram, "I love my father very much. This time around, I am choosing to prioritize my young children and the private life we are creating as a family. I do not plan to be involved in politics. While I will always love and support my father, going forward I will do so outside the political arena. I am grateful to have had the honor of serving the American people and I will always be proud of many of our Administration's accomplishments."

Melania Trump told advisers she was supportive of Trump but was also reluctant to give up her privacy and find herself scrutinized by the press. But she walked out into the ballroom all smiles and hand in hand with Trump, but notably dressed casually, at least for Mrs. Trump, in a white skirt and polka-dot top.

Fashion experts, who carefully cover her outfits and try to conjure up meaning from them, noted how it was a distinctly different look from that of Florida first lady Casey DeSantis, who wore a shimmering yellow ball gown the week before, when her husband won his race.

Trump's speech was supposed to turn the media narrative around, energize his base, and shut up the naysayers. But the main takeaways were that Trump came across "low energy" and that he was even bored by the speech, which was supposed to last for forty-five minutes but dragged on for over an hour.

Trump mostly stuck to his usual rally talking points. He painted his own administration as a roaring economic success—ignoring the pandemic—and he spoke darkly about an "invasion" of migrants at the southern border and blood in the streets. And while he compared America's election system to a "third world country," to the relief of advisers and allies who encouraged him to let up on talk of 2020, he did not fixate and obsess over the election results in the same way he would at midterm rallies.

"There has never been anything like it, this great movement of ours . . . And perhaps there will never be anything like it again," Trump declared. "America's comeback starts right now."

None of the three major broadcast networks—ABC, CBS, or NBC—took Trump's speech live. Instead, ABC aired *Bachelor in Paradise,* the lowbrow dating show. MSNBC did not air Trump's speech. CNN kept it on for twenty-five minutes before turning coverage over to a panel.

Fox News aired Trump's speech until it reached the ten o'clock hour and the start of Laura Ingraham's show. She cut into the event as Trump rambled on about how he and his family had been subpoenaed more than the Prohibition-era gangster Al Capone or the famous outlaws Billy the Kid and Jesse James.

"We're going to go back to former president Trump when news warrants," she said. "Just one week after the 2022 midterms, and look at this, we're already gearing up for 2024."

The next morning, Trump barely made the front page of the *New York Post,* which wrote at the bottom of the paper, "Florida Man Makes Announcement." The story about the event was found on page 26: BEEN THERE, DON THAT.

For Trump's advisers, the speech was okay. At the bare minimum, Trump mostly stuck to the script. They were able to launch his campaign and move on to building out his campaign operation.

But Trump's announcement was a political low point. He was dismissed by some of the conservative elite and the media, and after the midterm elections, Republicans were suddenly not shy about expressing that Trump was not the sole leader of the party. And hovering over his announcement were his mounting legal problems over his handling of classified documents, his actions on January 6, and his potential interference in Georgia's 2020 election recount.

Trump had found himself at all-time lows before and critics had counted him out before. While leaders of the Republican Party and the conservative elite were not enthusiastic about the relaunch of a twice-impeached former president who left the White House in disgrace and led Republicans to disappointing midterms, he remained popular among Republican voters, who had shown since he left office they were still willing to follow him, win or lose.

A *Politico*/Morning Consult poll taken around the time of Trump's announcement found that 47 percent of Republicans and Republican-leaning independents said they would back Trump in a Republican presidential primary, while 33 percent said they would back Florida governor Ron DeSantis. Among all voters, 65 percent said Trump should probably or definitely not run again.

But some of the Republican Party's biggest donors had seen enough, and they gave cover to others looking to break from Trump. Blackstone CEO Steve Schwarzman said he wouldn't help Trump during the 2024 primary. Ken Griffin, the founder and CEO of the hedge fund Citadel, called Trump a "three-time loser" and said he would support DeSantis. Billionaire Ronald Lauder, an heir to the Estée Lauder fortune, said he wouldn't donate to Trump's campaign. Billionaire Thomas Peterffy called for a "fresh face" to run.

If Trump's announcement was designed to stop other Republicans from running against him, there was no signs it worked at the Republican Jewish Coalition's conference in Las Vegas, where a parade of 2024 speeches by GOP stars showed how little influence he had days after he became the first declared candidate. Trump's former U.N. ambassador, Nikki Haley, who said in the spring of 2021 she would back Trump if he ran again, hinted at a run in her speech. So did DeSantis, Senator Tim Scott of South Carolina, Mike Pompeo, and former vice president Mike Pence, who had just released a book that described Trump as "reckless" on January 6.

Miriam Adelson, who was Trump's biggest donor during the 2020 election and the top supporter of the Republican Jewish Coalition along with her late husband, Sheldon, skipped out entirely on the event for a trip to Israel and indicated she would not be giving in the 2024 presidential primary.

Trump was agitated that some of his biggest donors were looking at DeSantis and Youngkin, but his team also saw an opportunity for him to run as an "outsider." They welcomed the idea of a crowded primary field that would benefit Trump just as it did in 2016.

It seemed ridiculous to assign outsider status to a former president whose campaign apparatuses had over $100 million in the bank and who acted as the leader of the party. And yet, after his announcement, Trump seemed almost as exiled and on the outside as he was when he left for Palm Beach.

THE MIDTERMS WERE DISAPPOINTING, AND the lackluster 2024 announcement did not provide Trump or his campaign with the kind of reset they were hoping for. And the wave of bad news kept coming. On November 18, the Justice Department appointed a special counsel to examine the January 6 riots and Trump's possession of classified government documents at Mar-a-Lago. And the Supreme Court denied Trump's last-ditch effort to keep six years of his tax returns out of Congress's hands, opening the door for the Treasury Department to hand the records over to the House Ways and Means Committee. Trump argued that the request was nothing more than a political fishing expedition meant to embarrass him and reveal private information.

Trump had a steady stream of meetings at Mar-a-Lago and political events on the horizon to keep him distracted from his laundry list of frustrations. And he looked forward to one event on his calendar over Thanksgiving—a dinner with the rapper Kanye West.

For weeks, Trump and West had tried to get dinner on the calendar. In October, West called up Trump after he announced he was buying the conservative app Parler—and after West made headlines for a series of anti-Semitic remarks. When West's Instagram account was restricted because he posted content that was viewed as anti-Semitic, he took his ranting to Twitter, where he appeared to threaten Jewish people. "I'm a bit sleepy tonight but when I wake up I'm going death con 3 On JEWISH PEOPLE The funny thing is I actually can't be Anti Semitic because black people are actually Jew also You guys have toyed with me and tried to black ball anyone whoever opposes your agenda," West wrote in a post that was taken down by the platform.

West had also recently worn a T-shirt at Paris Fashion Week that read WHITE LIVES MATTER, and he sat down for an interview with Fox News host Tucker Carlson during which he made a series of anti-Semitic comments. The rapper was immediately met with outrage, and he was dropped by almost all of his sponsors and professional collaborators, including Adidas.

Trump's team knew a dinner with West was a rotten idea. They tried to persuade Trump to cancel his plans. They showed him West's comments and made Trump aware of all the business deals West had lost. But Trump remained unconvinced.

Trump had long been fascinated with West for his status as a celebrity and cultural icon. West wore MAGA hats and publicly praised him, and Trump liked to have famous people on display at his club.

In an interview with radio host Chris Stigall shortly after West lost his business deals, Trump said that West sounded "very sharp and very smart." Trump briefly mentioned West's anti-Semitic comments, which he said were "rough." But he mostly seemed flattered by the praise West heaped on him during the interview with Carlson.

"I was very honored because I didn't know him that well. But I liked him. I always got along with him very well," Trump said. "I was very honored in a sense because he said all those great things about me on Tucker Carlson. He made some statements—rough statements on Jewish—you heard them and you know them well."

Trump and West had a long and strange history. In 2018, West visited Trump in the Oval Office of the White House for a bizarre and shocking media circus of a meeting.

"Trump is on his hero's journey right now. And he might not have expected to have a crazy motherfucker like [me]" supporting him, West said in a freewheeling ten-minute monologue.

Trump had also gotten to know West's ex-wife, Kim Kardashian, when she advocated for criminal justice reform during his administration and worked for the pardon of Alice Johnson.

Considering West's recent anti-Semitic outbursts and his open struggle with bipolar disorder and mental illness, which made him particularly unpredictable, Trump's advisers were not looking forward to a second Trump-West summit or the potential headlines and PR headaches.

But Trump thought he could help give some advice to West and plowed ahead with his plans. A dinner was scheduled for the Tuesday night before Thanksgiving when, conveniently for Trump, his advisers had gone home to be with their families for the holiday. They would come to regret leaving Trump without a minder, though. The pre-Thanksgiving dinner would become the biggest political nightmare of Trump's week-old 2024 presidential campaign.

West arrived at Mar-a-Lago on a rainy Tuesday evening wearing jeans and a sweatshirt and with an entourage in tow. Karen Giorno, who was a senior adviser on Trump's 2016 presidential campaign in Florida, was asked by Milo Yiannopoulos, a British far-right provocateur who had been working as a kind of political adviser to West, to pick West and his companions up from the Miami airport and make the ninety-minute drive to Palm Beach.

Even though Trump was a former president and had the protection of the Secret Service, security at his club was not tight. Guards would check for guests' names on an iPad at the front gate, after which members or their guests would be welcomed on the property.

When Giorno arrived in her car with West and his guests, she did not have her driver's license on her—she forgot it in her rush to get to the airport—and only had to flash her credit card with her name to get in. It helped that West was instantly recognizable and expected at the club that evening.

Trump greeted West and his entourage in the gilded foyer of Mar-a-Lago. Trump knew Giorno, who ran Florida for him in 2016 before Wiles stepped in, and she was a frequent guest at his club.

Giorno had just run right-wing activist Laura Loomer's failed congressional campaign in Florida. But Trump did not know the two other people with West. Even worse, neither Trump nor any of his staff thought to ask.

Even though only West and Trump were supposed to have dinner, Trump invited the entire group to join him at his table on the patio at Mar-a-Lago, where the entire crew would be on full display.

In addition to West and Giorno, Trump was joined by Jamar Montgomery, a Boeing employee from California who knew West and was invited to fly out for the dinner, and a young man named Nick Fuentes.

Fuentes was a twenty-four-year-old racist, anti-Semite, and Holocaust denier and one of the best-known white supremacists in the country, who had a reputation for sharing his racist and sexist views to his online following and hosting an annual white supremacist event, the America First Political Action Conference, that attracted lawmakers like Representatives Marjorie Taylor Greene and Paul Gosar. (Greene said she didn't know who the organizers were or their views.)

Trump had been left to his own devices over Thanksgiving. All of his advisers had gone home to spend the holiday with their families, and no one was at the club in the evenings with Trump except for Walt Nauta, his valet, who stayed behind to staff the former president at his club.

The news that Fuentes was with Trump set off a scramble among his campaign staffers, who immediately understood the category five political hurricane Trump had breezily waltzed into and were trying to get accurate information about how the dinner went down. Advisers were texting with Nauta and Mar-a-Lago staff to try to figure out who was with Trump at the dinner.

Over turkey and stuffing, Fuentes identified himself only as a Trump supporter. Trump and his advisers adamantly claimed later that he did not know who Fuentes was when he met him, but according to accounts of the dinner, Trump was gratified by his flattery.

During the dinner, Trump let West pick out music to play while they sat on the patio. West claimed in a posted video after the dinner that Trump was "impressed" by Fuentes. During the dinner, Fuentes praised the former president and his speeches from the 2016 campaign and encouraged Trump to support those who were charged in the January 6 riots. Fuentes had led "Stop the Steal" rallies in 2020 in support of Trump's false claims about a stolen election, and led a group of his supporters to the Capitol. Fuentes never entered the building, instead remaining outside, but later praised the attack as "awesome."

West in his video said Trump got annoyed when he said he was considering a run for president himself and wanted to know if Trump would be his vice president. "I think the thing Trump was most perturbed about [was] me asking him to be my vice president. I think that was lower on the list of things that caught him off guard," West claimed.

As Trump's senior staff frantically tried to figure out what happened, Milo Yiannopoulos gloated on the app Telegram about the dinner setup.

Yiannopoulos, a onetime *Breitbart* editor who was barred from Twitter and Facebook for harassing the comedian and actress Leslie Jones and had a history of incendiary remarks, was a Trump critic who wanted to embarrass the former president and knew that West would be a Trojan horse for Fuentes, whose presence would cause an uproar.

The blowback was swift and intense. Trump knew immediately he had walked into a trap. Trump was furious with West over the dinner that went sideways, and even more upset when he was told about his other dining companion. But it took Trump days to acknowledge the screw-up—and when he did, there was no disavowal of Fuentes's speech.

"This past week, Kanye West called me to have dinner at Mar-a-Lago," Trump wrote. "Shortly thereafter, he unexpectedly showed up with three of his friends, whom I knew nothing about. We had dinner on Tuesday evening with many members present on the back patio. The dinner was quick and uneventful. They then left for the airport."

In a subsequent post to Truth Social, Trump claimed West wanted to meet with him to get advice on personal and business matters, and that they also discussed politics. Trump told West not to run for president.

"Anyway, we got along great, he expressed no anti-Semitism, & I appreciated all of the nice things he said about me on 'Tucker Carlson.' Why wouldn't I agree to meet? Also, I didn't know Nick Fuentes."

Over the Thanksgiving holiday, Trump heard from some of his Jewish friends who were furious that Trump would take a meeting at his club with two of the nation's most vocal anti-Semites. Among those who called up Trump the weekend after was Roger Stone, who asked what happened.

"Why?" Trump asked. "Is it a big deal?" It was unclear to Stone whether Trump was actually unaware of the headlines or was just trying to downplay the public firestorm.

"Yeah. It's becoming a very big deal," Stone said.

"What am I supposed to say? No? They're standing there and everyone's hungry. I said, 'Okay, fine,'" Trump said of West's bringing Fuentes.

But as much as Trump tried to shrug off the event, he was surprised by the backlash from his friends in Palm Beach. Some of Trump's top Jewish donors reached out to Caroline Wren, who had been a fundraiser for Trump, and suggested they were done with Trump for good.

On Monday, the pile-on of criticism continued from donors and from lawmakers on Capitol Hill who denounced West's and Fuentes's anti-Semitism and called Trump's dinner foolish. And it underscored bubbling frustrations in the party over Trump's involvement in the midterms and his selection of candidates who repeated his election lies and were not embraced by independents and moderates.

David Friedman, Trump's ambassador to Israel, wrote on Twitter, "To my friend Donald Trump, you are better than this. Even a social visit from an antisemite like Kanye West and human scum like Nick Fuentes is unacceptable. I urge you to throw those bums out, disavow them and relegate them to the dustbin of history where they belong." The tweets were seen by Trump, who called up Friedman to try to smooth things over.

Trump's former vice president Mike Pence told NewsNation in an interview that Trump should apologize and "denounce [West and Fuentes] without qualification." Trump had shown poor judgment, Pence said, but "I don't believe he's a racist or a bigot. I would not have been his vice president if he was."

In a statement, Republican National Committee chairwoman Ronna McDaniel said that "white supremacy, neo-Nazism, hate speech and bigotry are disgusting and do not have a home in the Republican Party."

"Anyone meeting with people advocating that point of view, in my judgment, are highly unlikely to ever be elected president of the United States," said Senate Minority Leader Mitch McConnell.

President Joe Biden, on vacation with his family in Nantucket, Massachusetts, told reporters when asked about the dinner, "You don't want to hear what I think."

Trump's spokesperson Liz Harrington tried to brush aside concerns about the dinner by saying that Trump is "probably the most pro-Israel president we've ever had."

"Trump is not going to shy away from meeting with Kanye West," she said.

But Harrington's viewpoint was not shared by all of Trump's advisers, who recognized how embarrassing and politically damaging the dinner was for their week-old campaign, and how the lack of guardrails did not help Trump as he was under investigation for his handling and storage of classified documents at the club.

Wiles and Trump's staff got to work buttoning up the operation and making sure they were always aware of who was on Trump's calendar so that he could never have a dinner like that again.

THE KANYE WEST AND NICK Fuentes dinner only marked the beginning of a series of controversies, fumbles, and disappointments at the start of Trump's campaign. And for the next month, Trump seemed to hunker down at his own clubs. He rarely ventured beyond Mar-a-Lago or his golf club or made any public appearances. Instead, he made video appearances for a fundraiser for January 6 defendants and a tele-rally for Walker's runoff race, and dropped by events at his club.

After announcing a 2024 run, Trump appeared to be isolated and floundering. Trump's advisers wanted him to lay low until after holidays when his campaigning would begin in earnest. But instead he only ushered in new controversies.

In a shocking Truth Social post in early December, Trump called for the termination of the Constitution after emails from Twitter were released showing an internal debate over the company's decision to block links to stories about emails found on Hunter Biden's laptop in the fall of 2020.

"Do you throw the Presidential Election Results of 2020 OUT and declare the RIGHTFUL WINNER, or do you have a NEW ELECTION? A Massive Fraud of this type and magnitude allows for the termination of all rules, regulations, and articles, even those found in the Constitution," Trump wrote on Truth Social, and accused social media giants of being in cahoots with Democrats. "Our great 'Founders' did not want, and would not condone, False & Fraudulent Elections!"

It was an extraordinary statement from a former president and played into criticisms from President Joe Biden, other Democrats, and Trump critics that he was an antidemocratic threat.

Trump denied that he wanted to "terminate" the Constitution

after he received criticism from some fellow Republicans and the White House. "Anyone seeking the presidency who thinks the Constitution can somehow be suspended or not followed, it seems to me, would have a very hard time being sworn in as president of the United States," McConnell said in response. But what was perhaps just as shocking as Trump's original message was the fact that so few Republicans criticized Trump for his statement.

A week later, Trump teased a "BIG ANNOUNCEMENT."

The statement sparked speculation about what could warrant a big announcement—critics hoped he might be dropping out, while his supporters wondered if he might make a wildly premature declaration about his pick for vice president.

Some of Trump's own advisers did not know what Trump was talking about until he revealed in a video that the very big announcement was actually for an online store to sell $99 digital trading cards, or NFTs, featuring cartoon drawings of him as characters including a cowboy, a superhero with a "T" suit and laser beams coming from his eyes, and an astronaut.

The NFTs were the brainchild of entrepreneur Bill Zanker, a friend and former collaborator of Trump's who approached him about the idea. Trump liked the idea of making some quick money off the licensing deal, and he loved the art on the cards, which also promoted a contest to come to Mar-a-Lago.

The announcement was widely mocked. Whoever pitched the NFTs "ought to be fired," said Steve Bannon on his *WarRoom* podcast. "I can't do this anymore."

Others called the stunt an embarrassment. But for all the criticism, all forty-four thousand of the $99 cards sold out in less than a day.

But the final blow in what had been a nightmarish start to the campaign came when Herschel Walker, whom Trump personally recruited to run for office, lost the runoff race in Georgia for Senate against Raphael Warnock.

Trump helped with fundraising and held a tele-rally for Walker in the final stretch, but he did not make any campaign appearances in Georgia out of recognition from both Trump's and the football star's campaigns that his presence might not be helpful in the increasingly purple state, where Democrats, including President Joe Biden, had recently won statewide.

Walker's loss further diminished Trump's standing in the party. And it left the door open for Trump's 2024 challengers.

12

I'm Still Standing

DONALD TRUMP AND HIS FLEDGLING 2024 CAMPAIGN WERE FLOUNDERING.

Trump's involvement in the 2022 midterms was met with widespread criticism. His presidential announcement was seen as flat and uninspiring. He dined with a white supremacist and an anti-Semite. He launched a collection of NFTs that, while profitable, was widely mocked. His call for the termination of the Constitution over his lie that the 2020 election was stolen was met with widespread condemnation. Trump attacked "Jewish Leaders" for their perceived lack of loyalty to him. Herschel Walker, his handpicked Georgia Senate candidate, lost a runoff election after a series of scandals. A New York jury found the Trump Organization guilty of seventeen felony counts in a criminal tax fraud case. The House Ways and Means Committee released six years of Trump's tax returns. The January 6 committee called on the Justice Department to bring criminal charges against Trump for the 2021 attack on the Capitol, saying it was "a time of reflection and reckoning."

Instead of trying to get out in front of the bad news, Trump retreated further into his cosseted club life. He did not hold any campaign events after announcing his third presidential bid. On occasion, he went beyond the four-mile radius of Mar-a-Lago and his golf club to visit another of his golf clubs an hour south, in Miami. During one visit, he spoke to a group of Orthodox Jewish leaders at Trump National Doral in what was seen as a kind of clean-up following the Kanye West and Nick Fuentes fiasco.

The mountains of bad press left some of Trump's aides privately grumbling about what they signed up for. Top Republicans were questioning his political future and whether he actually had a shot in 2024. Once again, Trump found himself at a political nadir as he stumbled from one bad headline to the next.

The polling reflected their doubts. In mid-December, a poll by *The Wall Street Journal* found that Republican primary voters preferred Florida governor Ron DeSantis to Trump in a hypothetical matchup, 52 percent to 38 percent. The poll indicated DeSantis was better liked than Trump, too.

If Trump was going to have any shot in the 2024 election, and if he was going to get out of the political hole he had furiously dug for himself, his campaign needed to squash DeSantis. And early.

Luckily for Trump, many of the people working for him—Susie Wiles, Jason Miller, Taylor Budowich, Justin Caporale, James Blair, and Tony Fabrizio—had also once worked for the Florida governor and were not just well versed in his ways, but eager to help the former president take him down. For the next year Trump and his campaign would humiliate, emasculate, and mock the rising star of the Republican Party and the biggest threat to Trump's presidential aspirations.

AS TRUMP WAS FLAILING IN early December, the staff of Make America Great Again Inc., the super PAC supporting Trump's presidential run, met for the first time in a conference room in Alexandria to start sketching out plans for how they were going to take down DeSantis.

MAGA Inc. was created in September 2022 to spend on the midterm races but also to provide a potential vehicle for Trump's 2024 run. Taylor Budowich, Trump's former spokesperson, was the founder and CEO, and others on the committee included top campaign adviser Chris LaCivita, communications adviser Steven Cheung, Tony Fabrizio, a top Republican pollster and strategist for Trump, Alex Pfeiffer, a former Fox News producer and communications strategist, and James Blair, a political consultant who previously worked in DeSantis's governor's office. After the midterms, Cheung and LaCivita left for the campaign while the rest of the team stayed on to support Trump's presidential run from the PAC.

On the heels of Trump's disastrous Thanksgiving dinner, Fabrizio conducted research on the potential 2024 field. In a PowerPoint presentation, he laid out Trump's weaknesses, DeSantis's weaknesses, what was being said about DeSantis, and the general state of the race. The bottom line: DeSantis was a real threat.

MAGA Inc. hadn't started testing opposition research on the Florida governor yet, but it was trying to get a broad understanding of how much work they had to do to defeat DeSantis—who had not yet even entered the race.

Among those sitting around the conference room with Fabrizio were Budowich, Pfeiffer, Blair, Fabrizio's business partner, opposition researchers, and a lawyer for the PAC.

The meeting, as one of the staffers described it, was "grim," as they faced the reality that the former president was trailing DeSantis. Fabrizio noted in the presentation that Trump still had high job approval and high favorability, but there was a public perception that DeSantis was better positioned to win in 2024.

They decided right then and there that they needed to kill DeSantis—politically speaking—as fast as possible. "We needed to bomb the fleet while it was still on the ground," as one Trump adviser put it.

It was also a conclusion Trump had reached on his own. At Mar-a-Lago, Trump balked at criticism that he was being too hard on DeSantis. "Bullshit," he would respond when he was told to tone down his attacks. DeSantis wouldn't be Florida governor if it weren't for him, and now he had the audacity to be angling for the presidency.

As they sat around the conference room table reviewing Fabrizio's research, the MAGA Inc. team settled on a "squeeze strategy"—they would try to pinch the Florida governor from both the right and the left.

They saw an advantage in DeSantis's disparate coalition on the right. He had attracted the support of Alex Jones conspiracy theorists and antivaxxers who liked the skepticism he had shown toward Big Pharma and its vaccines. But he also had support from some of the readers at the *National Review*, who still had one foot in the Romney and Bush GOP of years past.

If DeSantis were to present a hawkish position on Ukraine, for example, the team at MAGA Inc. would flag that to the isolationist wing of the party, like *Breitbart* and Steve Bannon's *WarRoom* podcast. If he presented a stance that was viewed as sympathetic to Russia, they would push any criticism by the *Wall Street Journal* editorial board and mainstream Republicans.

The best way to "squeeze" DeSantis, their polling found, was on the Social Security and Medicare reforms he'd supported back when he was a young congressman. Later in the spring they launched an ad attacking DeSantis on Social Security and Medicare—except that that was not the lasting impression or message viewers took away from the ad.

KEVIN MCCARTHY HAD THROWN TRUMP a lifeline.

Almost two years earlier, when the California congressman breezed into Mar-a-Lago while in the neighborhood for fundraisers, he delivered Trump the first political victory of his post-presidency. McCarthy stood next to Trump, who gave a thumbs-up and a cat-that-caught-the-canary grin. The resulting photo, released by Trump's team, sent a message to the public that McCarthy, then the highest-ranking Republican in the House, was with the former president in spite of it all.

Of course, just weeks before that photo was taken, McCarthy had told his colleagues on Capitol Hill that he thought Trump's behavior was unacceptable on January 6—"Nobody can defend that and nobody should defend it"—and that he would recommend to Trump that he resign. McCarthy denied reports of those private comments as "totally false and wrong," until Jonathan Martin and Alex Burns produced tapes of him saying just that for their book *This Will Not Pass*.

Since the famous photo op, McCarthy had tried to delegitimize the investigation of the January 6 riots and worked alongside Trump to elect House Republicans. McCarthy, who was once described as a "golden retriever of a man," used his agreeable personality and ideological flexibility to help him survive the modern arc of the GOP from the Bush years to the Tea Party, and finally Trump's populist era, and he was one step closer to fulfilling his dream of being Speaker of the House.

The relationship between Trump and McCarthy had its ups and downs, and Trump blamed McCarthy for making a strategic blunder and refusing to keep Republicans on the January 6 committee. But in early January 2023, Trump rewarded McCarthy for his loyalty.

After Republicans narrowly won back the House, Trump started making calls to the anti-McCarthy wing of the party and gave his public support to McCarthy's bid for speaker in an interview with *Breitbart* in December. And he even warned members trying to take down McCarthy, like Representatives Matt Gaetz and Bob Good, that they were setting up a "doomsday scenario" in the House.

But Trump would go only so far. He knew that their opposition to McCarthy had nothing to do with their loyalty toward him. Gaetz, for example, was about as die-hard as they came. The first failed round of votes on McCarthy's Speaker bid in the House was a remarkable display of Republican dysfunction. It was the first time in more than a century that the party in power had failed to elect a leader on the first day of voting.

McCarthy had already bent to the rebellious wing of the party and announced new rules that would allow just five House members to vote the Speaker out if they were dissatisfied. But they stood their ground, leaving open the extraordinary possibility that their chaos could potentially open the door to the minority leader—Representative Hakeem Jeffries—becoming Speaker. It was embarrassing, chaotic, and emblematic of just how disjointed House Republicans were.

That night, Trump called up McCarthy for an update on where things stood, and the next morning he put out a Truth Social post in support that helped stave off some more GOP defections. But over the course of the next week, the deep divisions within the Republican Party and Trump's inability to control the hard-right Frankenstein's monster of a conference he had helped create were laid bare.

It was a humiliating path to leadership for McCarthy, as he was forced to manage the right wing of the party on live television.

The final night of McCarthy's speakership bid made for must-see television, with members pouting and shouting and dealing out in the open like a Renaissance painting come to life. Trump made phone calls to GOP holdouts, with Representative Marjorie Taylor Greene at one point dialing up "DT" on her iPhone and trying to pass it over to Representative Matt Rosendale, one of the anti-McCarthy hold-outs, on the House floor. Trump also got on the phone with other holdouts in the Republican conference, including Gaetz and Representative Andy Biggs. But they still wouldn't budge. During another contentious moment, an altercation almost broke out after Gaetz's "present" vote forced a fifteenth, and ultimately final, round of voting.

After all that, Trump took credit for McCarthy finally becoming Speaker of the House. "The Fake News Media was, believe it or not, very gracious in their reporting that I greatly helped Kevin McCarthy attain the position of Speaker of the House," Trump wrote on Truth Social. "Thank you, I did our Country a big favor!"

TRUMP WAS STILL GETTING BRONZED and ready for the day when a group of reporters joined him aboard his private jet. They were bound for New Hampshire and South Carolina, the first two political stops of his presidential campaign.

Trump was eager to show off his plane—the refurbished cream-colored seats, the sleeping quarters with a bed and Trump's crest spread out on a blanket, airplane bathrooms with gold trim, and the white leather sofas and big-screen TVs. Trump gave his Boeing 757 a makeover in 2021, which included a fresh paint job, an American flag on the tail, and TRUMP in gold lettering along the fuselage.

Trump was also eager to show off his campaign operation after months of stories that cast doubt on him. Trump wanted to make clear that he was in fact serious about a presidential run even if nothing he was doing—from golf outings to meetings with Kanye West—indicated that. And he wanted his potential rivals to step into the ring.

Just a few days before Trump's campaign swing, he received a call at Mar-a-Lago from his former U.N. ambassador and the former governor of South Carolina, Nikki Haley. "She called me and said she'd like to consider it. And I said you should do it," Trump told reporters on his plane.

Trump and Haley had a good working relationship while he was in the White House. In an unexpected move, Haley stepped down from her post in 2018. And unlike many of the "formers" in Trump's administration who publicly broke with Trump, she remained loyal to Trump—that is, until shortly after January 6. In an interview with the journalist Tim Alberta, Haley placed blame on Trump for the riots and said that she put some responsibility on Republicans who repeated Trump's false claims about the 2020 election. "He went down a path he shouldn't have, and we shouldn't have followed him, and we shouldn't have listened to him. And we can't let that ever happen again," Haley said.

The day after she announced her presidential campaign in February 2023, Trump taunted Haley on Truth Social:

Nikki Haley had a hard time making the decision to run for President because she very publicly stated that she "would never run against the President. He did a GREAT JOB, and was the best President in my lifetime." I told Nikki to follow her heart, not her ambition or belief. Who knows, stranger things have happened. She's polling at 1%, not a bad start!!!

Trump told reporters he received a handful of calls at the beginning of 2023 from other would-be Republican presidential hopefuls, reassuring him that they did not plan on trying to sabotage any run.

But Trump and his team understood early on that the more GOP challengers Trump had, like Haley, the better his chances were of securing the nomination.

Haley was an afterthought compared to DeSantis, who received the brunt of Trump's attacks. Trump accused him of "trying to rewrite history" over his response to the COVID-19 pandemic, and said he "promoted the vaccine as much as anyone."

"When I hear that he might [run] I think it's very disloyal," Trump said. "He won't be leading, I got him elected," he said. "I'm the one that chose him."

Trump would soon turn in his turret and do what comes naturally—with vicious nicknames, gestures, and ad-libbed, ad hominem attacks, he would obliterate a perceived threat from the face of the earth.

PRESIDENTIAL PRIMARIES OFTEN COME DOWN to very basic emotional responses and likability. There is the famous "beer question," which emerged out of the 2000 presidential election, that asked voters which candidate they would prefer to share a beer with: Republican George W. Bush or his Democratic opponent, Al Gore. Bush, like Trump, was a teetotaler, but Bush beat Gore, 40 percent to 37, in the nonscientific poll commissioned by the beermaker Sam Adams. The idea took hold, becoming shorthand in electoral politics for how well a candidate could connect with voters.

In January and February 2023, MAGA Inc. and Fabrizio held a

series of focus groups in Iowa, New Hampshire, and South Carolina—the first three nominating contests of the GOP primary. What they found in their field research was that Republican voters didn't have an issue with Trump's actions, Trump's policies, or Trump's bombastic personality. What they were concerned about was Trump's electability. Could he actually beat Joe Biden?

DeSantis was presented to the public as an ideological carbon copy of Trump, but without all the baggage. And the PAC was confident that the former governor of South Carolina, Nikki Haley, was not a threat because her policies were viewed as out of step with his base. If anything, they wanted Haley to surge in the polls and take voter attention away from DeSantis.

But on the beer question, Trump's campaign and super PAC staff believed that their candidate had a clear advantage. They had worked with both men up close, and those who went to work for Trump, like Wiles, Blair, Budowich, and Miller, understood that one of DeSantis's greatest vulnerabilities as a candidate was that he could be awkward and aloof, and when attacked, would become paranoid and lash out at his own staff. To capitalize on that weakness—and to chip away at the notion that DeSantis was more palatable and electable in the general election—they planned to deploy humiliating psychological warfare on the governor in the lead-up to DeSantis's eventual announcement.

When discussing their strategy, one Trump adviser referred to Saul Alinsky's *Rules for Radicals*. Rule number five: Ridicule is man's most potent weapon.

"There is no defense. It is almost impossible to counterattack ridicule. Also it infuriates the opposition, who then react to your advantage."

Whether or not Trump ever read Alinsky's advice, members of his team had, and it summed up how the former president—who ridiculed his opponents' appearances and their wives' appearances, mocked them onstage and assigned insulting nicknames to them—

viewed politics: All was fair in love and political war. Scratch that. For Trump, there was no love in public life—all was war.

In mid-March, the campaign launched a disgusting and clever ad campaign that went viral and became the defining political ad of the primary.

It started with a story leaked to *The Daily Beast*. Years ago, DeSantis had taken a flight from Tallahassee to Washington on a donor's private jet. As he sat with the donor and his team, including political adviser Adrian Lukis and his deputy chief of staff, James Blair, he opened a cup of pudding and, because there were no utensils, started eating it with his fingers. The incident—gross and funny and strange— was gossiped about after the flight and quickly became part of Talla- hassee lore as the story spread among Republican operatives at the state capitol.

DeSantis told Fox Nation's Piers Morgan that he never remem- bered eating pudding with his fingers.

"I don't remember ever doing that," DeSantis told Morgan. "Maybe when I was a kid, but it's interesting there's a lot of people who when they go at you, sometimes they have really good ammuni- tion like, 'You're a crook, you did this, you did that,'" he said. "For me, they're talking about pudding, and I'm like, 'Is that really the best you've got? Okay, bring it on!'"

Not long after that story went viral, the PAC decided to launch an ad. Their goal was twofold: get under DeSantis's skin and start signal- ing to the public that he was, well, *strange* and would not pass the "beer test."

Dean Petrone of Go BIG Media presented a script to the PAC: "Ron DeSantis loves sticking his fingers where they don't belong. And we're not just talking about pudding. DeSantis has his dirty fingers all over senior entitlements, like cutting Medicare and slashing Social Security, even raising our retirement age. Tell Ron DeSantis to keep his pudding fingers off our money. Oh, and somebody get this man a spoon."

In the ad, a nondescript man playing DeSantis stuck his fingers into a cup of chocolate pudding and smeared it on his face.

There was some initial hesitation among the group. Even for those who worked for Trump, maybe this was going too far? Trump, a famous germaphobe, might be grossed out by the premise.

The ad played for less than 24 hours on national markets before MAGA Inc. rotated a more traditional political spot in its place. But the media picked up on Trump's PAC having spent seven figures on an ad buy and assumed it was all going to be about DeSantis's pudding snack habits.

Just like that, the damage was done. The ad went viral. And DeSantis was suddenly being asked about the pudding story.

The team at MAGA Inc. decided they liked the pudding fingers ad so much they included it in their next ad as a kind of Easter egg. In the ad, a DeSantis supporter takes off his hat and throws it into the garbage. Next to it is a used pudding cup.

IN 2016, TRUMP PLEDGED TO be his supporters' voice. But as Trump kicked off his 2024 presidential campaign, his message took a decidedly darker turn.

"Today, I add: I am your warrior. I am your justice. And for those who have been wronged and betrayed, I am your retribution," Trump told a crowd at the Conservative Political Action Conference in Maryland in early March. "I am your retribution," he repeated to cheers from the crowd.

Even for Trump, whose inauguration speech talked of "American carnage" and who used dark, violent rhetoric in his speeches, the promise to make his return to the White House a chance to seek vengeance was shocking. And it was deliberate.

At CPAC, Trump called on his supporters to join him in what he described as the "final battle" for America. Two weeks later, Trump's campaign planned a rally in Waco, Texas, where in 1993 federal law enforcement agents had laid siege to the Branch Davidian compound where a cult leader preached about the apocalypse.

Trump's campaign fervently pushed back on the idea that Waco was chosen with the thirtieth anniversary of the Waco massacre— a deadly standoff between a religious cult and federal agents—in mind. Waco, they claimed, was simply a convenient middle point between Austin and Dallas on I-35.

"And you see all these stories that the president chose this town because of an anniversary of an event that happened thirty years ago. Well, let me tell you that is pure bullshit, fake news—I picked Waco," said Texas Lieutenant Governor Dan Patrick at the rally. Trump had called Patrick about holding a rally in Texas, and Patrick said it was his idea to hold a rally in the ruby-red center of the state.

But the comparisons were easy to make. Trump opened the rally by playing "Justice for All," a song that features a choir of men who were all imprisoned for their role in the January 6 riots at the U.S. Capitol singing the national anthem with a recording of Trump reciting the Pledge of Allegiance. Video of the insurrection played on large screens as Trump stood onstage, taking in the crowd's reaction.

"You will be vindicated and proud," Trump said, defending the insurrectionists who stormed the Capitol. "The thugs and criminals who are corrupting our justice system will be defeated, discredited and totally disgraced."

It was a jarring display. Just two years after a mob interrupted the peaceful transfer of power and violence spilled across the steps of the Capitol, Trump had managed to flip the script on January 6 among his supporters. He pushed conspiracies that it was an inside job. He met with the family members of rioters and he called those sent to jail "political prisoners."

In particular, Trump had turned Ashli Babbitt into a martyr. Babbitt was among the rioters who invaded the Capitol on January 6, and was fatally shot by a Capitol Police officer as she tried to break into the Speaker's Lobby. In the summer of 2021, Trump called Babbitt's mother, Micki Witthoeft, to extend his condolences, and he had frequently brought Babbitt's name up at rallies ever since. In Trump's telling, she was an innocent Air Force veteran who had made the ultimate sacrifice to overturn the stolen election. And he painted the Capitol Police officer who had fired the shot that killed her (after repeatedly warning the rioters to back off) as a "murderer," even though the officer had just been doing his job that day and had been cleared of any wrongdoing by the Justice Department and the Capitol Police.

As Trump faced charges in Georgia and Washington over his efforts to overturn the election, he banded together with January 6 defendants as he declared them all victims.

The crowd waved posters that read WITCH HUNT, and the former president used fiery language to frame his speech around his own legal problems and what he called the "weaponization" of the justice system, which he said was the "central issue of our time."

One week before Trump's rally in Waco, Trump surprised—and alarmed—his advisers when he unexpectedly posted to Truth Social that he expected to be arrested in a Manhattan criminal investigation over a $130,000 hush money payment that Trump's fixer, Michael Cohen, made during the 2016 presidential campaign to porn star Stormy Daniels.

"WILL BE ARRESTED ON TUESDAY OF NEXT WEEK. PROTEST, TAKE OUR NATION BACK!" Trump declared in an all-caps post from his Mar-a-Lago club. A lawyer for Trump said the former president likely sent out the post after seeing a news report about security measures law enforcement in New York had planned around Trump's potential indictment.

But he had also been given a hint by former White House counselor Kellyanne Conway, who had testified in New York as part of Alvin Bragg's investigation into the payment made to Daniels, that he was likely to be indicted in the case.

Conway was in town for a book event and speech with the 45 Club, a Trump fan club that frequently met in South Florida and attracted conservative stars to its meetings, and met with her former boss for dinner at his golf club on March 12.

"Why do you think I'm going to get indicted?" Trump asked.

"Just the questions they're asking," Conway replied. "My testimony is solid. I never paid any of these women."

Conway testified to the grand jury that she believed Cohen was trying to "please the boss" by making the payment.

"Some people say it would help me if I got indicted," Trump said.

"Well, Mr. President," Conway replied, "in your life, if the question is to be indicted or not to be indicted, always pick door number two."

"I know, I know," Trump said.

But Trump and his team had been preparing for an indictment, which would make Trump the first current or former American president to face criminal charges. At least outwardly—and perhaps in an effort to put on a strong face—Trump seemed wholly unbothered by the potential of an indictment. He played golf at his Florida clubs, met with political advisers and continued to hold court each night at Mar-a-Lago, iPad in hand to curate the playlist.

Behind the scenes Trump's team had been preparing for the possibility Trump would be indicted and in March discussed the potential logistics. Would Trump have his mugshot taken? Would he be fingerprinted? Would they encourage supporters to line the streets of Manhattan as Trump's motorcade made its way to court? And while they did not like Trump's calls for protesters, they took advantage of the attention and fundraised off his potential arrest.

"Per CBS NEWS: MANHATTAN D.A. COULD BE CLOSE TO CHARGING TRUMP," read one fundraising email. "Friend— With the Deep State gunning for President Trump with phony witch hunts like never before, we had to be sure you saw the *private and secure* message he wrote for YOU."

DONALD TRUMP WAS AT HIS Mar-a-Lago club on the evening of March 30 when he was told by one of his attorneys that he had been indicted by a Manhattan grand jury.

The news itself was not surprising to Trump or his team. But the timing was. They had anticipated that the grand jury would make its decision at the end of April and had to suddenly scramble to plan his surrender. That evening, in an effort to play it cool, Trump had dinner at Mar-a-Lago with Melania Trump on the club's grand patio where all of his guests could see.

Trump's people had spent weeks laying the groundwork for the indictment, and just minutes after the news broke, the campaign released a statement describing it as "Political Persecution and Election Interference at the highest level in history." They then blasted out statements from supporters and allies rushing to Trump's defense, talking points for surrogates going on television to try to turn lemons into lemonade, and more fundraising appeals. His aides noted that it was lucky timing for fundraising, just ahead of Friday's end-of-first-quarter fundraising deadline and boosting his totals for the next month as well.

And they were preparing for what would be a media circus. One Trump adviser likened the Manhattan arraignment to "O.J. Simpson on steroids," referring to the infamous car chase down the highway in California, when news choppers followed his car chase from the sky. Trump's team had been in touch with news channels in New York that planned a TV bonanza with helicopters dramatically following Trump's motorcade route to Lower Manhattan.

Trump and his team were also keeping tabs on which Republicans were coming to his defense. When Florida governor Ron DeSantis appeared to mock Trump's legal issues in a press conference, Trump lashed out on Truth Social and insinuated that DeSantis would soon experience false accusations of his own. Unsatisfied with that Truth Social post, Trump deleted it and replaced it with another that went even further, suggesting without evidence that DeSantis could be faced with allegations from not only a woman but a man, too, and that it could also come from someone "underage."

It was a shocking and slanderous display. But this was the kind of New York gutter fighting that was second nature to Trump. Under the klieg lights of a fledgling high-profile campaign, any responsible adult target of such an attack would respond with incredulity, and never recover. And that wasn't all. As he had with so many more worthy opponents before, Trump and his team began to pile on the nicknames.

Ron DeSanctimonious.

Meatball Ron.

Rob.

It was juvenile. It was disrespectful. It was vicious and stupid.

Also incredibly effective. A surgically precise spine removal, with no anesthesia.

Trump benefited from having many of those punches taken by a spokesperson who literally came from the world of professional fighting, Steven Cheung. Cheung, who worked in communications on Trump's two previous presidential campaigns, was a former spokesman for the mixed-martial-arts franchise Ultimate Fighting Championship. And although he was known for being a well-liked, easygoing person by Trump team members and journalists alike, he mimicked Trump's ruthlessness in his statements from the campaign.

The pile-on from Trump and his team made the message to DeSantis clear: Defend me or else. The Florida governor then obediently called Alvin Bragg's indictment of Trump "un-American."

ON TUESDAY, APRIL 4, 2023, Trump, the only former president ever to be indicted, pleaded not guilty to thirty-four felony counts over allegations he and his associates falsified business records in an effort to cover up Trump's extramarital affair with a porn star.

"During and in furtherance of his candidacy for President, the Defendant and others agreed to identify and suppress negative stories about him," read the charging documents from Manhattan district attorney Alvin Bragg.

According to Bragg, the scheme began when Trump was running for president in 2016. Michael Cohen was contacted by the publisher of the tabloid magazine *National Enquirer*, who revealed that an adult film actress, Stormy Daniels, had come forward alleging an extramarital affair with Trump.

Hush money payments to a porn star was not a great campaign story, Trump's advisers admitted. But considering all the legal charges Trump was staring down—inciting an insurrection, squirreling away classified documents, and plotting to overthrow an election—they were grateful that this was the first case. It was, in their eyes, blatantly political and a mere bookkeeping issue that Trump would use to claim he was being unfairly targeted.

Trump's day in court set off a media spectacle that began when the former president had landed in New York the day before.

Trump flew from Palm Beach with a large crew of his aides, including Susie Wiles, Chris LaCivita, Jason Miller, Steven Cheung, Boris Epshteyn, and Dan Scavino. Trump, according to one of the people who flew with him to Manhattan, was "resolute" on the flight and "ready for the challenge." But Trump was also very angry. All evening he fired off Truth Social posts taking aim at Bragg and the Justice Department's special counsel investigation.

The next morning, Trump was stone-faced as he walked through the hallways of the courthouse and sat down next to his lawyers inside the courtroom to plead not guilty. Trump was uncharacteristically quiet for the proceedings, but his statements outside the courthouse were reprimanded by the judge—in particular his Truth Social post calling Bragg an "animal" and a cartoon he shared of himself standing with a baseball bat next to the district attorney.

Outside the courthouse, Georgia representative Marjorie Taylor Greene spoke at a rally across the street in protest of the indictment as helicopters buzzed overhead.

But more press cameras and random gawkers appeared to show up than protesters and counterprotesters who screamed at each other across metal barricades lining the street. New York representative George Santos, who was under investigation by the House Ethics Committee, showed up to peacock in front of the cameras; meanwhile, another New York representative, Democrat Jamaal Bowman, briefly appeared to tell Greene to "go back to your district."

Trump planned to end the unprecedented day in court in an unusual way: with a party at Mar-a-Lago.

Back at his beach club, hundreds of his allies, aides, club members, and press packed into the large gilded ballroom to sip champagne and hear Trump give a statement on his arraignment.

And the club itself became a strange catwalk for Trump's campaign team, allies, and his own family. Before Trump walked onstage, the crowd applauded as Donald Trump Jr. and Kimberly Guilfoyle, Tiffany Trump and her new husband, Michael Boulos, and Representative Matt Gaetz and his wife, Ginger Gaetz, walked two by two to the front of the room.

"It's pretty wild to see these people here celebrating," remarked Caroline Wren, an adviser to Kari Lake, who was also at the event. "Who has a baby shower when you can have an arraignment party?" she joked.

Trump walked out onstage defiant, with Johnny Cash's "Ring of Fire" blasting over the speakers, and ticked through a list of all the scandals he had endured and the opponents he faced, from Alvin Bragg to Jack Smith.

I fell into a burning ring of fire
I went down, down, down
And the flames went higher

Just four months earlier, Trump had walked out to an entirely different set of circumstances to announce his 2024 campaign. He was blamed for a lackluster midterm performance. DeSantis was the name on everyone's lips. Republicans were openly questioning whether he could run a presidential campaign.

Tuesday night's post-arraignment event felt like a campaign reset and relaunch. In polling, Trump had shifted from being behind DeSantis to being more than 20 percentage points ahead. He sucked all the oxygen out of the room for his presidential rivals, including DeSantis and Haley.

Once again, Trump made his controversies work to his benefit.

MAY 24, 2023, WAS SUPPOSED to be Ron DeSantis's day. The Florida governor had done all of the right things, at least in theory: He launched a book tour, collected donors, and delivered speeches meant to portray him as the best alternative to Trump. He tried to appear controlled and low-drama.

Except it was all for nothing. By the time he made his wobbly, self-conscious, and glitch-filled launch on Twitter, the Republican primary might as well have been over. Just as in 2016, Trump's rivals had waited to start punching back until the fight was long over.

Over the next several months, Trump's team would wage a piti-less war on their by-now-hapless opponent, who had once seemed so imposing. They shared photos of DeSantis appearing to wipe his nose before shaking hands with veterans at the Iowa State Fair. They jumped on comments he made to a child for eating too much sugar. They made fun of the white rain boots he wore while surveying hur-ricane damage in Florida, and they alleged that he was wearing lifts in his cowboy boots to make him look taller. Trump took that one step further by alleging that DeSantis's footwear was an indication he was gay, and he even appeared to suggest DeSantis could be a pedophile. When the weather was hot in central Iowa and DeSantis chose to wear a jacket, they accused him of dressing strangely. Trump claimed that DeSantis had begged "on his knees" for an endorsement.

DeSantis had his obvious weaknesses. He tried to patch together a coalition that included the far right and Bush Republicans. He lacked charisma or a sense of humor. He shunned the mainstream media. He signed a strict abortion ban in his state.

By the day DeSantis announced, MAGA Inc. had dumped almost $20 million in attack ads against DeSantis. GOP voters recognized Trump's preferred nickname for DeSantis—"Ron DeSanctimonious"— and thought it was hilarious.

After the pro-Trump MAGA Inc. released the pudding fingers ad, cleverly wrapped in critiques of DeSantis's Social Security and Medicare policies, DeSantis allies at Never Back Down, the super PAC supporting his presidential campaign, pushed back with an ad fact-checking Trump.

"Trump should fight Democrats, not lie about Governor DeSantis," the ad said.

A fine point, perhaps. But DeSantis had missed the point entirely. He was running a campaign from a different time.

Trump was barreling toward the nomination of a party that for a brief moment had considered leaving him behind, for the sake of its own survival. But by the time he had dispatched his opposition to the great political beyond, Donald Trump and the Republican Party were one and the same. Like his slogan, Make America Great Again, Trump was reaching out to the future while anchored in the past, in an alternate reality where he won the 2020 election. This time, though, he was determined to return to the White House, no matter what.

EPILOGUE

A BLIZZARD SWEPT THROUGH IOWA DAYS BEFORE THE 2024 REPUBLICAN caucus, bringing bone-chilling temperatures that reached minus 45 degrees Fahrenheit. The rolling farmland of Iowa—a state that prided itself on being first in the presidential nominating process— was frozen. And so was the entire presidential field.

Florida governor Ron DeSantis. Nikki Haley. Vivek Ramaswamy. For months, not one candidate had gained meaningfully on Donald Trump. Despite the best efforts of his twelve would-be rivals, he would never be knocked off his perch at the top of the polls. No one would even come close.

In a typical election year, candidates would fan out across the state in a final barnstorming rush before caucus night; in 2024, they were forced to cancel events from Dubuque to Des Moines as highways turned into icy, dangerous slip-and-slides that left crashed semi trucks abandoned in ditches. When candidates did make it to their events, they were often met with just as many journalists—bored by the hotel bar scene and the lack of any tension in the race—as supporters.

In a sign of the public apathy toward the entire event, one of the buzziest news stories of the caucus wasn't even the caucus itself, the results of which seemed predetermined despite the optimism of some Republican strategists and voters who desperately looked for a non-Trump mirage out in the snowy tundra. Moments before Chris Christie dropped out of the race at an event hundreds of miles from Iowa in New Hampshire, he was caught on a hot mic saying Haley was going to "get smoked."

"She spent sixty-eight million dollars so far," the former governor of New Jersey said. "And we spent twelve dollars. I mean, who's punching above their weight and who's getting a return on their investment?"

"She's going to get smoked, you and I both know," he added. "She's not up to this."

DeSantis called him, he said, and sounded "petrified."

Christie, a former Trump ally who had been one of the first major political players to endorse him in 2016, was the only candidate who was willing to take Trump head-on for much of the race. And he criticized his competitors on the debate stage for tiptoeing around the former president.

"Maybe it's because they have future aspirations. Maybe those future aspirations are now, or maybe they're four years from now," Christie said. "But the fact of the matter is, the truth needs to be told. Trump is unfit to be president."

But before the first nominating contest even kicked off, Christie said he had seen enough. Just like Senator Tim Scott and North Dakota governor Doug Burgum, Christie decided it was time to bow out.

In retrospect, the outcome of the Republican nomination had truly been decided almost a year earlier when Manhattan district attorney Alvin Bragg announced his indictment of Trump.

One by one in early 2023, Trump's political rivals jumped to his defense and echoed Trump's claims that the charges were political and a weaponization of the justice system.

In December 2023, two months before the Iowa caucuses, DeSantis seemed to recognize the devastating role the indictment played in his immediate political future in an interview with David Brody of the Christian Broadcast Network.

"I would say if I could have one thing change, I wish Trump hadn't been indicted on any of this stuff," DeSantis admitted. "It's just crowded out, I think, so much other stuff and it's sucked out a lot of oxygen."

Despite the millions of dollars DeSantis and his super PAC had poured into Iowa, he had failed to connect with voters on a personal level and sometimes sounded more like a right-wing podcaster than a presidential candidate. He threw around niche terms like "ESG" when more down-to-earth matters like inflation and high grocery prices were top of voters' minds.

Meanwhile, the Trump campaign ran what strategists said was an organized turnout operation that included incentives for volunteers like white trucker hats with TRUMP CAUCUS CAPTAIN embroidered in gold across the front. His more professional campaign operation, led by Susie Wiles and Chris LaCivita, was also paying off.

Ever since Trump had walked onstage at Mar-a-Lago to a dubious national audience after the MAGA movement was battered in the midterm election, he had acted as if he was the runaway front-runner, and nothing that happened in the ensuing campaign would cast doubt on that strategy. He would never give any of his Republican opponents a chance to lay a glove on him, refusing to participate in Republican National Committee–sanctioned debates with the rest of the field—one of the final blows to his relationship with Chairwoman Ronna McDaniel. The lack of substantive debates was a loss for voters but tactically smart for Trump.

In Iowa, even Trump was surprised by how quickly the caucus was decided. "How did I win the caucus? I just got here," Trump remarked to his team after he arrived at the Iowa Events Center in downtown Des Moines. It was so early that the convention room where Trump was going to make his victory speech to supporters was still half empty. Before Trump went onstage, he received a call from Ramaswamy, who told him he was dropping out and wanted to offer his endorsement.

"I want to congratulate Ron and Nikki for having a good time

EPILOGUE | 259

together," Trump said once the Associated Press decided he had won the caucus. "We don't even know what the outcome of second place is."

DeSantis lost to Trump by a devastating 30 points and barely squeaked past Haley, who came in third.

During the speech, Trump ally Representative Matt Gaetz turned around to note that the former president's "conciliatory tone" was notable—and an invitation for his rivals to drop out. It was the most magnanimous Trump would be for the rest of the race.

DeSantis had once appeared the best positioned to take down Trump and take up his mantle. But now his campaign was stumbling to its death. "May he rest in peace," Trump said about DeSantis at a New Hampshire rally after Iowa.

When DeSantis dropped out of the race in a video posted on social media, he obediently endorsed Trump. Susie Wiles, whose career DeSantis had once tried to destroy, dispatched the Florida governor with a sharp message on social media: "Bye, bye."

Haley, Trump's former U.N. ambassador, decided to forge ahead to New Hampshire—where she lost—and then on to her home state of South Carolina, where she lost once more before announcing that she was ending her bid for president.

Shortly after January 6, Haley had told Tim Alberta for *Politico* that she didn't believe Trump was "going to be in the picture" in 2024 because "he's fallen so far." She called the second impeachment of Trump a waste of time.

Haley was the first to challenge Trump in the primary and the last to drop out. But like the rest of the primary field, she struggled when it came to Trump himself. She claimed that she was not a Never Trumper and yet questioned Trump's mental fitness and age, said "chaos" followed him, and raised concerns about his ability to abide by the Constitution if he became president. Her message landed with a thud in the MAGA wing of the party.

Haley represented the last gasp of the "establishment" wing of the party to stop Trump in 2024.

But beyond Liz Cheney and a select few in the party, the pre-Trump conservative remnant of the Republican Party never did put up much of a fight. Just as in 2016, Trump benefited from a fractured field and politicians whose egos were too big to allow them to step aside in time to make a meaningful difference in the outcome. And for all the ink spilled about the anxieties of wealthy financiers and where they were putting their money, the Republican base was wholly with Trump.

The belief by some in his party that January 6 marked the end of the Trump era in America was plainly foolish. Trump was forgiven by the Republican Party, even as evidence mounted of the coordinated multistate effort that he had led from the White House to overturn the election. A whitewashing of January 6 began as a grassroots movement spurred by those who participated in the riots and faced legal consequences, and it ultimately spread to Trump. By the time Trump clinched the nomination in mid-March 2024, only 14 percent of Republicans held him responsible for January 6, compared to 56 percent of independents and 86 percent of Democrats, according to a *Washington Post*/University of Maryland poll.

Most of the Republican lawmakers who had once criticized Trump eventually fell back into line. Senate Minority Leader Mitch McConnell—who said shortly after Trump was acquitted in a Senate trial that "there's no question, none, that President Trump is practically and morally responsible for provoking the events of the day," and whose wife, former cabinet secretary Elaine Chao, was mocked and targeted during Trump's post-presidency—became one of the last Republican holdouts to endorse Trump.

Trump's former attorney general Bill Barr, who once called Trump a "consummate narcissist" who "constantly engages in reckless conduct that puts his political followers at risk and the conservative and Republican agenda at risk," essentially endorsed him on Fox News. "Given two bad choices, I think it's my duty to pick the person I think would do the least harm to the country, and in my mind I will vote the Republican ticket," Barr said.

And Trump's former political rivals became allies in his race against Biden.

In late April 2024, Trump and DeSantis met face to face in Florida, for what was described as a "friendly" conversation to make peace and discuss fundraising efforts. The next month, DeSantis convened his network of donors to encourage them to donate to Trump. "Ron, I love that you're back," Trump told DeSantis over speakerphone at the event.

Meanwhile Scott, Ramaswamy, and Burgum became Trump's top surrogates and shot to the top of his vice president shortlist, which also included Senator J. D. Vance.

Even Haley, who declined to endorse Trump upon dropping out, eventually said she would be voting for him. Her reasoning, like that of Barr, McConnell, and others who had once criticized Trump, was that "Biden has been a catastrophe" on issues like the economy, immigration, and the wars in Ukraine and Gaza.

Even as the party continued to fall in line, loyalty to Trump did not always pay off. Kevin McCarthy, who carefully managed his relationship with Trump for years and stuck his neck out for the former president just days after Trump arrived at Mar-a-Lago to begin his exile, did not get bailed out by the former president when he battled to keep his job as Speaker of the House in October 2023 and ultimately lost.

Ronna McDaniel, after loyally serving Trump and the Republican National Committee as chair for seven years, eventually succumbed to pressure from the former president and his allies to step aside. Trump was frustrated by the RNC's primary debates, and his top advisers heard from donors who were unhappy with the state of the party's finances. Michael Whatley, who was chair of the North Carolina GOP and had endorsed Trump's baseless claims about massive voter fraud and a stolen election, and Lara Trump, Trump's daughter-in-law, were handpicked by Trump to replace McDaniel. They were elected chair and co-chair. Chris LaCivita, one of his top campaign advisers, was moved over to a top role at the RNC to ensure that the Trump campaign and the Republican Party were officially one and the same going into 2024.

There were a few holdouts to Trump's takeover of the Republican Party, including Mike Pence. Trump's former vice president, who was targeted by a mob on January 6, had a strained relationship with Trump after the White House; he unsuccessfully tried to run for president and was ultimately shunned by Trumpworld and the MAGA movement. It was not surprising that Pence would not endorse Trump. But it was remarkable—and historic—that a former vice president would not support his former running mate. "Donald Trump is pursuing and articulating an agenda that is at odds with the conservative agenda that we governed on during our four years, and that is why I cannot in good conscience endorse Donald Trump in this campaign," Pence said on Fox News.

For decades to come, historians will be debating how Trump got to this moment. How a man who had sought to remain in power despite losing an election, who had been a political pariah in exile, became the champion of his party once again. How large swaths of Americans were shocked and horrified by what happened on January 6, but then forgave or downplayed or excused or simply moved on. How one man was able to recreate and rebuild himself over and over again.

One answer could be found in the FBI search of Mar-a-Lago, followed by his four criminal indictments in New York, Florida, Washington, D.C., and Georgia, which turbocharged Trump's determination to return to power.

By the time he became the Republican nominee, he faced eighty-eight felony charges ranging from mishandling classified documents to claiming hush money payments to a porn star as legal expenses.

Trump would turn the mugshot taken at the Fulton County Jail in Georgia into a pop culture moment and parlay it into a record-breaking fundraising haul. He would be known as a former president and also inmate number P01135809. Trump, according to advisers, wanted to get his scowling look at the camera just right—

acutely aware of how it would become instantly iconic among his fans.

As the spring of 2024 unfolded, there would be more mugshots in Trumpworld, as more pillars of the former president's legal defense—political operative Mike Roman and attorneys John Eastman, Christina Bobb, Boris Epshteyn, and Jenna Ellis—were indicted for their roles in the fake electors scheme in Arizona.

At the end of May 2024, Trump became the first sitting or former president to be convicted of a felony when a jury in New York City found him guilty on all thirty-four counts in the Stormy Daniels hush money case.

Since his first indictment, Trump had attacked prosecutors, judges, and other court officials involved in his cases in previously unthinkable terms. But after his conviction, his congressional allies joined him in declaring war. Even some of his detractors in the party called the case a misuse of the law. In another sign of support, Trump's campaign said it raised an eye-popping $53 million in the twenty-four hours after the verdict was handed down.

"If they can do this to me, they can do this to anyone," Trump claimed as he stood in the gold and marble lobby of Trump Tower on Fifth Avenue, where he had announced his 2016 campaign for president nine years earlier. The former president declared that his conviction was evidence that the U.S. was now a "fascist state."

We don't yet know how this story ends. If Trump loses in 2024, how will he and his supporters respond to defeat once again? If he wins, will he govern as radically as his ramped-up rhetoric suggests that he will? Recent history tells us to take him at his word.

Before Donald Trump, a cardinal rule of American politics was that a candidate for president of the United States must articulate a positive vision for the future of the country. Instead, Trump has spoken like no president or candidate for the office in American history. At campaign rallies, he has vowed to restore American strength at home and abroad, and yet his path to "making America great again" is paved with revenge and apocalyptic consequences if he is not elected.

"This is the final battle," Trump said repeatedly on the campaign trail. "With you at my side, we will demolish the deep state. We will expel the warmongers from our government. We will drive out the globalists; we will cast out the communists, Marxists, and fascists. We will throw off the sick political class that hates our country, we will rout the fake news media. And we will liberate America from these villains once and for all."

Trump even took to prognosticating the end of America as we have known it, saying over and over again, at high-dollar fundraisers and rallies, "This could very well be the last election this country ever has." When Trump left the White House for Mar-a-Lago, he vowed he would be back. As he has emphasized at rallies, Donald Trump has "unfinished business."

ACKNOWLEDGMENTS

WHEN KEITH URBAHN, MATT LATIMER, AND THE TEAM AT JAVELIN INI-
tially approached me about this project—pitched as a crash book on
Trump's post-presidency in Palm Beach—I was hesitant to dive in. I
had never written a book before and was concerned about being able
to keep up the pace, especially as I balanced it with my full-time job
at *Politico*. I frankly wasn't sure I could pull this off, but I thank Keith
and the Javelin team for seeing something in me and in the importance of telling this story.

This book was written at a remarkable pace, even with several
generous delays in the deadline. I could never have done any of this
without the brilliance, kindness, and patience of Mark Warren, my
editor, and Cameron Peters, my right-hand man. I am so grateful for
Mark's and Cameron's sharp edits, contributions, research, and col-
laboration. I will miss our weekly meetings, our conversations about
current events and our ideas for this book. I could not have asked for
a better team and am eternally grateful to you both.

My sources for this book were generous with their time and knowl-
edge, and made this story come to life. I appreciate your insights and
trust in me.

Thank you to the team at Random House, who worked hard to shepherd this project from the beginning to the end and at lightning speed: Random House editor in chief Ben Greenberg, deputy publisher Alison Rich, publicist Greg Kubie, marketer Michael Hoak, editorial assistant Leila Tejani, production editor Evan Camfield, and copy editor Emily DeHuff.

I thank my colleagues and the leadership at *Politico* for allowing me to take on this book project. Thank you to my editors, in particular Sam Stein, who was obliged to badger me daily about scoops and stories but would at times allow me space to focus on book writing and reporting. Some of my favorite stories from Trump's post-presidency involved Gabby Orr, whom I worked with at *Politico* before she left for CNN and then to raise a beautiful family, and I thank her for her helpful edits and suggestions for this book.

I could not have written this book without the support of my colleagues at *Politico,* among them Natalie Allison, Sally Goldenberg, David Siders, Daniel Lippmann, Adam Wren, Rachel Bade, Jonathan Martin, Steve Shephard, Zach Montellaro, Michael Kruse, Josh Gerstein, Lisa Kashinsky, Kyle Cheney, Jonathan Lemire, Melissa Cooke, Claire Barkley, Olivia Beavers, Burgess Everett, Alex Burns, Anita Kumar, Mike Zapler, David Kihara, Kay Steiger, Gary Fineout, Kimberly Leonard, and Alex Isenstadt. Alex was working on a book of his own at the same time, and I appreciated his near-daily support as we both juggled our day jobs with the demands of a book project.

I owe a debt of gratitude to my colleagues and journalists who also covered Trump's post-presidency and his presidential campaign. Throughout this era, they cranked out scoops and sharp and insightful reporting that formed a foundation for this book, and many of them have become friends over the course of our many hours together in Bedminster, New Jersey, and Palm Beach, Florida. They include my dear friends Josh Dawsey at *The Washington Post,* Kaitlan Collins at CNN, Nancy Cook at *Bloomberg,* and Tara Palmeri at *Puck,* who were constant sources of encouragement during this process. And the talented reporters on the Trump beat whose bylines I never miss, including Jill Colvin at Associated Press; Kristin Holmes, Kate Sullivan and Alayna Treene at CNN; Vaughn Hillyard, Matt Dixon, and Jonathan Allen at NBC News; Jacqueline Alemany, Ashley Parker, Marianne Levine, and Isaac Arnsdorf at *The Washington Post;* Marc Caputo at *The Bulwark;* Shelby Talcott at *Semafor;* Alex Thompson at *Axios;* Olivia Nuzzi at *New York;* Alex Leary at *The Wall Street Journal;* Jonathan Karl and Rachel Scott at ABC; Robert Costa and Finn Gomez at CBS; Brooke Singman and Paul Steinhauser at Fox News; and Maggie Haberman, Jonathan Swan, and Mike Bender at *The New York Times.*

My parents, Dan and D'Ann, my sisters, Madeline and Margaret, and my grandmother Ethel were support systems for me when I felt like I was drowning in transcripts, clips, and self-doubt. My parents first sparked my love of reading, writing, and generally being curious about the world, and throughout my life they have believed in me when I didn't believe in myself. I love you all. You are my rock.

My boyfriend, John Beasley, was patient, encouraging, and loving throughout this entire project. When I was buried in my laptop working on this project in my free time, he never complained and was always a cheerleader for me. I look forward to making up for lost time with you.

I feel lucky to have incredible friends (among them the DICS crew), and I owe you all for the many times I had to cancel plans as I worked away on this book during the weekends and evening hours. You were always understanding during this time and gave me something to look forward to when I stepped away from my laptop. Thank you.

Finally, I would like to thank Daisy, my beloved basset hound, who is a dog and cannot read and did not contribute anything to this project, but was a constant companion snoring at my side and reminding me that fresh air and a walk around the block cures writer's block and just about any blues in life.

SOURCES

THIS BOOK IS THE RESULT OF YEARS SPENT COVERING DONALD TRUMP, through the end of his presidency, a norms-shattering post-presidency, and his ascension as the Republican nominee for president for a third and final time. In that time, I had a front-row seat to the former president at his lowest ebb, and to the people who make up Trumpworld and worked to bring him back to the forefront of American political life.

In the course of my reporting, I spoke with current and former Trump advisers, aides, and attorneys, who have had an intimate view of his fall and his return; current and former members of Congress, including leaders in both parties; Republican Party officials; members of Trump's Mar-a-Lago and Bedminster clubs; and a wide universe of Trump-allied pundits and activists. I reported from nine states and the District of Columbia, and I also drew on my own source notes, interviews, and reporting for *Politico* from 2021 to 2023 on Trump's post-presidency.

I am grateful for the time my sources afforded me to help tell this story.

Additionally, I relied on the following sources and reporting:

CHAPTER 1

Bennett, Kate. "Ivanka Trump and Jared Kushner to Head South as She Explores Political Future." CNN, December 11, 2020.

Burns, Alexander, and Jonathan Martin. "'I've Had It With This Guy': G.O.P. Leaders Privately Blasted Trump After Jan. 6." *The New York Times*, April 21, 2022.

Clement, Scott, Emily Guskin, and Dan Balz. "Post-ABC Poll: Overwhelming Opposition to Capitol Attacks, Majority Support for Preventing Trump from Serving Again." *The Washington Post*, January 15, 2021.

Cloutier, M. M. "Nixon Checked out Mar-a-Lago to Be Southern Camp David When U.S. Owned the Property." *Palm Beach Daily News*, March 21, 2024.

Davies, Emily, and Alex Horton. "Washingtonians Navigate New Normal: Razor-Tipped Wire Fences and Armed Soldiers." *The Washington Post*, January 29, 2021.

Dawsey, Josh, and Manuel Roig-Franzia. "RNC Chairwoman Ronna McDaniel Is Trying to Hold Together a Party That Donald Trump Might Want to Tear Up." *The Washington Post*, January 29, 2021.

Dawsey, Josh, and Michael Scherer. "Trump Jumps into a Divisive Battle over the Republican Party—with a Threat to Start a 'MAGA Party.'" *The Washington Post*, January 23, 2021.

Din, Benjamin. "Trump Issues Last-Minute Pardon to Albert Pirro, Ex-Husband of Jeanine Pirro." *Politico*, January 20, 2021.

Draper, Kevin, and Bill Pennington. "Trump Golf Club Loses 2022 P.G.A. Championship." *The New York Times*, January 10, 2021.

Ferguson, Ellyn. "TRUMP TAKES OVER MAR-A-LAGO." *Miami Herald*, December 29, 1985.

The Five. "Joe Biden's Inaugural Address Put Under the Microscope on 'The Five.'" Fox News, January 20, 2021.

Gaudiana, Nicole, and Michael Stratford. "Education Secretary Betsy DeVos Resigns, Citing Violence at the Capitol." *Politico*, January 7, 2021.

Godfrey, Elaine. "Among the Guardsmen." *The Atlantic*, January 19, 2021.

Hannity. "Biden Calls for Unity, but Party's Recent Past Tells Different Story." Fox News, January 20, 2021.

Hill, Evan, Arielle Ray, and Dahlia Kozlowsky. "'They Got a Officer!': How a Mob Dragged and Beat Police at the Capitol." *The New York Times,* January 11, 2021.

Inside Edition. "Anthony Scaramucci Says Even He Got Invited to Trump Military Sendoff: 'Trust Me That Had to Be a Mass Email.'" January 18, 2021.

Izadi, Elahe. "Watch President Trump and the First Lady Have Their First Dance to Frank Sinatra's 'My Way.'" *The Washington Post,* January 20, 2017.

Kumar, Anita, Gabby Orr, and Meridith McGraw. "'Like a Ghost' in the White House: The Last Days of the Trump Presidency." *Politico Magazine,* January 20, 2021.

Lippman, Daniel. "Trump Staffers Are Worrying About Their Next Job." *Politico,* January 7, 2021.

McGraw, Meridith, and Daniel Lippman. "Trump 'Going Crazy' over Impeachment Legacy." *Politico,* December 18, 2019.

Montanaro, Domenico. "GOP Leader McCarthy: Trump 'Bears Responsibility' for Violence, Won't Vote to Impeach." NPR, January 13, 2021.

Nadworny, Elissa. "Nearly 200,000 Flags on National Mall Represent Those Who Cannot Attend Inauguration." NPR, January 20, 2021.

The Palm Beach Post. "PHOTOS: Building Mar-a-Lago: History of Trump's Winter White House." December 28, 2017.

Peters, Jeremy W. "'They Have Not Legitimately Won': Pro-Trump Media Keeps the Disinformation Flowing." *The New York Times,* January 20, 2021.

Reinhard, Beth, Rosalind S. Helderman, and Marc Fisher. "Donald Trump and Jeffrey Epstein Partied Together. Then an Oceanfront Palm Beach Mansion Came Between Them." *The Washington Post,* July 31, 2019.

Schmidt, Michael S., and Maggie Haberman. "Trump Is Said to Have Discussed Pardoning Himself." *The New York Times,* January 7, 2021.

Siegler, Mara. "Melania Trump Fuels Rumors of Mar-a-Lago Move After Touring Florida School." *Page Six,* December 13, 2020.

Snyder, Tanya. "Chao Resigns from Transportation Department, Citing 'Traumatic,' 'Avoidable' Capitol Riot." *Politico*, January 7, 2021.

Treene, Alayna. "Trump Departs on Final Air Force One Flight." *Axios*, January 20, 2021.

Trump, Donald, and Kate Bohner. *Trump: The Art of the Comeback*. Times Books, 1997.

Weiner, Rachel, and Tom Jackman. "Proud Boy Who Broke Capitol Window: 'I Got Caught Up in All the Craziness.'" *The Washington Post*, April 18, 2023.

Woodward, Bob, and Robert Costa. *Peril*. Simon & Schuster, 2021.

CHAPTER 2

ABC News. "The Bushes Buy New Home in Dallas." December 4, 2008.

Agiesta, Jennifer, and Ariel Edwards-Levy. "CNN Poll: Percentage of Republicans Who Think Biden's 2020 Win Was Illegitimate Ticks Back up near 70%." CNN, August 3, 2023.

The Arizona Republic. "How We Got Here: An Arizona Election Audit Timeline." September 24, 2021.

Associated Press. "Obamas Join Richard Branson for Private Island Getaway." February 7, 2017.

Barr, Jeremy. "CNN Pro-Trump Contributor Jason Miller Departs Amid Legal Accusations." *The Hollywood Reporter*, September 22, 2018.

Barragán, James. "Despite His Victory in Texas and No Credible Evidence of Widespread Fraud, Donald Trump Calls for Election Audit Legislation." *The Texas Tribune*, September 23, 2021.

Bennet, James. "'I Never Dreamed It Would Turn Out This Way.'" *The Atlantic*, October 2014.

Betz, Bradford. "Trump Adviser Claims Former President Has No Plans for Third Political Party." Fox News, January 24, 2021.

Bluestein, Greg. "Meet Donald Trump's New Georgia-Bred Political Guru." *The Atlanta Journal-Constitution*, February 11, 2019.

Brennan Center for Justice. "Voting Laws Roundup: December 2021." December 21, 2021.

Caputo, Marc, Josh Dawsey, and Alex Isenstadt. "Trump Pick Backs Out of White House Job After Affair Allegations." *Politico,* December 25, 2016.

Carnevale, Mary Lu. "Bush Jokes About Being a 'Type A' Retiree." *The Wall Street Journal,* January 20, 2009.

CBS News. "$300M Legacy: Bush Plans Texas Funds." March 14, 2009.

Cheney, Liz. *Oath and Honor: A Memoir and a Warning.* Little, Brown, 2023.

Collins, Eliza. "Trump: 'I'm the Ernest Hemingway of 140 Characters.'" *Politico,* November 20, 2015.

Cooper, Jonathan J. "Arizona Republicans Censure Cindy McCain, GOP Governor." AP, January 23, 2021.

Corley, Cheryl, and Amita Kelly. "Obama Presidential Center Design Unveiled." NPR, May 3, 2017.

Coscarelli, Joe. "Lil Wayne and Kodak Black Among 4 Hip-Hop Figures Trump Pardoned." *The New York Times,* January 20, 2021.

Craggs, Ryan. "Obama Arrives in Bali for a Family Vacation." *Condé Nast Traveler,* June 23, 2017.

Crummy, Brianna. "Trump Clings to False Election Claims at Arizona Rally." *Politico,* July 24, 2021.

Dawsey, Josh, and Robert Costa. "Kevin McCarthy Relishes Role as Trump's Fixer, Friend and Candy Man." *The Washington Post,* January 15, 2018.

Dawsey, Josh, Tom Hamburger, and Amy Gardner. "Trump's Legal Team Exited After He Insisted Impeachment Defense Focus on False Claims of Election Fraud." *The Washington Post,* January 31, 2021.

Dawsey, Josh, and Michael Scherer. "Trump Jumps into a Divisive Battle over the Republican Party—with a Threat to Start a 'MAGA Party.'" *The Washington Post,* January 23, 2021.

Din, Benjamin. "Trump Did Not Provoke Capitol Riots, McCarthy Says." *Politico,* January 21, 2021.

Everett, Burgess, Marianne LeVine, and Meridith McGraw. "Trump Sends a Message to Senate Republicans Ahead of His Trial." *Politico*, January 25, 2021.

Fahrenthold, David A., Tom Hamburger, and Rosalind S. Helderman. "The Inside Story of How the Clintons Built a $2 Billion Global Empire." *The Washington Post*, June 2, 2015.

Field, Jeff. "Mitch McConnell 'Absolutely' Would Support Trump if GOP Nominee in 2024." Fox News, February 25, 2021.

Fineout, Gary. "DeSantis Signs Bill Creating One of the Nation's Only Election Police Units." *Politico*, April 25, 2022.

Fingerhut, Hannah. "AP-NORC Poll: Most Republicans Doubt Biden's Legitimacy." Associated Press, February 5, 2021.

Gardner, Amy. "'I Just Want to Find 11,780 Votes': In Extraordinary Hour-Long Call, Trump Pressures Georgia Secretary of State to Recalculate the Vote in His Favor." *The Washington Post*, January 3, 2021.

Haberman, Maggie. *Confidence Man: The Making of Donald Trump and the Breaking of America*. Penguin Press, 2022.

———. "McCarthy Seeks Thaw with Trump as G.O.P. Rallies Behind Former President." *The New York Times*, January 28, 2021.

———. "Trump Replaces Brad Parscale as Campaign Manager, Elevating Bill Stepien." *The New York Times*, July 15, 2020.

Harwell, Drew. "Co-Founder of Trump's Media Company Details Truth Social's Bitter Infighting." *The Washington Post*, October 15, 2022.

Harwell, Drew, and Josh Dawsey. "Trump Ends Blog After 29 Days, Infuriated by Measly Readership." *The Washington Post*, June 2, 2021.

———. "Trump Is Sliding Toward Online Irrelevance. His New Blog Isn't Helping." *The Washington Post*, May 21, 2021.

Heil, Emily. "The Obamas Vacation Under the Tuscan Sun as the Trumps Work Abroad." *The Washington Post*, May 23, 2017.

Helderman, Rosalind S., Amy Gardner, and Tom Hamburger. "With Impeachment Trial Looming, Trump Taps New Lawyers Who Drew Spotlight in Past Work." *The Washington Post*, February 1, 2021.

Holcombe, Madeline, and Theresa Waldrop. "January Has Been the Deadliest Month for Covid-19 with Nearly 80,000 Lives Lost So Far in the US." CNN, January 27, 2021.

Isenstadt, Alex. "Trump Poll Shows Impeachment Backlash Hitting Cheney." *Politico,* January 27, 2021.

Karl, Jonathan. *Betrayal: The Final Act of the Trump Show.* Dutton, 2021.

Klein, Rick. "George W. Bush: 'Painting Has Changed My Life.'" ABC News, April 24, 2013.

Kruse, Michael. "The Antipope of Mar-a-Lago." *Politico Magazine,* January 29, 2021.

Kunzelman, Michael, and Michelle Smith. "Pandemic's Deadliest Month in US Ends with Signs of Progress." AP, February 1, 2021.

Mac, Ryan, and Rosie Gray. "Parler Wanted Donald Trump on Its Site. Trump's Company Wanted a Stake." *BuzzFeed News,* February 5, 2021.

Markay, Lachlan. "Trump Political Team Disavows 'Patriot Party' Groups." *Axios,* January 25, 2021.

Martin, Jonathan, Maggie Haberman, and Nicholas Fandos. "McConnell Privately Backs Impeachment as House Moves to Charge Trump." *The New York Times,* January 12, 2021.

Mauger, Craig. "Judge Rules Against Legal Push Targeting Michigan Election in Antrim County." *The Detroit News,* May 18, 2021.

Mazzei, Patricia, and Maggie Haberman. "Brad Parscale, Ex-Campaign Manager for Trump, Is Hospitalized in Florida." *The New York Times,* September 27, 2020.

McPherson, Lindsey. "Trump Conviction Unlikely After Most GOP Senators Vote to Dismiss Impeachment Trial." *Roll Call,* January 26, 2021.

Monmouth University Poll. "Majority Support Trump Impeachment." January 25, 2021.

Parker, Ashley. "From 'My Generals' to 'My Kevin,' Trump's Preferred Possessive Can Be a Sign of Affection or Control." *The Washington Post,* September 16, 2019.

Rathe, Adam. "Did Marjorie Merriweather Post Inspire *The Great Gatsby?*" *Town & Country*, February 15, 2022.

Rogers, Alex, Lucy Kafanov, and Jason Kravarik. "Matt Gaetz Rails Against Liz Cheney in Wyoming." CNN, January 29, 2021.

Rucker, Philip, Josh Dawsey, and Ashley Parker. "Trump Is Isolated and Angry at Aides for Failing to Defend Him as He Is Impeached Again." *The Washington Post*, January 13, 2021.

Santucci, John, Josh Margolin, Katherine Faulders, and Aaron Katersky. "Secret Service Members Asked About Protecting Soon-to-Be-Former President Trump Full Time in Florida: Sources." ABC News, November 23, 2020.

Shear, Michael D., and Maggie Haberman. "From Trump's Mar-a-Lago to Facebook, a National Security Crisis in the Open." *The New York Times*, February 13, 2017.

Smith, Allan. "Liz Cheney Calls on GOP to Stop 'Embracing' Trump Ahead of Senate Impeachment Trial." NBC News, February 7, 2021.

Terkel, Amanda. "Kevin McCarthy: 'Everybody Across This Country' Is to Blame for Capitol Attack." *HuffPost*, January 22, 2021.

Thompson, Krissah, and Juliet Eilperin. "Two Months out of Office, Barack Obama Is Having a Post-Presidency like No Other." *The Washington Post*, March 26, 2017.

Weaver, Jay. "Behind the Scenes of How Trump's Truth Social Was Born, and How It Could Fall Apart." *Miami Herald*, October 7, 2022.

Wingett Sanchez, Yvonne. " 'He Told Me That I Needed to Run': Kelli Ward to Run Again for Arizona GOP Chair at Trump's Urging." *The Arizona Republic*, January 5, 2021.

Wolff, Michael. *Landslide: The Final Days of the Trump Presidency*. Henry Holt, 2021.

Youssef, Nancy A., Vivian Salama, and Michael C. Bender. "Trump, Awaiting Egyptian Counterpart at Summit, Called Out for 'My Favorite Dictator.'" *The Wall Street Journal*, September 13, 2019.

CHAPTER 3

Alemany, Jacqueline, Josh Dawsey, and Beth Reinhard. "Backstage Drama at Jan. 6 Rally for Trump Draws Interest of House Committee." *The Washington Post*, February 26, 2022.

Allen, Jonathan, and Matt Dixon. "'She Sits in a Tough Chair': Meet Susie Wiles, the Operative Trying to Guide Trump Through Four Indictments to the White House." NBC News, March 1, 2024.

Bade, Rachel, and Tara Palmeri. "POLITICO Playbook: Scoop: Trump Sends Legal Notice to GOP to Stop Using His Name." *Politico*, March 6, 2021.

Bender, Michael C. *Frankly, We Did Win This Election: The Inside Story of How Trump Lost*. Twelve Books, 2021.

Blitzer, Ronn. "Pence Declined CPAC Invitation: Source." Fox News, February 21, 2021.

Choi, Matthew, Marianne LeVine, Meridith McGraw, and Gabby Orr. "Trump Attacks McConnell in Fiery Statement." *Politico*, February 16, 2021.

Contorno, Steve. "Ron DeSantis' Political Team Planned $25K Golf Games, $250K 'Intimate Gatherings,' Memos Say." *Tampa Bay Times*, September 12, 2019.

Dawsey, Josh. "RNC Chairwoman Ronna McDaniel Comes Under Pressure to Show More Independence from Trump." *The Washington Post*, April 17, 2021.

———. "RNC Moves Portion of Its Spring Donor Retreat to Trump's Mar-a-Lago Club." *The Washington Post*, March 8, 2021.

———. "Trump Slashes at McConnell as He Reiterates Election Falsehoods at Republican Event." *The Washington Post*, April 11, 2021.

Dawsey, Josh, Ashley Parker, Michael Scherer, and Anu Narayanswamy. "Trump Helped the GOP Raise $2 Billion. Now Former Aides and Allies Are Jockeying to Tap into His Fundraising Power." *The Washington Post*, March 27, 2021.

Dixon, Matt. "Florida GOP Hired Marvel-Linked Security Consultant for Internal Probe." *Politico*, October 31, 2019.

Flegenheimer, Matt, Maggie Haberman, and Michael C. Bender. "DeSantis Tried to Bury Her. Now She's Helping Trump Try to Bury Him." *The New York Times*, April 18, 2023.

Forgey, Quint. "All Living Former Presidents, First Ladies Appear in New Vaccine PSAs—Except the Trumps." *Politico*, March 11, 2021.

Haberman, Maggie. "CPAC to Trump: You're Hired!" *Politico*, February 10, 2011.

———. "Trump and His Wife Received Coronavirus Vaccine Before Leaving the White House." *The New York Times*, March 1, 2021.

Hamel, Liz, Lunna Lopes, Grace Sparks, Ashley Kirzinger, Audrey Kearney, Mellisha Stokes, and Mollyann Brodie. "KFF COVID-19 Vaccine Monitor: September 2021." Kaiser Family Foundation, September 28, 2021.

Hanna, John. "Trump Endorses Kansas Sen. Moran; Primary Fight Less Likely." AP, February 26, 2021.

Helderman, Rosalind S., Josh Dawsey, Ashley Parker, and Jacqueline Alemany. "How Trump Jettisoned Restraints at Mar-a-Lago and Prompted Legal Peril." *The Washington Post*, December 18, 2022.

Holmes, Kristen, and Jeremy Herb. "Newly Released Emails Debunk Trump and Allies' Attempts to Blame the GSA for Packing Boxes That Ended Up in Mar-a-Lago." CNN, October 10, 2022.

Isenstadt, Alex. "Haley Criticizes Trump over Capitol Riot, Election Claims in RNC Speech." *Politico*, January 7, 2021.

———. "Lewandowski Cast Out of Trump Operation After Allegation of Unwanted Sexual Advances." *Politico*, September 29, 2021.

———. "RNC Brushes Back Trump Team on Cease-and-Desist Demand." *Politico*, March 8, 2021.

———. "Trump Shares Plans for New Super PAC in Mar-a-Lago Meeting." *Politico*, February 25, 2021.

———. "Trump to Attend RNC Spring Donor Summit." *Politico*, February 22, 2021.

Isenstadt, Alex, and Matt Dixon. "Trump Campaign Cuts Ties with Top Adviser in Florida." *Politico*, September 17, 2019.

Karni, Annie, and Zolan Kanno-Youngs. "As Biden Confronts Vaccine Hesitancy, Republicans Are a Particular Challenge." *The New York Times*, March 15, 2021.

Kruse, Michael. "The True Story of Donald Trump's First Campaign Speech—in 1987." *Politico Magazine*, February 5, 2016.

Lippman, Daniel. "What a Photo of Trump's New Office Reveals About How He Wants to Be Remembered." *Politico*, April 6, 2021.

LoBianco, Tom. "SCOOP: The Top Trump Political Fundraiser Who Helped Plan His January 6 Rally Is out of Trumpworld." *Business Insider*, June 8, 2021.

Martin, Jonathan, and Maggie Haberman. "Trump's Republican Hit List at CPAC Is a Warning Shot to His Party." *The New York Times*, February 28, 2021.

Mauger, Craig. "Trump Recorded Pressuring Wayne County Canvassers Not to Certify 2020 Vote." *The Detroit News*, December 21, 2023.

Merica, Dan. "Sarah Huckabee Sanders Announces Bid for Arkansas Governor." CNN, January 25, 2021.

Orr, Gabby, and Steve Contorno. "She Helped Trump Win Florida Twice. Now She Could Lead His Expected 2024 Campaign." CNN, August 8, 2022.

Plott, Elaina. "At CPAC, a Golden Image, a Magic Wand and Reverence for Trump." *The New York Times*, February 28, 2021.

Plott, Elaina, and Shane Goldmacher. "Trump Wins CPAC Straw Poll, but Only 68 Percent Want Him to Run Again." *The New York Times*, February 28, 2021.

Rove, Karl. "Peril and Opportunity for Trump at CPAC." *The Wall Street Journal*, February 24, 2021.

Schmidt, Michael S. *Donald Trump v. The United States: Inside the Struggle to Stop a President*. Random House, 2020.

Schmidt, Michael S., and Maggie Haberman. "Trump Ordered Mueller Fired, but Backed Off When White House Counsel Threatened to Quit." *The New York Times*, January 25, 2018.

Schorsch, Peter. "Citing Health Issue, Susie Wiles Leaves Ballard Partners." *Florida Politics*, September 17, 2019.

Summerall, Pat. *Summerall: On and Off the Air.* Thomas Nelson, 2008.

Tapper, Jake. "Former White House Chief of Staff Tells Friends That Trump 'Is the Most Flawed Person' He's Ever Met." CNN, October 16, 2020.

CHAPTER 4

The Arizona Republic. "How We Got Here: An Arizona Election Audit Time-line." September 24, 2021.

Barragán, James. "Despite His Victory in Texas and No Credible Evidence of Widespread Fraud, Donald Trump Calls for Election Audit Legislation." *The Texas Tribune,* September 23, 2021.

Barragán, James, and Patrick Svitek. "Gov. Greg Abbott's Pick for Top Texas Election Post Worked with Trump to Fight 2020 Results." *The Texas Tribune,* October 21, 2021.

Berman, Dan. "Supreme Court Allows Defamation Lawsuit against MyPillow CEO Mike Lindell to Proceed." CNN, October 3, 2022.

Blest, Paul. "Mike Lindell's Election Fraud Movie 'Absolute Proof' Has Absolutely No Proof." Vice News, February 5, 2021.

Briggs, Ryan, and Katie Meyer. "New Video Appears to Show State Sen. Mastriano Closer to Capitol Riot than He Said." WHYY, May 25, 2021.

Bump, Philip. "The Great Bamboo Hunt: Arizona's Bizarre Vote-Examination Effort Gets More Bizarre." *The Washington Post,* May 6, 2021.

Cassidy, Christina A. "Report Shows Big Spike in Mail Ballots During 2020 Election." AP, August 16, 2021.

Cooke, Charles C. W. "Maggie Haberman Is Right." *National Review,* June 3, 2021.

Cooper, Jonathan J. "Arizona GOP Election Audit Draws More Republican Politicians." AP, June 2, 2021.

———. "'Botched': Arizona GOP's Ballot Count Ends, Troubles Persist." AP, July 31, 2021.

———. "What's Wrong with Arizona's 2020 Audit? A Lot, Experts Say." AP, August 22, 2021.

Coulter, Ann. "Dinesh's Stupid Movie." *Unsafe,* June 15, 2022.

Crummy, Brianna. "Trump Clings to False Election Claims at Arizona Rally." *Politico,* July 24, 2021.

D'Anna, John. "Man Behind Vote Fraud Conspiracy Theory Previously Pushed Debunked Info with CIA, Joe Arpaio." *The Arizona Republic,* November 13, 2020.

Farhi, Paul, and Elahe Izadi. "One America News Is the Face of the Arizona Election Audit. Its Reporter Is Also Helping Pay for It." *The Washington Post,* June 18, 2021.

Fifield, Jen, and Robert Anglen. "Hand Count in Audit Affirms Biden Beat Trump, as Maricopa County Said in November." *The Arizona Republic,* September 23, 2021.

Gardner, Amy, and Rosalind S. Helderman. "Inspired by Arizona Recount, Trump Loyalists Push to Revisit Election Results in Communities Around the Country." *The Washington Post,* May 19, 2021.

Gerstein, Josh. "Judge Refuses to Toss Out Dominion Defamation Suits Against Powell, Giuliani and Lindell." *Politico,* August 11, 2021.

Godfrey, Elaine. "The Kari Lake Effect." *The Atlantic,* October 9, 2022.

Haberman, Maggie. "Photos of Trump Ally Who Visited the White House Capture Notes About Martial Law." *The New York Times,* January 15, 2021.

Hansen, Ronald J., and Dan Nowicki. "Trump Returns to Arizona, Attacks Doug Ducey and Predicts Ballot Review Will Vindicate Him." *The Arizona Republic,* July 24, 2021.

Harris, Craig. "Why an Ex-CEO with a Ph.D. Is Helping Cyber Ninjas and Trump Challenge the Election in Arizona." *USA Today,* September 24, 2021.

Helderman, Rosalind S. "Arizona Senate President Says 2020 Recount Will Proceed, Despite Angry Objections from Maricopa County Officials." *The Washington Post,* May 18, 2021.

———. "Michigan Judge Dismisses Lawsuit Seeking New Audit of Antrim County Vote, One of the Last Remaining 2020 Legal Challenges." *The Washington Post,* May 18, 2021.

———. "'Our Democracy Is Imperiled': Maricopa County Officials Decry 2020 Recount as a Sham and Call on Arizona Republicans to End the Process." *The Washington Post,* May 17, 2021.

Karl, Jonathan. *Tired of Winning: Donald Trump and the End of the Grand Old Party.* Dutton, 2023.

Karni, Annie, and Maggie Haberman. "Fox's Arizona Call for Biden Flipped the Mood at Trump Headquarters." *The New York Times,* November 4, 2020.

Lake, Kari. *Unafraid: Just Getting Started.* Winning Team Publishing, 2023.

Lippman, Daniel, and Tina Nguyen. "Trump Has Been Nudging MyPillow CEO Mike Lindell to Run for Office." *Politico,* March 30, 2020.

Marks, Joseph. "The Cybersecurity 202: My Pillow Cyber Symposium Is yet Another Font of Election Fraud Lies." *The Washington Post,* August 11, 2021.

Mauger, Craig. "Judge Rules Against Legal Push Targeting Michigan Election in Antrim County." *The Detroit News,* May 18, 2021.

Mayer, Jane. "The Big Money Behind the Big Lie." *The New Yorker,* August 2, 2021.

Petrizzo, Zachary. "Mike Lindell Held Secret Meeting with Trump on 'Reinstatement Day.'" *Salon,* September 10, 2021.

Reuters/Ipsos. "Ipsos/Reuters Poll: The Big Lie." May 21, 2021.

Tucker Carlson Originals. "The Candidate: Blake Masters." Fox Nation, October 25, 2022.

Wines, Michael. "The Arizona Vote Review Winds Down amid Disclosures That It Was Paid For Almost Entirely by Trump Supporters." *The New York Times,* July 29, 2021.

Zeidman, Bob. "How I Won $5 Million from the MyPillow Guy and Saved Democracy." *Politico Magazine,* May 26, 2023.

Zuidijk, Daniel, and Kartikay Mehrota. "Trump Lashes Voting Tech Firm with Barrage of Debunked Claims." *Bloomberg,* November 17, 2020.

CHAPTER 5

Arkin, James. "Trump Backs Budd in North Carolina Senate Race." *Politico,* June 5, 2021.

Barr, Jeremy. "Fox News Hires the Former President's Daughter-in-Law, Lara Trump, as a Pundit." *The Washington Post,* March 29, 2021.

Dawsey, Josh, and David A. Fahrenthold. "GOP Candidates Are Flocking to Mar-a-Lago to Pay Trump for the Privilege of Hosting Their Events." *The Washington Post,* December 16, 2021.

Dawsey, Josh, and Rosalind S. Helderman. "Trump's PAC Collected $75 Million This Year, but So Far the Group Has Not Put Money into Pushing for the 2020 Ballot Reviews He Touts." *The Washington Post,* July 22, 2021.

Diamond, Dan, Daniel Lippman, and Nancy Cook. "Trump Team Launches a Sweeping Loyalty Test to Shore Up Its Defenses." *Politico,* July 15, 2020.

Eavis, Victoria. "US House Candidate Bouchard Says He Impregnated 14-Year-Old When He Was 18." *The Casper Star-Tribune,* May 21, 2021.

Ferris, Sarah, and Nicholas Wu. "Cheney Joins Dems on Jan. 6 Probe, Defying McCarthy Threat." *Politico,* July 1, 2021.

Gangel, Jamie, Jeremy Herb, and Elizabeth Stuart. "CNN Exclusive: Mark Meadows' 2,319 Text Messages Reveal Trump's Inner Circle Communications Before and After January 6." CNN, April 25, 2022.

Gardner, Amy. " 'I Just Want to Find 11,780 Votes': In Extraordinary Hour-Long Call, Trump Pressures Georgia Secretary of State to Recalculate the Vote in His Favor." *The Washington Post,* January 3, 2021.

Grisham, Stephanie. *I'll Take Your Questions Now: What I Saw at the Trump White House.* Harper, 2021.

Haberman, Maggie. "Trump Forms PAC in Hopes of Keeping Hold on G.O.P." *The New York Times,* November 9, 2020.

Helderman, Rosalind S., Michelle Ye Hee Lee, Josh Dawsey, Shane Harris, Ashley Parker, and Devlin Barrett. "The Aide Who Stayed: Walt Nauta, Key Witness in Trump Documents Case." *The Washington Post,* March 18, 2023.

Herb, Jeremy. "Exclusive: CNN Obtains the Tape of Trump's 2021 Conversation About Classified Documents." CNN, June 26, 2023.

Isenstadt, Alex. "'Full of S—': Candidates Warned Not to Fake Trump Endorsement." *Politico,* June 14, 2021.

———. "Mo Brooks Nabs Trump Endorsement in Alabama Senate Race." *Politico,* April 7, 2021.

———. "Trump Endorses Primary Rival Challenging Republican Impeachment Supporter." *Politico,* February 26, 2021.

———. "Trump Super PAC to Hold First Fundraiser at Bedminster." *Politico,* May 10, 2021.

———. "Trump's Secret Sit-down with Ohio Candidates Turns into 'Hunger Games.'" *Politico,* March 25, 2021.

Isenstadt, Alex, and Meridith McGraw. "Jason Miller to Head Tech Startup That Could Become Trump Platform." *Politico,* June 10, 2021.

———. "Trump Political Groups Have over $100M in the Bank." *Politico,* July 31, 2021.

Isenstadt, Alex, and Zach Montellaro. "Trump Looks to Take Down Raffensperger in Georgia." *Politico,* March 21, 2021.

Kim, Soo Rin. "Fresh from 2020 Election, Big Donors Are Already Jumping Back In to Support Pro-Trump and Pro-Biden PACs." ABC News, August 10, 2021.

Korte, Lara. "A Sacramento Kid Grew Up to Be a Voice for Donald Trump. Now He's Fighting Jan. 6 Subpoenas." *The Sacramento Bee,* February 16, 2022.

Orr, Gabby, and Meridith McGraw. "How to Mess Up a Possible Trump Endorsement in One Easy Step." *Politico,* March 21, 2021.

Orr, Gabby, and Michael Warren. "Trump Endorses Ted Budd in North Carolina Senate GOP Primary." CNN, June 5, 2021.

Schiffer, Zoë. "Salesforce Says It Has Taken Action Against the RNC, but Won't Say How." *The Verge,* January 11, 2021.

Zanona, Melanie, and Olivia Beavers. "Cheney Booted from Republican Leadership Spot." *Politico,* May 12, 2021.

CHAPTER 6

ABC News. "Majority of Products Trump Boasted About Last Night No Longer Available." March 9, 2016.

Baker, Peter. "Trump Denies Talking to Ambassador About Moving British Open to His Resort." *The New York Times,* July 22, 2020.

Beaton, Andrew. "Trump Says LIV Golf Has Been Worth 'Billions of Dollars' in Publicity for Saudi Arabia." *The Wall Street Journal,* July 26, 2022.

Bennett, Kate. "Trump Ditches Florida and Heads North for the Summer." CNN, May 19, 2021.

Bernstein, Jacob. "At Ivana Trump's Funeral, a Gold-Hued Coffin and the Secret Service." *The New York Times,* July 20, 2022.

Blest, Paul. "Donald Trump and Bill O'Reilly's 'History Tour' Isn't Going So Great." Vice News, March 28, 2024.

Blinder, Alan, and Maggie Haberman. "Trump Embraces LIV Golf, Backing a New Saudi Strategy." *The New York Times,* July 27, 2022.

Cassidy, John. "The Serial Golf Cheat in the White House." *The New Yorker,* April 3, 2019.

Deak, Mike. "At Trump National, the President Is Just a Good Neighbor." *Courier News,* June 9, 2017.

Draper, Kevin, and Bill Pennington. "Trump Golf Club Loses 2022 P.G.A. Championship." *The New York Times,* January 10, 2021.

Goldmacher, Shane, and Eric Lipton. "Selling Trump: A Profitable Post-Presidency Like No Other." *The New York Times,* February 12, 2022.

Haberman, Maggie, and Emily Steel. "Jared Kushner Talks of a Trump TV Network with a Media Deal Maker." *The New York Times,* October 17, 2016.

Harwell, Drew. "Co-Founder of Trump's Media Company Details Truth Social's Bitter Infighting." *The Washington Post,* October 15, 2022.

———. "Trump's Truth Social's Disastrous Launch Raises Doubts About Its Long-Term Viability." *The Washington Post,* February 22, 2022.

Landler, Mark, Lara Jakes, and Maggie Haberman. "Trump's Request of an Ambassador: Get the British Open for Me." *The New York Times*, July 21, 2020.

Lippman, Daniel. "Ticket Sales Are Moving Slowly for the Coming Trump-O'Reilly Stadium Tour." *Politico*, July 16, 2021.

Lippman, Daniel, and Meridith McGraw. " 'He's Screwed Over So Many Publishers': Trump Confronts a Skeptical Book Industry." *Politico*, June 15, 2021.

Mac, Ryan, and Rosie Gray. "Parler Wanted Donald Trump on Its Site. Trump's Company Wanted a Stake." *BuzzFeed News*, February 5, 2021.

Newport, John Paul. "A Matter of Golf and Death." *The Wall Street Journal*, June 26, 2015.

The New York Times. "POSTINGS: Part of Stalled Development in New Jersey; Trump Buys Golf Course." September 22, 2002.

Nobles, Ryan. "Devin Nunes Says He's Leaving Congress by the End of the Year." CNN, December 7, 2021.

Palazzo, Anthony. "Penguin Random House Wins Bidding War for Obamas' Memoir Rights." *Bloomberg*, March 1, 2017.

Pennington, Bill. "Greg Norman Takes Aim at PGA Tour with New Saudi-Backed Golf League." *The New York Times*, October 29, 2021.

Radden Keefe, Patrick. "How Mark Burnett Resurrected Donald Trump as an Icon of American Success." *The New Yorker*, December 27, 2018.

Reilly, Rick. *Commander in Cheat: How Golf Explains Trump*. Hachette Books, 2019.

Scherer, Michael, and Josh Dawsey. "Books, Speeches, Hats for Sale: Post-Presidency, the Trumps Try to Make Money the Pre-Presidency Way." *The Washington Post*, January 28, 2022.

Weaver, Jay. "Behind the Scenes of How Trump's Truth Social Was Born, and How It Could Fall Apart." *Miami Herald*, October 7, 2022.

Whitcomb, Dan. "Former U.S. President Donald Trump Launches 'TRUTH' Social Media Platform." Reuters, October 21, 2021.

CHAPTER 7

Allison, Natalie, and Meridith McGraw. "How Trump Threw Mo Brooks Under the Bus." *Politico*, March 23, 2022.

Allison, Natalie, and Holly Otterbein. "Dr. Oz Announces Senate Bid to His Millions of Followers," *Politico*, November 30, 2021.

———. "Trump Endorses Oz in Key Senate Race," *Politico*, April 9, 2022.

Arkin, James. "J.D. Vance Joins Already Chaotic Ohio Senate Primary." *Politico*, July 1, 2021.

Bosman, Julie, and Monica Davey. "Former Gov. Eric Greitens: How His Downfall Unfolded." *The New York Times*, May 15, 2018.

Dixon-Hamilton, Jordan. "Chaos in Ohio GOP Senate Debate: Gibbons, Mandel in Heated Altercation as Vance Berates Them for Conduct Unbecoming." *Breitbart*, March 18, 2022.

Garrity, Kelly. "Trump Advised Tudor Dixon to Soften Her Line on Abortion During Michigan Governor's Race." *Politico*, August 30, 2023.

Gerstein, Josh, and Alexander Ward. "Supreme Court Has Voted to Overturn Abortion Rights, Draft Opinion Shows." *Politico*, May 2, 2022.

Haberman, Maggie. *Confidence Man: The Making of Donald Trump and the Breaking of America*. Penguin Press, 2022.

Isenstadt, Alex. "Inside the Wild Bedminster Lobbying Spree That Led to Trump's Double Missouri Endorsement." *Politico*, August 2, 2022.

———. "Mo Brooks Nabs Trump Endorsement in Alabama Senate Race." *Politico*, April 7, 2021.

———. "Trump Gives Vance Coveted Endorsement in Ohio Senate Race." *Politico*, April 15, 2022.

Kelly, Kate, and Trip Gabriel. "David McCormick, Hedge Fund Chief, Joins Pennsylvania G.O.P. Senate Fray." *The New York Times*, January 12, 2022.

McCormick, David. *Superpower in Peril: A Battle Plan to Renew America*. Center Street, 2023.

Olander, Olivia, and Alice Miranda Ollstein. "Michigan Governor Debate Features Accusations of Lies, with Abortion Front and Center." *Politico*, October 13, 2022.

Pietsch, Bryan. "Top GOP Governor Candidate: Mich. Abortion Ban Should Cover Rape, Incest." *The Washington Post*, July 21, 2022.

Slodysko, Brian, Bill Barrow, and Jake Bleiberg. "As Herschel Walker Eyes Senate Run, a Turbulent Past Emerges." AP, July 23, 2021.

Smyth, Julie Carr. "Trump Becomes Target of New Ad After Ohio Senate Endorsement." AP, April 27, 2022.

Tamari, Jonathan. "Pa. Senate Candidate Sean Parnell's Wife Testified That He Choked Her and Hit Their Children." *The Philadelphia Inquirer*, November 2, 2021.

Vigdor, Neil, and Jonathan Weisman. "Ex-Wife of Eric Greitens, Senate Candidate in Missouri, Accuses Him of Abuse." *The New York Times*, March 21, 2022.

Weigel, David. "Trump Endorses 'ERIC' in Missouri Primary, a Name Shared by Rivals." *The Washington Post*, August 1, 2022.

CHAPTER 8

Alemany, Jacqueline, Josh Dawsey, Tom Hamburger, and Ashley Parker. "National Archives Had to Retrieve Trump White House Records from Mar-a-Lago." *The Washington Post*, February 7, 2022.

AP. "Trump Says He Had the Right to Tweet Iran Satellite Photo." August 30, 2019.

Bellware, Kim. "There Will Be 'Riots in the Street' If Trump Is Prosecuted, Graham Says." *The Washington Post*, August 29, 2022.

Betz, Bradford, Jon Street, David Spunt, and Brooke Singman. "Trump Says Mar-a-Lago Home in Florida 'Under Siege' by FBI Agents." Fox News, August 8, 2022.

Bromwich, Jonah E., Ben Protess, and William K. Rashbaum. "Manhattan Prosecutors Move to Jump-Start Criminal Inquiry into Trump." *The New York Times*, November 21, 2022.

Bromwich, Jonah E., William K. Rashbaum, and Ben Protess. "N.Y. Attorney General Accuses Trump of 'Staggering' Fraud in Lawsuit." *The New York Times*, September 21, 2022.

Fahrenthold, David A., Josh Dawsey, Isaac Stanley-Becker, and Shayna Jacobs. "RNC Agrees to Pay Some of Trump's Legal Bills in N.Y. Criminal Investigation." *The Washington Post*, November 22, 2021.

Fausset, Richard, and Danny Hakim. "Georgia Prosecutors Open Criminal Inquiry into Trump's Efforts to Subvert Election." *The New York Times*, February 10, 2021.

Gardner, Amy. "'I Just Want to Find 11,780 Votes': In Extraordinary Hour-Long Call, Trump Pressures Georgia Secretary of State to Recalculate the Vote in His Favor." *The Washington Post*, January 3, 2021.

Gerstein, Josh, and Kyle Cheney. "Garland Names Jack Smith Special Counsel for Trump Criminal Probes." *Politico*, November 18, 2022.

Haberman, Maggie, Ben Protess, and Adam Goldman. "F.B.I. Searches Trump's Florida Home, Signaling Escalation of Inquiries." *The New York Times*, August 8, 2022.

Izadi, Elahe. "How a Former Florida Political Operative Broke the Mar-a-Lago FBI Story." *The Washington Post*, August 9, 2022.

Izaguirre, Anthony. "NY Attorney General Letitia James Has a Long History of Fighting Trump and Other Powerful Targets." Associated Press, September 28, 2023.

McCaskill, Nolan D. "Trump: No Politician 'Has Been Treated Worse or More Unfairly.'" *Politico*, May 17, 2017.

Myre, Greg, and Wynne Davis. "The Reason Why Presidents Can't Keep Their White House Records Dates Back to Nixon." NPR, August 13, 2022.

Orr, Gabby, Kristen Holmes, Evan Perez, and Jeremy Herb. "Inside Trump's Public Bravado and Private Resistance over Mar-a-Lago Documents." CNN, August 25, 2022.

Parker, Ashley, Jacqueline Alemany, Josh Dawsey, and Tom Hamburger. "15 Boxes: Inside the Long, Strange Trip of Trump's Classified Records." *The Washington Post*, February 12, 2022.

Protess, Ben, and William K. Rashbaum. "Judge Imposes Gag Order on Trump in Manhattan Criminal Trial." *The New York Times*, March 26, 2024.

Reid, Paula, Kristen Holmes, Kaitlan Collins, Jeremy Herb, and Katelyn Polantz. "Trump's Legal Team Hopes to Appeal Directly to Attorney General Garland to Close Criminal Probes into Former President." CNN, May 24, 2023.

Thrush, Glenn, Charlie Savage, Alan Feuer, and Maggie Haberman. "Documents at Mar-a-Lago Were Moved and Hidden as U.S. Sought Them, Filing Suggests." *The New York Times*, August 31, 2022.

CHAPTER 9

Allen, Mike. "Scoop: Trump Trashes Barr in Rant to Lester Holt." *Axios*, March 7, 2022.

Barr, William P. *One Damn Thing After Another: Memoirs of an Attorney General*. William Morrow, 2022.

Bender, Michael C. *Frankly, We Did Win This Election: The Inside Story of How Trump Lost*. Twelve Books, 2021.

Gedeon, Joseph. "10 House Republicans Voted to Impeach Trump. Cheney's Loss Means Only 2 Made It Past Their Primaries." *Politico*, August 13, 2022.

Gruver, Mead. "Wyoming Lawmakers to Debate Trump-Backed Primary Changes." AP, February 17, 2022.

Hutchinson, Cassidy. *Enough*. Simon & Schuster, 2023.

Isenstadt, Alex. "How Team Trump Systematically Snuffed Out Liz Cheney's Reign in Congress." *Politico*, August 16, 2022.

Kane, Paul. "Liz Cheney Went Against the 'Clear' Path. Now She Leads an Anti-Trump Movement." *The Washington Post*, August 17, 2022.

Kaplan, Anna. "Exclusive: Liz Cheney Says She'll 'Make a Decision in the Coming Months' About Running for President." *Today*, August 17, 2022.

Karl, Jonathan. *Tired of Winning: Donald Trump and the End of the Grand Old Party*. Dutton, 2023.

Koblin, John. "At Least 20 Million Watched Jan. 6 Hearing." *The New York Times,* June 10, 2022.

Lizza, Ryan, and Eugene Daniels. "Cheney to Launch Anti-Trump Organization After Primary Defeat," *Politico,* August 17, 2022.

Meadows, Mark. *The Chief's Chief.* All Seasons Press, 2021.

Schmidt, Michael S. *Donald Trump v. The United States: Inside the Struggle to Stop a President.* Random House, 2020.

Sciutto, Jim. *The Return of Great Powers: Russia, China, and the Next World War.* Dutton, 2024.

Wallace-Wells, Benjamin. "Liz Cheney's Kamikaze Campaign." *The New Yorker,* August 10, 2022.

CHAPTER 10

Allen, Jonathan. "Trump on the Brink?" NBC News, June 5, 2022.

Allen, Mike. "Ron DeSantis' 'God Ad' Invokes God 10 Times in 96 Seconds." *Axios,* November 5, 2022.

AP. "Pennsylvania Governor's Race Breaks Campaign Finance Record." October 15, 2022.

Breitman, Kendall. "Trump to Form Exploratory Committee for Possible 2016 Presidential Bid." *Politico,* March 18, 2016.

Carney, Jordan. "Fetterman Fends Off Oz in Pennsylvania Senate Showdown." *Politico,* November 9, 2022.

Epstein, Reid J. "Mastriano's Sputtering Campaign: No TV Ads, Tiny Crowds, Little Money." *The New York Times,* September 26, 2022.

Goldmacher, Shane, Maggie Haberman, and Jonathan Swan. "Why Ron DeSantis Is Limping to the Starting Line." *The New York Times,* May 13, 2023.

Hester, Wesley P. "Powhatan's LaCivita a Political Warrior on National Stage." *Richmond Times-Dispatch,* June 12, 2011.

Isenstadt, Alex. "Trump to Unleash Millions in the Midterms in Possible Prelude to 2024." *Politico,* September 23, 2022.

Lonas, Lexi. "Majorities in New Poll Say Biden, Trump Should Not Run Again in 2024." *The Hill*, July 12, 2022.

McFadden, Robert D. "Citing Public Support, Trump Forms Exploratory Committee on Presidency." *The New York Times*, October 8, 1999.

Nuzzi, Olivia. "Donald Trump on 2024: 'I've Already Made That Decision.'" *New York*, July 14, 2022.

Olander, Olivia, and Kelly Hooper. "'Do You Care About Family Values?': Walker's Son Denounces Father's Campaign." *Politico*, October 3, 2022.

Otterbein, Holly. "Where in the World Is Dr. Oz?" *Politico*, July 7, 2022.

Scherer, Michael, and Josh Dawsey. "Trump Eyes Longtime Virginia Operative for Senior 2024 Campaign Role." *The Washington Post*, October 25, 2022.

Sollenberger, Roger. "Herschel Walker, Critic of Absentee Dads, Has Yet ANOTHER Secret Son—and a Daughter." *The Daily Beast*, June 16, 2022.

———. "Herschel Walker Ex Comes Forward: He Attacked Me in a Rage." *The Daily Beast*, December 1, 2022.

———. "Herschel Walker Says He's a Model Dad. He Has a Secret Son." *The Daily Beast*, June 14, 2022.

———. "'Pro-Life' Herschel Walker Paid for Girlfriend's Abortion." *The Daily Beast*, October 3, 2022.

Suebsaeng, Asawin. "Trump Family Dunks on DeSantis: You're 'Stealing' Our Bit!" *Rolling Stone*, August 28, 2022.

Swan, Jonathan. "Scoop: Trump Team Eyes Nov. 14 Announcement." *Axios*, November 4, 2022.

Toobin, Jeffrey. "The Dirty Trickster." *The New Yorker*, May 23, 2008.

CHAPTER 11

Allison, Natalie, and Meridith McGraw. "Walker to Trump: Please Phone It In." *Politico*, November 29, 2022.

Arnsdorf, Isaac, and Michael Scherer. "Trump, Who as President Fomented an Insurrection, Says He Is Running Again." *The Washington Post*, November 15, 2022.

Barr, Jeremy. "Broadcast Networks Take a Pass on Trump Campaign Announcement." *The Washington Post*, November 15, 2022.

Bender, Michael C., and Maggie Haberman. "Trump Sells a New Image as the Hero of $99 Trading Cards." *The New York Times*, December 15, 2022.

———. "Trump Under Fire from Within G.O.P. After Midterms." *The New York Times*, November 9, 2022.

Bennett, Kate. "Tiffany Trump's Wedding Assembles a Family Divided over Its Patriarch's Political Future." CNN, November 11, 2022.

Bensinger, Ken. "Selling Trump Isn't What It Used to Be." *The New York Times*, February 4, 2023.

Blake, Aaron. "How Bad the 2022 Election Was for the GOP, Historically Speaking." *The Washington Post*, November 10, 2022.

Brasch, Ben, and Jacob Bogage. "These Brands Have Dropped Kanye West amid Antisemitism Controversy." *The Washington Post*, October 25, 2022.

Breuninger, Kevin. "Trump Made a Bundle of Cash Selling NFTs, Financial Filings Show." CNBC, April 14, 2023.

Cadelago, Christopher, Meridith McGraw, and Alex Isenstadt. "Unbowed by Midterms Fiasco, Trump Tries for President Again." *Politico*, November 15, 2022.

Caputo, Marc. "The Inside Story of Trump's Explosive Dinner with Ye and Nick Fuentes." NBC News, November 29, 2022.

Friedman, Vanessa. "Many Flags but No Ivanka." *The New York Times*, November 16, 2022.

Gibson, Brittany, and Natalie Allison. "Warnock Beats Walker in Georgia, Padding Dems' Senate Edge." *Politico*, December 6, 2022.

Isenstadt, Alex. "Club for Growth Steps on Trump Relaunch with Polls Showing DeSantis Beating Him." *Politico*, November 14, 2022.

Ivanova, Irina. "Donald Trump's First NFT Collection Sells Out in Less than a Day." *CBS MoneyWatch*, December 16, 2022.

Mascaro, Lisa. "GOP's Stefanik Backs Trump '24 as Other Republicans Decline." AP, November 11, 2022.

Mazzei, Patricia. "With Runaway Win, DeSantis's Political Career Becomes Supercharged." *The New York Times,* November 9, 2022.

McGraw, Meridith, and Christopher Cadelago. "It's Still Trump's Party and He'll Run if He Wants to . . . Run If He Wants to, Run If He Wants To." *Politico,* November 15, 2022.

Navarro, Aaron, and Robert Costa. "Marjorie Taylor Greene Downplays Speaking at a Conference Founded by White Nationalist." CBS News, February 28, 2022.

Ollstein, Alice Miranda. "Kansas Voters Block Effort to Strip Abortion Protections from State Constitution." *Politico,* August 2, 2022.

Orr, Gabby, Kristen Holmes, and Veronica Stracqualursi. "Former President Donald Trump Announces a White House Bid for 2024." CNN, November 15, 2022.

Rogers, Katie. "Kanye West's White House Rant Steals Trump's Spotlight." *The New York Times,* October 11, 2018.

Samuels, Brett. "Jason Miller: Trump Should Wait for Georgia Senate Runoff Before Making 2024 Announcement." *The Hill,* November 10, 2022.

Savage, Mark. "Kanye West's Twitter and Instagram Accounts Locked over Anti-Semitism." BBC, October 10, 2022.

Scott, Eugene. "McConnell: Anyone Meeting with Antisemites Is 'Unlikely to Ever Be Elected President.' " *The Washington Post,* November 29, 2022.

Singman, Brooke. "Ivanka Trump Says She Loves Her Father but Does 'Not Plan to Be Involved in Politics.' " Fox News, November 15, 2022.

Vozzella, Laura, and Gregory S. Schneider. "Virginia's GOP Lieutenant Governor Calls Trump 'Liability to the Mission.' " *The Washington Post,* November 10, 2022.

Wang, Amy B. "GOP Lawmakers Largely Silent after Trump Suggests 'Termination' of Constitution." *The Washington Post,* December 4, 2022.

The WSJ Editorial Board. "Donald Trump's Presidential Reru." *The Wall Street Journal,* November 14, 2022.

———. "Trump Is the Republican Party's Biggest Loser." *The Wall Street Journal,* November 9, 2022.

CHAPTER 12

Adragna, Anthony, Nicholas Wu, Meredith Lee Hill, and Marianne LeVine. "McCarthy Claims Speakership on 15th Ballot." *Politico,* January 7, 2023.

Alberta, Tim. "Nikki Haley's Time for Choosing." *Politico Magazine,* February 12, 2021.

Allen, Mike. "Scoop: DeSantis Super PAC Strafes Trump in First TV Ad." *Axios,* April 16, 2023.

Bender, Michael C., and Nicholas Nehamas. "The Emasculation of Ron DeSantis by the Bully Donald Trump." *The New York Times,* January 22, 2024.

Burns, Alexander, and Jonathan Martin. "'I've Had It with This Guy': G.O.P. Leaders Privately Blasted Trump After Jan. 6," *Politico,* April 21, 2022.

Dawsey, Josh, Shayna Jacobs, Carol D. Leonnig, and Justine McDaniel. "Trump Calls for Protests of What He Claims Is His Imminent Arrest." *The Washington Post,* March 18, 2023.

Durkin, Erin. "Trump Org. Guilty on All Counts in New York Criminal Tax Fraud Trial." *Politico,* December 6, 2022.

Grayer, Annie, and Jeremy Herb. "McCarthy Pulls His 5 GOP Members from 1/6 Committee After Pelosi Rejects 2 of His Picks." CNN, July 21, 2021.

Guggenheim, Benjamin. "Trump's Tax Returns Released, Launching Fresh Scrutiny of His Finances." *Politico,* December 30, 2022.

Haberman, Maggie, Mark Landler, and Edward Wong. "Nikki Haley to Resign as Trump's Ambassador to the U.N." *The New York Times,* October 9, 2018.

Hartmann, Margaret. "Donald Trump's Nasty Ron DeSantis Nicknames, Ranked." *New York,* May 31, 2023.

Hirschfeld Davis, Julie. "What's an Election Loss When He's 'My Kevin'? McCarthy Appears Set to Lead House G.O.P." *The New York Times,* November 13, 2018.

Homans, Charles. "A Trump Rally, a Right-Wing Cause and the Enduring Legacy of Waco." *The New York Times,* March 24, 2023.

Hooper, Kelly. "Nikki Haley Announces 2024 White House Run." *Politico*, February 14, 2023.

Isenstadt, Alex, and Meridith McGraw. "'O.J. Simpson on Steroids': Team Trump Preps for a Post-Indictment Frenzy." *Politico*, March 30, 2023.

Jalonick, Mary Clare, Eric Tucker, and Farnoush Amiri. "Jan. 6 Panel Urges Trump Prosecution with Criminal Referral." AP, December 19, 2022.

Lahut, Jake, and Zachary Petrizzo. "The GOP Campaign Trail Is Already Getting DeSantis-Proofed." *The Daily Beast*, March 16, 2023.

Malone, Clare. "The Face of Donald Trump's Deceptively Savvy Media Strategy." *The New Yorker*, March 25, 2024.

Martin, Jonathan, and Alexander Burns. *This Will Not Pass: Trump, Biden, and the Battle for America's Future.* Simon & Schuster, 2022.

McCann Ramírez, Nikki. "Trump Bashes Jewish Leaders for Not Being 'Loyal' After His Dinner with Holocaust Deniers." *Rolling Stone*, December 9, 2022.

McCormick, John. "Ron DeSantis Holds Early Lead over Donald Trump Among GOP Primary Voters, WSJ Poll Shows." *The Wall Street Journal*, December 14, 2022.

McGraw, Meridith, and Alex Isenstadt. "Trump's First '24 Rally Has a Familiar Feel: Anger and Attacks on His Tormentors." *Politico*, March 25, 2023.

McGraw, Meridith, and Nicholas Wu. "Trump's Spell over GOP Breaks with McCarthy Meltdown." *Politico*, January 4, 2023.

Petrizzo, Zachary. "DeSantis Doesn't 'Remember' Eating Pudding with Three Fingers." *The Daily Beast*, March 23, 2023.

Protess, Ben, Jonah E. Bromwich, William K. Rashbaum, Kate Christobek, Nate Schweber, and Sean Piccoli. "Trump Is Indicted, Becoming First Ex-President to Face Criminal Charges." *The New York Times*, March 30, 2023.

Rasmussen Reports. "Would You Rather Have a Beer With Clinton or Trump?" June 15, 2016.

Swan, Jonathan, and Maggie Haberman. "Trump Allies Pressure DeSantis to Weigh In on Expected Indictment." *The New York Times*, March 19, 2023.

EPILOGUE

Alberta, Tim. "Nikki Haley's Time for Choosing." *Politico Magazine*, February 12, 2021.

Allison, Natalie. "RNC Installs New Leadership as Trump Tightens Hold on GOP." *Politico*, March 8, 2024.

Arnsdorf, Isaac, and Josh Dawsey. "How the GOP's Rewriting of Jan. 6 Paved the Way for Trump's Comeback." *The Washington Post*, January 6, 2024.

Hawkins, Derek, and Nick Mourtoupalas. "Breaking Down the 88 Charges Trump Faces in His Four Indictments." *The Washington Post*, March 14, 2023.

Isenstadt, Alex, and Meridith McGraw. "Trump Allies and MAGA Luminaries Move to Kill off the Haley-for-VP Buzz." *Politico*, December 22, 2023.

Mascaro, Lisa. "Kevin McCarthy Endorses Trump for President and Would Consider Serving in His Cabinet." AP, December 8, 2023.

INDEX

Barr, Bill, 136, 179, 180, 182, 188, 260
Bartiromo, Maria, 68, 148
Bartos, Jeff, 149
Bedminster
    fundraising at, 101
    LIV Golf tournament, 127–28
    PGA Championship tournament
        (2022) and, 15, 138
    as Republican pilgrimage
        destination, 116, 123
Bender, Michael, 180
Benessere Capital Acquisition
    Corporation, 128
Biden, Joe
    Afghanistan withdrawal, 193
    inauguration of, 4–6, 7
    legitimacy of presidency according
        to Republicans, 28
    popularity of, xvi
    reinstatement of Trump as
        president conspiracy theory and,
        79–82
    as Republicans' hoped for 2024
        candidate, 64
    Republican support of, in 2020, 26
    Trump and MAGA as threats to
        democracy and, 212–13
    Trump's dinner with West and
        Fuentes and, 232
    win in Arizona, 83, 87
Biggs, Andy, 241
"big lie." See stolen election conspiracy
    theory
"birtherism" conspiracy, 30
Biteman, Bo, 122, 123–24
Black, Charlie, 204
Blair, James, 237, 238, 244, 245
Blanchard, Lynda, 101, 116–17
Bobb, Christina
    basic facts about, 85–86, 170
    fundraising for Arizona ballot audit
        by, 87
    presidential documents at Mar-a-
        Lago and, 161–62, 163, 165, 170
Bolduc, Don, 210
Bolton, John, 6–7, 178

Bondi, Pam, 53, 102, 186
Bongino, Dan, 85, 93, 128–29, 148,
    165
Borgum, Doug, 257
Bossie, David
    election of 2022 and, 59, 211
    MAGA Inc. and, 102
    Rigged and, 88–89, 90, 91–92
    Timken and, 146
Bouchard, Andy, 122
Boulos, Michael, 10, 216, 253
Bowers, Butch, 40
Bowman, Jamaal, 253
Bragg, Alvin
    charges against Trump, 251–52
    criminal investigation of Trump,
        176, 248
    indictment of Trump, 248–50,
        252–54, 257–58
    Trump's attacks on, 177, 252
Branigan, Laura, x
Branson, Richard, 23
Bratt, Jay, 161–62, 169–70
Britt, Katie, 210
British Open golf championship, 138
Brooks, Mo, 101, 117, 141–42, 144
Budd, Ted, 105, 210
Budowich, Taylor, 196
    announcement of Trump's 2024
        candidacy and, 196
    basic facts about, 111–13, 216
    as former DeSantis staffer, 237, 244
    on Lewandowski, 77
    MAGA Inc. and, 199, 237–38
Burnett, Mark, 34
Burns, Alex, 240
Burr, Richard, 44, 104
Bush, George H. W., 55
Bush, George W., 22–23, 68, 243
Bush, Jeb, 219
Butina, Maria, 86
Byrne, Patrick, 86–87

Campaign Monitor, 102
Campaign Nucleus, 31–32
Cannon, Alex, 69–70

ABOUT THE AUTHOR

MERIDITH MCGRAW is a national political correspondent at *Politico*, where she has worked since 2019. After starting her career as a White House reporter and producer at ABC News, she is now a regular contributor on television and has appeared on MSNBC, Fox News, CNN, CBS, NBC, and ABC. She holds a bachelor's degree from the University of Texas at Austin and a master's degree from the Columbia University Graduate School of Journalism. She grew up in West Virginia and now resides in Washington, D.C.